Why Good Things Happen to Good People

✤

More Praise for
Why Good Things Happen to Good People

"People want to be generous; they just don't dare risk it. Now they can, knowing that real benefits come to people who live generously. This is truly good news for everybody. Lives will change for the better as a result of this book."

> —**Rev. Peter J. Gomes**, Plummer Professor of Christian Morals and Pusey Minister in the Memorial Church, Harvard University

"This is encouraging news indeed! The scientific studies in this book bring to light the human capacity for goodness, for caring, and for love. They prove that we have the capacity to change this world just by giving."

> —**Sharon Salzberg**, author of *Lovingkindness: The Revolutionary Art of Happiness*

"As someone who has long believed that giving of oneself is essential to good health, I was delighted by the theoretical and practical support for my belief found in this book by Stephen Post and Jill Neimark. I would suggest reading this book before ever dismissing the idea that giving is good medicine."

> —**Dr. Tim Johnson**, medical editor, ABC News

"Prepare to be uplifted and transformed by Stephen Post and Jill Neimark's remarkable book. The authors bring courage and joy to their readers in their inspiring description of the human capacity for love."

> —**Susannah Heschel**, Eli Black Professor of Jewish Studies, Dartmouth College, editor of *Moral Grandeur and Spiritual Audacity: Essays by Abraham Joshua Heschel*

"Stephen Post and Jill Neimark have brought sophisticated survey research techniques to the task of exploring such supposedly elusive topics as compassion and love. In this book they examine the extraordinary benefits of giving. Their focus is practical, and encourages readers to make giving a driving force in their lives, leading to positive thoughts and actions. Appearing at a time of growing public angst about the state of society and the world, this book offers a timely message of hope and restoration."

—**George Gallup, Jr.**, founder, the George H. Gallup
International Institute

"This work converts the currency of today's sciences into a capital account that can be invested in a universe of Love."

—**Joan Konner**, Professor and Dean Emerita, Columbia University,
The Journalism School

"This unique book should be exceptionally well received for bringing new science to what we physicians know from clinical practice—positive emotions are good for your health. Learn about ten different ways of giving unselfishly to others . . . and the good news is that in the process, we give to ourselves too!"

—**Dr. Eric J. Topol, MD**, Chief Academic Officer of Scripps Health
and Chief of the Scripps Translational Science Institute and
Genomic Medicine Program

"As a psychologist who works with families around their personal struggles, I will now recommend Stephen Post and Jill Neimark's new book as critical reading. It will help me convince adults and adolescents alike that the best path to a good and happy life is within their grasp. *Why Good Things Happen to Good People* is inspiring to me, and I hope it will reach millions of others, because reading it will help to make the world a better place."

—**Sylvia Rimm, PhD**, clinical professor of psychiatry and pediatrics,
Case Western Reserve University School of Medicine, and author
of *See Jane Win*

Why
Good Things
Happen to
Good People

❧

The Exciting New Research That Proves
the Link Between Doing Good
and Living a Longer, Healthier, Happier Life

❧

Stephen Post, PhD, and Jill Neimark

BROADWAY BOOKS
NEW YORK

BROADWAY

PUBLISHED BY BROADWAY BOOKS

Published in the United States by Broadway Books, an imprint of
The Doubleday Broadway Publishing Group, a division of
Random House, Inc., New York.
www.broadwaybooks.com

BROADWAY BOOKS and its logo, a letter B bisected on the diagonal,
are trademarks of Random House, Inc.

Book design by Jennifer Ann Daddio

Library of Congress Cataloging-in-Publication Data
Post, Stephen Garrard, 1951–
Why good things happen to good people : the exciting new research that
proves the link between doing good and living a longer, happier,
healthier life / Stephen Post and Jill Neimark.—1st ed.
p. cm.
1. Altruism—Psychological aspects. 2. Helping behavior. I. Neimark,
Jill. II. Title.

BF637.H4P665 2006
177'.7—dc22
2006024040

ISBN: 978-0-7679-2017-9

PRINTED IN THE UNITED STATES OF AMERICA

1 3 5 7 9 10 8 6 4 2

First Edition

To those beacons of good who inspire me always:
Joseph Foley, Cathy M. Lewis,
Richard Watson, and Sir John Templeton.

— S . P .

For Thomas Usher,
who always gives but
never sacrifices.

— J . N .

Contents

Preface

BY REVEREND OTIS MOSS JR.

L ove is the most radical, life-altering force in the universe. In the book you are about to read, Dr. Stephen Post and Jill Neimark communi-cate the science and the spirit of genuine love. I've spent many hours with Dr. Post, since he lives in my own city of Cleveland. He brings to the academy and community here a special calling to unite the scientific and the spiritual in a triumphant synthesis. The words in this book show you how to be powerful, courageous, forgiving, and *completely* human—while at the same time going above and beyond the accustomed boundaries of hu-man behavior.

I know about the forces that fight love. It was during my college years that the lynching of Emmett Till took place in Mississippi and that Rosa Parks refused to give up her seat on a bus in Montgomery, Alabama, and above all, it was during my college years that the Reverend Dr. Martin Luther King Jr. mentored me and I became a disciple and leader in the nonviolent sit-in movement in Atlanta. I learned then, so long ago, that the world needs apostles of love and ambassadors of peace. As Robert Kennedy said often in his days of campaigning, quoting Tennyson: "Come, my friends, 'tis not too late to seek a newer world."

All great men and women have known this about love: it is not too late, and it is the way to a new world. To Mahatma Gandhi, love was Satyagraha (truth force). And so Gandhi broke the yoke of British colonialism in India without a gun. To Jesus and his disciples, love was redemption. For the Holocaust survivor Viktor Frankl, love is the one reality that gives meaning to life in all dimensions.

There is a beautiful message in the book of Isaiah, chapter 35, verse 1, and part of that verse reads, "The desert shall rejoice and blossom like a rose." This idea has guided my ministry in times of highest joy and deepest pain, suffering, and sorrow. Just five words capture what I would like to say to introduce the book that follows: *the desert and the rose.*

Life brings to us many deserts, many desert experiences. And if we are pilgrims rather than tourists in life, our journey will always take us through the desert, through the wilderness. Yes, life is filled with deserts.

Sometimes there are relational deserts. Relationships that have been built across many years and have passed through many seasons come to moments in time when they seem to be nothing but a desert—dry, parched, negative. Sometimes the garments we wear, the vehicle in which we ride, the house where we reside, are all quality products, but underneath it all is a scorching heat, a burning desert that leaves our relationships empty of meaning, empty of content, empty of substance.

Sometimes there are economic deserts on our journey. Deserts of recession and unemployment. And we can count in our own nation tens of millions of individuals who stand in desert places uninsured.

Sometimes sickness can become a desert. I remember many years ago when I was the pastor of a wonderful church in Cincinnati, Ohio. It became my responsibility to go to the hospital to visit one of our members. As I entered the hospital room of Sister Leola McNair, she greeted me with great enthusiasm, then told me, "When I entered the hospital, I was prepared for one leg to be amputated. I knew I would lose one of my legs. But since I have been in the hospital I have discovered that I must have both legs removed."

And I stood there frozen, wondering, *What can I say?* All of my seminary training had not prepared me adequately for this moment. As I paused, waiting for some meaningful word to come, she spoke, literally, for me. She looked at me and confided, "I have been here in my bed thinking about all the wonderful things I'm going to do with my hands when I go home from the hospital."

Now, Sister McNair did not say, "*If* I go home" but "*when* I go home" from the hospital. And then she said, "From my early childhood I learned to sew, to knit, to crochet, to cook, and to do remarkable things with my hands. I have been going over in my mind all of the marvelous things I will do with my hands." She paused and added, "I think I will bake you a cake."

Here, in this challenging, profound, almost overwhelming moment, she not only brought wisdom and a sense of purpose, but she brought a sense of humor. In the desert of her sickness, she planted a rose. I will never forget her and what she gave to me in that instant. Her future as a double amputee did not mar her view of life or break her spirit. If anything, it caused her to pull up from the great spiritual well inside her a greater and more profound witness to true courage and love. She went home, where she lived alone on Social Security income. She did just as she proclaimed. She began to do wonderful things with her hands. And in her wheelchair we saw the power of love at work. Nobody could feel sorry for Sister Leola McNair because she was so busy, so engaged in bringing help and hope to others.

There are Sister McNairs everywhere. Perhaps you are one. From Sunday to Sunday I look out into a sea of faces, and some have gone through triple bypass surgery, or witnessed death in untimely ways, or simply endured the daily struggles of life, and yet they sing "Hallelujah" in a new key. These are remarkable witnesses to what can happen in an individual's life through the power of love. Love remarkes us and gives us new courage and new strength.

And so, as you read this book, think about the desert and the rose. When you are in a desert, plant a rose. Plant a rose of liberation. Plant a rose of peace, a rose of reconciliation, and a rose of faith, hope, and love. And the desert will blossom. I hope this book will change your life.

❧

One

❧

Find the Fire

If I could take one word with me into eternity, it would be "give."

For the past eighteen years I've taught medical ethics at Case Western University Medical School, and since 2001 I've run a research institute dedicated to exploring the extraordinary power of giving. We've
funded over fifty studies at forty-four major universities.

I have one simple message to offer and it's this: giving is the most potent force on the planet. Giving is the one kind of love you can count on,
because you can always choose it: it's always within your power to give.
Giving will protect you your whole life long.

Most of us can recall with radiant clarity those moments when giving
was receiving, when another's happiness was our own. After fifty-five years
on this earth, I, like you, hold those moments as my most precious. But I
also know about the power of giving because, as head of the Institute for
Research on Unlimited Love (IRUL), I've funded studies and seen scientific proof. Pioneering scientists across many disciplines are pursuing a

whole new topography of research focused on the traits and qualities that create happiness, health, contentment, and lasting success in life. These scientists are discovering the deep, remarkable impact of benevolent behavior on mental and physical health. Personally, I am now convinced that giving is the answer to the malaise that corrodes many lives today, a malaise born of too much "bowling alone," as the sociologist Robert Putnam describes our fragmented lives.

You wish to be happy? Loved? Safe? Secure? You want to turn to others in tough times and count on them? You want the warmth of true connection? You'd like to walk into the world each day knowing that this is a place of benevolence and hope? Then I have one answer: give. Give daily, in small ways, and you will be happier. Give and you will be healthier. Give, and you will even live longer.

Generous behavior shines a protective light over the entire life span. The startling findings from our many studies demonstrate that if you engage in helping activites as a teen, you will *still* be reaping health benefits sixty or seventy years later. And no matter when you adopt a giving lifestyle, your well-being will improve, even late in life. Generous behavior is closely associated with reduced risk of illness and mortality and lower rates of depression. Even more remarkable, giving is linked to traits that undergird a successful life, such as social competence, empathy, and positive emotion. By learning to give, you become more effective at living itself.

As psychiatrist Dr. Karl Menninger wrote, "Love cures—both the ones who give it and the ones who receive it." This book will show you why giving is scientifically sound advice, and by the time you're finished reading these pages, you'll have many tools for embarking on a healthier, more giving lifestyle yourself.

Romance of a Different Kind

This book has one purpose: to inspire you to a healthier, more giving lifestyle. It offers:

- The latest scientific findings connecting generous behavior and happiness, health and longevity, as well as a look toward future science

- A practical roadmap detailing the distinctly different ways of giving available to all of us every day that will allow you to think about daily giving concretely, chapter by chapter
- Stories of giving, for what is life but a tapestry of stories? We are meaning-making creatures, and stories inspire us
- A new and unique Love and Longevity Scale, developed by top scientists, with which you can self-rate your own strengths and gifts
- Simple, practical suggestions and exercises to help you shift easily and gradually to a life of greater giving

You'll notice, as you read this book, that when I speak of giving and love, I rarely mention romantic infatuation. What of the face that launched a thousand ships? The rose that, by any other name, would smell as sweet? The troubadours, music, poetry, art, and wars waged because of love?

Romantic attraction is a pleasure-driven passion that carries its own unique brain chemistry, marked by fevered highs and, at times, wrenching lows. When we "fall" in love, infatuation propels us to ride a tidal wave of overwhelmingly positive feelings, so that we see our beloved as perfection incarnate. This early bliss helps propagate the species—but it tends to be fleeting. Though falling in love is an experience we all cherish, it is not the kind of love that does the heavy lifting in life. Staying in love requires the many expressions of generous behavior that are the core of this book. I have been married for twenty-five years. It's fair to say that my marriage began with romantic infatuation. Friendship emerged because it had to. After the birth of our daughter, cooperation and tolerance became essential; in fact, the transition to parenthood was one of the most maturing events of my life. But even the new, cooperative friendship that developed as we became parents would not have been enough to hold us together over the decades. A deeper kind of love emerged, one grounded in compassion, hope, forgiveness, loyalty, tolerance, respect.

In every marriage that begins with the dizzying highs of romance, it is the deeper, quieter ways of love that ultimately sustain it. The Harvard psychiatrist George Vaillant, who has followed the lives of Harvard graduates for half a century, gives the example of a judge who met his wife in high school. At age sixty-five, he reported that his love was "much deeper than at the beginning." At age seventy-seven, he said, "As life gets shorter, I

love Cecily even more." This book is about that kind of love. And it is giving that renews and sustains love over time.

How Did a Bioethicist End Up Running an Institute on Love?

One evening in the year 2000, at Duke University, a philanthropist named
Sir John Templeton sat with me over a friendly cup of tea and suggested
that I start an institute to study love, and love alone. Sir John is legendary
in the investing world for creating one of the most successful mutual funds
of the last century. His specialty was to identify emerging markets so that
stimulating business could benefit the local economy. Knighted in 1987 for
his achievements, Sir John retired to the Bahamas and began a unique
kind of philanthropy. His foundation gives away $60 million a year for
both spiritual and scientific endeavors and achievement. His annual Templeton Prize for Progress Toward Research or Discoveries About Spiritual
Realities offers about $1.5 million a year and has been awarded to every-
body from Mother Teresa to Aleksandr Solzhenitsyn to the physicist Paul
Davies.

I was a bit floored by Sir John's suggestion. When I came to Case Western Reserve University School of Medicine in 1988, I chose to focus on the
needs of Alzheimer's sufferers and their families. I was drawn to these people I call the "deeply forgetful" because I had seen my own grandmother die
of Alzheimer's. I knew that even in the haze of dementia, she could still
give and receive love—in fact, it was the only language left to her. These
patients revealed to me the simple truth that love is our core. I learned a
lot about giving from the deeply forgetful and their families as I traveled
around the country holding focus groups. Sir John knew this, and he himself had long been captivated by the idea of unselfish love.

A few months after we'd shared tea, Sir John wrote me to continue the
conversation; he asked that I establish a first-class scientific institute to
study the impact of love and giving on our lives. Soon after, I sat down
with the dean of Case Medical School, Nathan A. Berger, to discuss it.
"Nate," I said, "public health is about more than the flu and lead paint and

obesity. It's also about benevolence and generosity and hope. Love is actually powerful medicine. We all know that—Harry Harlow told us that half a century ago—but we don't study it enough."

In 1951 the psychologist Harry Harlow had offered an extraordinary presidential address to the American Psychological Association. Harlow was one of the first scientists to bring love into the lab. His controversial studies of baby monkeys clinging to cloth-and-wire "moms" are unforgettable—they showed us how deep and hardwired the need for affection and warmth is. "Love," Harlow said, "is a wondrous state, deep, tender and regarding . . . [and yet] psychologists tend to give progressively less attention to a motive which pervades our entire lives." He challenged the entire audience of his peers, asking why we study hatred, violence, fear, pornography, but not positive emotions.

Nate got my point. Visionaries like Nate Berger and Sir John Templeton are rare. And so, in 2001, with a generous start-up grant from the John Templeton Foundation, the Institute for Research on Unlimited Love was founded as an independent entity located at Case Medical School.

Many colleagues of mine, even good friends, have been amused by the name of the Institute. When you accept a challenge like Sir John's, you've got to shore up a lot of nerve to push it forward. And so I embrace the skepticism I encounter. It's one of the delightful challenges of this kind of work, and increasingly, people have come to take the Institute seriously.

When people ask me what the Institute does, I have three answers. The first: we fund pioneering, high-level, empirical research on unselfish love in every aspect from human development and genetics to positive psychology and sociology. The second: Remember what Mr. Rogers said after the September 11, 2001, terrorist attacks? He was asked on television what parents should tell their children about the terrorist attacks and his simple answer was: "Keep your eye on the helpers." That is what this institute does: it keeps an eye on the helpers, literally studying their good hearts, good works, and good lives, and distills lessons for the rest of us to live by.

And the third answer? In the giving of self lies the unsought discovery of self. In other words, when we give, we find our true selves. At the Institute, we aid that discovery as we can.

Though we are all flawed in a thousand ways, giving can guide our lives. The philosopher Ruth Groenhout of Calvin College recently asked me, "What would it take to generate a true revolution in scientific and evolutionary thinking so that love could be acknowledged openly and unabashedly?"

How about scientific proof for starters? The evidence is mounting, and as you will discover in this book, it is hard not to be swayed by the new research. Let's replace *cogito ergo sum* ("I think, therefore I am") with the far more benevolent notion, "I love, therefore I am." Love is not so much taught as transmitted, from good neighbors to parents, children, strangers, and saints. What message could be more important?

Consider the story of Katherine Meyers. In the winter of 1996 she met a homeless man named Marvin on the streets of Chicago, and he told her:

"Don't call me homeless. I have a home and it's in my heart." Meyers had just dropped money in Marvin's cup on her morning walk down Michigan Avenue, often called the "Magnificent Mile" because of its imposing stores and architectural splendor. "As I passed him I felt as if my feet weighed two hundred pounds," she recalls. "I couldn't keep walking. I was being pulled back." She turned around and introduced herself. Marvin was born blind, and yet he walked without a cane. "You have eyes in your feet and hands," Meyers said, and he reached for her hand and put it on his heart. "And your heart," she added. She sat down and they began to talk. Soon she put her arms around him, and as she did so she noticed that people walking by them were turning away. Meyers says, "They were missing out on this man's wisdom. He sat there without judgment or bitterness." She has been working with the homeless ever since. "I've learned that an outstretched hand doesn't always mean, 'Put money here.' Sometimes it means, '*Take* my hand. See me in my humanity. Acknowledge me.'"

Giving is a great equalizer. Whatever your background—privileged or impoverished, blessed or difficult—the starting place for a life of greater love is within your reach. I think of the life of Susie Valdez, nicknamed the "Queen of the Dumps." Valdez was born in the slums of Mexico, dropped out of school in the tenth grade, and had four babies in quick succession. Packing just a few possessions, she moved with her children to El Paso, Texas, and spent the next forty years caring for dirt-poor Mexicans. Valdez founded a mission, raised funds for two medical centers, mobilized prominent politicians, subsidized schools, and fed as many as three thousand poor people a day. Many who have met her marvel at her charismatic radiance in the face of so much suffering.

Give love, and you'll discover life in all its force, vitality, joy, and buoyancy. In generosity lies healing and health.

The New Science of Love and Health

The remarkable bottom line of the science of love is that giving protects overall health twice as much as aspirin protects against heart disease. If giving weren't free, pharmaceutical companies could herald the discovery of a stupendous new drug called "Give Back"—instead of "Prozac"—and run TV ads about love. The findings of the Institute build on the work of pioneers who have come before me—from great philosophers of love like Pitirim Sorokin to pathbreaking psychologists of happiness like Martin Seligman, the former head of the American Psychological Association and author of *Learned Optimism*.

The study of love leaves no person or field of science untouched. For those of us sharing the unfolding of this new field, it is an inspiring time. We are seeing the scientific confirmation of lifelong intuitions. The new research encompasses everybody from Afro-American teenagers to middle-aged Vietnam veterans to churchgoers, atheists, and the elderly. It draws on the insights of scientists from diverse fields—psychology, evolutionary biology, cross-cultural anthropology, gerontology, epidemiology, public health, religion, and human development. Some researchers are even trying to bring love into the doctor's office, asking physicians to prescribe generous behavior. Adam Hirschfelder is one such pioneer: he heads a new program, called Rx: Volunteer, in which patients recruited from the Medicare practice of a large HMO in California receive a volunteerism "prescription" from their physicians.

Giving protects the giver at all ages and stages of life. They say only the good die young. Of course, sometimes the good *do* die young, and we all eventually face sickness from causes that are completely beyond our control or responsibility. But the remarkably good news is that, over the past ten years, we have about five hundred serious scientific studies that demonstrate the power of unselfish love to enhance health, and our new IRUL-funded studies render the picture even more vivid.

Here are some of the exciting, fresh scientific findings that I will detail throughout this book:

Giving in high school predicts good physical and mental health all the way into late adulthood, a time interval of over fifty years. This finding comes from perhaps the most impressive and powerful new study that our institute has funded, by psychologist Paul Wink of Wellesley College. Wink studied nearly two hundred individuals who have been followed ever since the 1920s, when some of them were born. They were part of a special study initiated in conjunction with the University of California at Berkeley, and every decade these individuals were interviewed for four to five hours by clinicians. Longitudinal studies like this are the platinum standard of psychological research, because they are so richly detailed and have been carried out over so many decades. They truly allow us to see a life unfolding.

Giving reduces mortality significantly in later life, even when you start late. This new study comes from Doug Oman of the University of California at Berkeley. Oman has followed almost two thousand individuals over the age of fifty-five for five years. Those who volunteer for two or more organizations have an impressive 44 percent lower likelihood of dying—and that's after sifting out every other contributing factor, including physical health, exercise, gender, habits like smoking, marital status, and much more. That reduction in mortality is truly impressive considering that it is stronger than that associated with mobility (39 percent), exercising four times a week (30 percent), or attendance at religious services (29 percent). The only activity with a slightly higher effect is to stop smoking (which reduces mortality by 49 percent).

Giving reduces adolescent depression and suicide risk. The Institute sponsored four special studies on teens and found that generous behavior has a significant impact on teens' mental health. In new research from Peter Benson of the Search Institute in Minneapolis, boys in particular benefit markedly from feelings of love and from generous behavior. Just as intriguing is a study from David Sloan Wilson, one of the great evolutionary biologists of our time, and Mihaly Csikszentmihalyi, the psychologist who famously coined the word *flow* to describe certain highly creative states. Wilson has found that teen girls are more giving than teen boys and that teens who are giving, hopeful, and socially effective are also happier and more active, involved, excited, and challenged than their less engaged counterparts.

Giving is more powerful than receiving in its ability to reduce mortality. A large scientific literature has already found that both control and self-esteem are beneficial for health and well-being, and Neal Krause of the School of Public Health and Institute of Gerontology at the University of Michigan tested this in a new study of 976 churchgoing adults over a period of three years. Krause found that offering social support to others reduces people's anxiety over their own economic situation when they are under economic stress. He suspects that this extends to other stress as well—that giving reduces stress about your own life and thus lengthens your life.

Giving to others helps us forgive ourselves for our own mistakes, which is key to a sense of well-being. In this study, Krause found that a special type of giving was potent, and particularly for African Americans. Krause and his colleagues interviewed 989 older Americans whose average age was seventy-four; 46 percent were white and 54 percent were African American. He found that providing emotional support to others—rather than simply participating in formal volunteering programs—enhanced African Americans' ability to forgive themselves for their own mistakes.

Helping friends, relatives, and neighbors, along with providing emotional support to a spouse, reduces mortality, although receiving the same kind of help does not. Psychologist Stephanie Brown of the University of Michigan spent five years studying 423 older couples. After adjusting for age, gender, and physical and emotional health, Brown found that those who provided no significant support to others were more than twice as likely to die in that five-year period. These surprising findings ruled out other factors like personality, health, mental health, and marital relationship variables.

Even the simple act of praying for others, Neal Krause found, reduces the harmful impact of health difficulties in old age for those doing the praying. Other research by the sociologist Marc Musick of the University of Texas at Austin and his colleagues found that for people age sixty-five and older, volunteer work substantially reduces symptoms of depression. According to another study by Musick and his colleagues, individuals over sixty-five who volunteer are significantly less likely to die over the next eight years than those who do no volunteer work. Musick found that simply adding the volunteering role itself is protective.

Why Is Giving Good Medicine?

When we give, it's likely that we turn off the fight-or-flight response. Giving pushes aside the brooding negative emotions, like rage and spite and envy, that clearly contribute to stress-induced psychological and physical illness.

The "helper's high" was named by Allan Luks as far back as 1988. A full 50 percent of helpers reported feeling "high" when they helped others, while 43 percent felt stronger and more energetic. An astonishing 13 percent even experienced fewer aches and pains. Despite these fascinating reports, science has not yet conducted in-depth studies on the impact of giving on our neurological, hormonal, and immune systems, either short-term or long-term. We do have evidence that states like compassion are hardwired and can be identified with functional magnetic resonance imaging (fMRI) of the brain and that cultivating appreciation and gratitude for life lowers stress hormones like cortisol. We also know that older adults who give massages to infants have lower levels of stress hormones. But a future direction for research lies in pinpointing the precise neurobiology of generous behavior.

Giving may also be potent because, as Paul Wink discovered in his research, it is actually built of three important qualities: a giving disposition, empathy, and competence, particularly social competence. These qualities reverberate across many domains of life, leading to success in work, friendship, and love—and resulting in happiness and health.

It's fascinating to discover that giving may be so beneficial, because to give requires, in its own way, the ability to live well. In the words of Neal

Krause: "One person cannot provide effective help to another without entering another's mind sympathetically and with compassion." Giving may also help us gain a sense of control over our lives. One very important factor in health is the belief that the environment will respond to your efforts, says Krause. "Helping others increases your sense of control and counteracts low self-esteem."

Like a resonant bell, giving reverberates all the way down a lifetime. Consider the life of Teri Pipe, director of nursing research at the Mayo Clinic Hospital in Phoenix, Arizona—a position with a great deal of responsibility and innumerable interactions with hospital staff and patients. Two decades earlier she was head nurse at a rural nursing home. One spring day a new patient named Mr. K was admitted. Mr. K gave her a gift that, "amazingly, even after all these years, is inside me still," Pipe says.

That gift didn't come right away. Mr. K was cantankerous at best, Pipe recalls. He shouted, swore, and struck out at all of the nurses and aides. "The only tool we had available was love. I instructed all of the aides to treat Mr. K with love and respect, no matter what he said to them." Slowly, painstakingly, Mr. K began to respond to the outpouring of kindness. After a few weeks he was willing to take a shower. He began to comb his hair and stopped wearing pajamas all the time. "It felt good to see him changing, so we stepped up our loving care. About six months after his admission, Mr. K walked without assistance to the nurses' station and greeted me by name," says Pipe. "We both had a quiet moment as I took his hands in mine and told him he was an unforgettable reminder of the power of love. Caring for him when he was most unlovable had been hard and sometimes felt hopeless, and yet there he was before me ready to reach out because we had first reached out to him. This is all we have to give: ourselves one to another. What a gift and what a responsibility once you realize how powerful that gift is. Twenty years later I still am warmed by that feeling of being humbled and blessed by his transformation."

How to Become Good at Giving

Most days, love is both little and large. Little in that it is often as simple as a reassuring smile, a moment of patience, a gentle touch, and a small thing given with an open heart. Large because a life well lived is really the sum of thousands of small, ordinary acts of kindness. Can those acts, that life well lived, be quantified somehow for the rest of us to learn from?

In twenty-five years of studying generous behavior, I've found a very effective approach to the research: I look at ten different ways of giving in four areas of life, or "domains." Relying on this approach, the Institute asked top psychologists at the University of Miami to develop a *Love and Longevity Scale*. It contains two hundred questions and has been tested on hundreds of individuals. Each chapter of this book addresses one of the ten ways of giving and contains a section of the scale for that particular way. You will be able to self-rate your own strength and chart yourself as you change and grow. (Of course, I say this with the strong caveat that love is ineffable—or in the words of Emily Dickinson, "That Love is all there is,/Is all we know of Love.")

You will learn more about the scale and the domains and ways of giving in chapter 1. For now, suffice it to say that with practice and encouragement, individuals can become very good at it. Doug Oman, a close colleague of mine at the University of California at Berkeley, trained sixty-one nurses in eight spiritually based coping tools for two hours a week over an eight-week period. All the nurses who were given this training reported significantly greater inner peace, energy, and balance and less stress at the end of the eight weeks, as well as greater competence in everything from handling patients' families to bonding with patients.

But here's the surprise: when Oman interviewed the nurses again after another eight weeks, and yet again after another nineteen, their mental well-being had increased even more. Stress continued to decrease, and empathy to increase. With a little help and structure, these nurses were able to apply helpful tools on their own and benefit even more, long after the study had concluded. Says Oman, "We were astonished to discover that almost all of the outcomes had increased in their effect sizes."

It's my hope that the exercises and guidelines offered in this book will have the same impact on your own life that Doug's study had on those sixty-one nurses. Think of the chapters that follow as a buffet of possibilities. You have the freedom to pace yourself and choose what appeals to you. The person sitting next to you at this very moment can be delighted by a small kindness—a gentle word or touch, a thoughtful gesture.

Mother Teresa once said, "We can do no great things; only small things with great love."

Here is what giving can do, as described in a letter sent to me by a twenty-two-year-old health psychology researcher: "The call was at 6:00 A.M. on October 8, 2003," writes Jocelyn. "My dear friend and former partner was in the hospital, having attempted suicide the night before by reenacting his father's death: he had driven into a telephone pole at eighty-five miles per hour, holding a rosary in his right hand and hoping to go headfirst through the windshield, just like his dad, whom he worshiped. The following two weeks after his suicide attempt were the most heart-wrenching days of my life, but miraculously, one of the most healing and constructive periods of this young man's, yes, *life*. In those two weeks at the hospital, he spoke openly of the thoughts of suicide that had been haunting him over the years, of his bitter drift from the love we once held sacred, of the excruciating shame and hatred he bore in trying to be someone he was not. And while listening to the person I once thought I knew best in the world relate all these new things to me, what I did then was simply *hold* him. I held him with every atom of my soul, and realized for a fleeting moment the meaning of unconditional, unselfish love—of accepting the entirety of another human being without judgment, want, or expectation. I did not care who he was, but simply *that* he was. Wrapping him in my arms, bruised and broken on the hospital bed, I had never before felt something so alive and human, a miracle in material form made up of an infinite number of factors stretching back into the birth of time. I did not want just the best parts of him, the illuminated parts of him; for once, I wanted nothing of him, but to embrace every precious piece of him, light and dark, strong and weak, nurtured and neglected, and stitch them all together in a mandalic tapestry woven with the silk threads of compassion.

"He felt it too, I could tell—the gift of having every piece of himself held as one. It's one of the greatest gifts I've ever given. And for the past twelve weeks since his suicide attempt, he has started to extend tiny bits of compassion towards himself, thread by thread, weaving his soul back together again. Alongside this process, for the past twelve weeks every night before I go to sleep, I, the former no-nonsense, in-the-world agnostic, thank the Infinite for his life, for my life, for the lives of those close to me, far from me, before me, and ahead of me yet to come."

On the Bus to Where?

Most lives, mine included, are on a steep learning curve when it comes to generosity and giving. Last year I missed my flight from New York to Cleveland and had to take the Trailways bus home so I could teach my class the next morning. It was a sweltering summer night and the bus's air-conditioning was broken. The driver heaved to his feet and said apologetically, "We can leave, but I warn you, you're all gonna be warm tonight." He was right—I was about to be warmed in body and soul.

Behind me was a young man with mild Down's syndrome. He had the flat head, slanting eyes, and unusually large tongue typical of such individuals. I desperately wanted to sleep that night, but about every fifteen minutes the young man tapped me hesitantly on the shoulder and asked:

"Are we in Cleveland yet?"

And I would answer, "No, we'll be traveling most of the night."

At the same time, the man in front of me—who was cognitively intact—was in a rage. Every so often he'd rise up from his seat and pound the ceiling of the bus furiously, as if he were a trapped prisoner and could somehow punch through the metal and escape. He'd yell, "Why is it so damned hot in here? Why is this bus so slow? Why can't that guy back there shut up?" He had two young sons with him, and each time he exploded in rage they'd shrink back instinctively in their seats, gazing up at him in fear. One of the boys would start to cry silently, and the other would follow suit. The bus driver would stop the bus, ask the man to calm down, and we'd resume traveling—and if I was lucky enough to start to nod off, the inevitable tap came on my shoulder. I'd turn around and there was my Down's friend, somehow looking like a grown-up version of those two boys, with his wide, childlike stare. He needed reassurance.

This doesn't sound like a recipe for love, does it? We finally got to Milesburg, Pennsylvania, a little town in the middle of the Appalachian Mountains. The bus pulled into a parking lot, ground to a stop, and the driver turned off the engine. He then firmly escorted the man and his children off the bus and refused to let them back on. We resumed our journey, and the remaining four hours were, of course, punctuated by my Down's friend's hesitant tapping:

"Are we in Cleveland yet?"

"No, we're not there yet, but we will be soon."

At 6:30 A.M. the bus finally reached Cleveland and we disembarked. My young friend followed me and tapped me on the shoulder one last time. Then, with the typical uninhibited effusiveness one often finds in the mildly retarded, he gave me a big hug.

"We are here! Good night," he beamed.

A good night indeed. I often drive by Milesburg on Route 80, and every time I pass that town I remember two men on a bus. One man was cognitively intact, but he chose rage, again and again, until he and his unfortunate sons were left in the parking lot at Milesburg. The other man was cognitively impaired and needy, but he was remarkably loving. In giving to him, I received back—great joy and thanks. I'm glad I took that bus.

You don't have to leap from bed at dawn to dole out sandwiches at the soup kitchen in the middle of an icy winter, or take up the torch of social activism and march in the streets, in order to reap the lifelong benefits of giving. You will find the style that is right for you.

So, take my hand. And then give your hand to someone else. Come search for fire with me. You don't have to have lived an exemplary life to be warmed by love. You don't need a Nobel Peace Prize or songs and poems and biographies memorializing you. All you need to realize is that for your own happiness and fulfillment it really is good to be good, and science says it is so.

Are we in Cleveland yet? The bus is hot, but are we warm? We may not be home just yet, but I hope this book can help you begin the journey.

Two

The Love and Longevity Scale: Learn Ten Ways of Giving

G *ive* is a simple but amazingly versatile word—kind of like *snow* in Inuit. Living in an arctic world of white powdery stuff, Eskimos have invented separate words for fine snow like rain, snow that clings, soft and deep snow, snow that crusts, snow that forms a cornice, snow that floats on water, snow that drifts. *Give* has a similar number of meanings. Even a quick look at the word in *Webster's* dictionary shows a long column of definitions—from "bestow" to "offer" to "award," "devote," "entrust," "consent," "yield," and "care." I have immersed myself in the many "snows" of giving, so to speak. We each have unique capacities—just as one snowfall may be a crisp crust of powder perfect for a ski buff, and another so pillowy that your golden retriever ecstatically rolls her way through it.

Celebration is one way of giving. Consider Maggie Smith, a Newport, Washington, massage therapist who is married with two children. In 1998 she read a story in *Family Circle* magazine about donating bone marrow and registered to donate with the Puget Sound Blood Center. A few years later

Maggie's husband was diagnosed with malignant melanoma and was lucky enough to make a complete recovery. The night he was given a clean bill of health, Maggie told him, "We have to do something huge to celebrate." When they got home, there was a message on their answering machine: Maggie was a possible bone marrow match for Michael, a twelve-year-old boy with leukemia. She turned to her husband: "This is what I'll do to celebrate."

"How could I not take two weeks out of my life to possibly save a little boy?" Maggie recalls. "I remember waking up out of anesthesia and looking at the bag of my bone marrow hanging there and giving it a little blessing and falling back asleep." On the one-year anniversary of Michael's successful transplant and cure, his family invited Maggie to come celebrate with them. They met her at the airport gate, and Michael handed her a dozen roses. "When we got back to their home, there was a crowd of sixty people standing outside waiting, all wearing matching T-shirts that they had worn to support Michael during his illness. I was overwhelmed by hugs from his friends, family, even the priest who married his parents. Michael's fourth-grade basketball coach came up to me and said, 'You don't know what this community would have lost if Michael wasn't here. . . . You just don't know.' It wasn't until all these people were standing there that it hit me how many lives Michael has affected. Michael and I have an amazing connection, and I just love him, I adore him, and his family are just like family to me now."

Loyalty is another way of giving. In Loretto, Pennsylvania, a woman named Rosemary Bertocci gave money to a friend, but in truth, she gave her friendship. When she heard that a mutual friend was about to lose her house because she owed over $6,500 in back taxes, she invited the woman over to dinner and listened to her story. "My husband and I wrote her a check, saying, 'We are so proud of you, we know how hard you work.'" The woman's eyes filled with tears, and at that moment Bertocci felt the simple joy of being a loyal friend.

Generativity is yet another way of giving. A man named Henry wrote me this story about his mom, who died thirty-eight years ago. As a boy he wanted a new baseball mitt. On his mom's birthday, *her* mom sent her some money to buy herself a gift. "That year," Henry says, "Mom bought herself the gift of a baseball mitt, to give to me. I begged to go out and play catch. The exercise made her cough until her face grew red." She reassured her son that she was okay, and went on playing. "Mom still communicates to me through that act of giving. I was nine that last morning she told me to have a good day at school, just before my sisters and I went out the door to meet the school bus. By the end of the school day she had completed her journey on earth as our mom. But every day, through memories like the baseball mitt, she speaks to me of love. Her love is the reason that I walk to my neighbor's house during a snowstorm and join him in silence as we work to clean his drive." Generativity is like that: it is a torch passed down the generations.

Four Domains

Why did I decide to create a Love and Longevity Scale? First of all, scales are a powerful tool in the social sciences and they capture the tremendous variation in human behavior. Once a robust scale has been created, researchers in many different domains can apply it and discover how certain traits link to a whole range of behaviors. Scales can also be used to diagnose the degree and quality of an individual's health, and they help in developing treatment protocols. "Scales can change lives," says Giacomo Bono, one of the researchers who helped develop this scale. "They can help people learn about themselves and overcome problems. They help us discover which behaviors are useful for coping or for finding happiness." Scales allow us to chart the ways in which people change over time and the factors that are most relevant to big-picture traits like love, gratitude, forgiveness, and happiness. I hope the Love and Longevity Scale, and elements of it, will be applied in studies to come over the years, helping us to develop a truly robust measure of giving and health in many different populations.

Another reason grew out of a project I took part in a few years ago. I co-authored a section on kindness with my friend Michael McCullough, an associate professor of psychology and religious studies at the University of Miami, for a remarkable book called *Character Strengths and Virtues: A Handbook and Classification*. This book was edited by the positive psychology gurus Martin Seligman and Christopher Peterson, and it became an instant classic in the field. It is a direct blow to the famous *DSM* (*Diagnostic and Statistical Manual*), which classifies human behavior by pathologies. In contrast, this pioneering book classifies all the human qualities and strengths that help each of us flourish, and it supports each classification with research.

When Mike and I began our work, we looked at the research literature and found scales to measure gratitude, forgiveness, and volunteer behavior. Mike himself had developed a gratitude scale, called the GQ6, with the psychologist Robert Emmons of the University of California and Jo Ann Tsang of Baylor University's Department of Psychology and Neuroscience. But there was no scale that captured giving across the whole of everyday life. Mike and I wanted to develop something that would encompass an overarching spectrum of giving behaviors and then to test it over the years.

And so we developed the Love and Longevity Scale and offer it in this book so that you can test your own gifts of giving. Most likely, you'll find yourself scoring higher on certain ways of love than others, as they reflect your inborn talents and personality. Other ways, and domains for practicing them, may not come as naturally, but you may find that practice brings unexpected rewards. One useful aspect of this scale is that you can retest yourself after making lifestyle changes.

I first conceived of four domains, or spheres, in the early 1990s, when I wrote a rather dry, philosophical book entitled *Spheres of Love*. I'd read through all the existing scholarship on love, and I realized with a shock that almost every writer selected only one domain of life to focus on—one might write of marriage, another of the neediest in humanity. Nobody had yet written fully of the connections between the various domains; nobody had mapped the geography of love. Here is a step in that direction.

FAMILY

In everyday life most of us encounter the first sphere of love every morning and evening. Our spouse may be a few inches from us, still asleep. Our children may climb into bed with us, or our pets may nuzzle our noses as a way of asking for their morning meal. Our parents, if they don't live with us, might be in touch by phone or in our thoughts. Family is the inner sphere, the one that encompasses and defines the core of our being, where our most profound, challenging, and sustaining love is experienced. "I remember when I was on maternity leave," says the scientist Carolyn Schwartz, the principal investigator on one of our important studies on youth and giving, "and went to a first-time moms' group. A woman my age said the love she felt for her daughter was so much bigger than she'd ever imagined. You don't know you have that much love in you until it happens."

FRIENDS

We're taking a bite from toast with jam or packing the kids' lunchboxes as we rush them off to school, we're on the cell phone in the car, we're at work checking e-mail—and we hear from a friend of twenty years. Friendships sustain us throughout life and form the second sphere of love. Beth Kephart, a National Book Award nominee, puts it this way: "Throughout our lives, friends enclose us, like pairs of parentheses. They shift our boundaries, crater our terrain. They fume through the cracks of our tentative houses, and parts of them always remain. . . . Friendship asks and wants, hollows and fills, ages with us and we through it, cradles us, finally, like family. It is ecology and mystery and language, all three."

COMMUNITY

From city to suburb, high-rise to country cottage, our community weaves a web that sustains us. We chat with neighbors, form block associations, arrange playdates for our children. At work we're enmeshed in a community of colleagues that is often national and global. For those in the helping professions, community often extends to those we mentor and help as they become closer to us than a stranger, but perhaps not quite as close as a true friend. This community in all its varied colors is vital to a rich life.

HUMANITY

As Gandhi said, "Humanity is an ocean; if a few drops of the ocean are dirty, the ocean does not become dirty." All humanity represents the fourth sphere of love. This could be the person on the street selling carnations; the stranger on a plane we talk intimately with and wave good-bye to forever as we part; perhaps an individual we'll never even know of who is inspired by our work; or the anonymous recipient of a donation we make to the victims of a natural disaster.

Ten Ways

Within these four domains, there are myriad ways to give. Our scale captures ten of them: celebration, generativity, forgiveness, courage and confrontation, humor, respect, compassion, loyalty, listening, and creativity.

"How do I love thee?" penned Elizabeth Barrett Browning. "Let me count the ways." My favorite way of giving is *celebration*, which wells up from gratitude for life in all its infinite variety. Celebration is pure fun, palpable and effervescent, and its rituals are innumerable—a birthday, graduation ceremony, baby shower, or housewarming party, a thank-you card, a special present for a loved one, a wilderness trek, a blissful meditation, or a cheer for your team as they win.

GENERATIVITY

Giving is *generative* in deep and lasting ways. Generativity has been extensively studied in the social sciences and is a hallmark of well-being. The great, if clichéd, truism behind generativity is: "Give a man a fish and he eats for a day; teach a man to fish and he eats for a lifetime." When we nurture others so that their lives develop in unexpected and beautiful ways, we are passing on the torch of love.

FORGIVENESS

One of the most studied ways of giving is *forgiveness*. Forgiveness brings an inner freedom, serenity, and peace that sets the tone for an entire life. Forgiveness sets us free from our burden of guilt and yet, paradoxically, frees us from pain. Sometimes it simply means privately letting go of our rumination and bitterness and moving on. Though there are certainly times when forgiveness is not appropriate, more often than not it is healing.

COURAGE

From Joan of Arc to Martin Luther King, giving can take the form of *confrontation*—tempered by caring. It takes *courage* to confront harmful behavior, and no discussion of love is complete without an acknowledgment of how confrontation with evil has changed history—from Rosa Parks to Gandhi. Confrontation can take the form of questioning, example setting, suggestion, and guiding influence, and yet there are times when it requires absolute, unflinching directness and social activism.

HUMOR

I myself am a bit in love with *humor* (and am known for regaling others with ridiculous jokes that they tolerate with their own good humor). Humor is the fastest, fleetest form of giving—it can change pain to joy in a mere millisecond. A good joke can sometimes lift a person out of pain when no other way of love is effective. The exemplar of healing humor is Patch Adams, who dons a clown suit and red clown nose in hospitals.

RESPECT

Respect comes from the Latin *respectare*, which means "to look again." We must look again and again, look deeply, look past our natural biases and judgments. Respect allows love to breathe, allows us to accept another's choices in life even if they clash with our own. Respect offers tolerance, civility, acceptance, and even reverence. Yes, there is a sense of wonder and quiet awe in having deep respect for another person, even an appreciation for the miracle of being.

COMPASSION

Giving can take the form of *compassion*—love's response to suffering. The outpouring of empathy is the essence of much Buddhist thought and is now the subject of new, fascinating scientific research in brain imaging. Researchers have actually seen the parts of the brain that light up when a mother hears her baby cry or sees him smile, or when a monk meditates. Compassion is so common and engrossing that I see it as the emotional core of morality.

LOYALTY

Loyalty is love through time. Love in its highest form endures through difficulties. As I write this I am playing a 1970s hit song by Glenn Frey with this refrain: "You're a part of me, I'm a part of you, wherever we may travel, whatever we go through." No marriage can flourish without the trust that loyalty engenders. Loyal parents continue to take care of a child with severe disabilities over a lifetime, good friends remain our friends no matter what transpires, and people who love and care for the neediest usually remain loyal to their causes always.

LISTENING

We quietly give the gift of caring simply by *listening*. This form of attention is a skill and a gift. Those who listen deeply do not attempt to fix a single thing. They are simply present in a reassuring way. Attentive listening is the foundation of good therapy, leadership, parenting, friendship, and even meaningful politics. The need to be heard, understood, and truly known is universal.

CREATIVITY

And finally, *creativity* is the most spontaneous, joyful expression of life itself—from the stunning creativity of the cosmos to the unthinkable genius of a Beethoven, Einstein, Michelangelo, or Edison. Thomas Edison is, of course, my own favorite because he lived near Cleveland and woke early each morning for years to experiment tirelessly until he found a filament to light the world.

Ten ways of giving, in four domains, give you at this very moment a cornucopia of forty different ways to give.

What the Scale Can Do for You

The Love and Longevity Scale was tested on 339 undergraduates at the University of Miami in Coral Gables, Florida. This test group included both men and women from a melting pot of cultures and races—Caucasian, African American, Hispanic, Asian—that provided a nice cross-section of the population. Your score will tell you whether you are in the top, second, third, fourth, or fifth percentile in each way of love as compared to the sample group who took the scale. This is a very useful measure to help you understand your strengths.

Each chapter of this book contains the twenty questions of the scale that address that chapter's particular way of giving in the four domains (family, friends, neighbors and colleagues, and humanity at large). You can answer those twenty questions, add up your score, and see where you stand on that particular form of giving. The highest you can score on the entire scale (in theory) is 240, though I've never seen a perfect score yet. (And I hope I won't! After all, we're all human.) If you score in the eighteth percentile, that means you are more giving than 80 percent of folks out there; you are a high giver. If you score in the twentieth percentile, you are a low giver.

However, as you'll soon see, the scale can quickly reflect changes in your life. In just eight weeks of doing volunteer yard work for his family and neighbors, one teenager went from being a low to a moderate giver. If you find out where you are now and then take the scale again in three months, you may be pleased to see your own progress in certain ways of giving and in your overall score.

The Scale Is a Useful Mirror

Curious to see what it would reveal, I asked two famous givers to take the scale. I also asked a few teens to take the scale, carry out a self-designed program of giving two hours a week for eight weeks, and take the scale again, to see if their scores improved. I tested youth because they are at risk today, and research has shown that giving is highly protective for adolescents, reducing risky behaviors while increasing well-being and self-esteem.

Sir John Templeton, one of the most famed mutual fund managers of all time, whose generous grant enabled me to start the Institute, was the first to take the scale. Now ninety-four years old, Sir John has devoted the last twenty years of his life to funding research on spirituality, science, and human potential. I was fascinated by the particulars of his score. Not surprisingly, on a question like "I think it's better for me to try to leave this world better than when I found it," Sir John responded with "strongly agree." Yet, though he scored as a high giver, he is a self-made man who grew up in rural Tennessee and went to Yale University, and so he only slightly agreed with the statement "I would not be where I am in life if it were not for the support of my friends." He disagreed with the statement "I drop everything to care for people when they are feeling sad, in pain, or lonely." His investment strategy has focused on emerging markets— allowing poorer economies a chance to get on their feet. He does not overindulge even those close to him. After taking the scale, Sir John said to me, "As a philanthropist, I feel that love can mean helping people discover their own abilities, including thrift, responsibility, and character."

Millard Fuller is the world-famous founder of Habitat for Humanity, a nonprofit organization that builds affordable housing in partnership with families in need. Fuller gave away his considerable wealth when he was thirty years old. A few years later he founded Habitat, along with his wife, Linda. When asked in 1981 about the goal of Habitat for Humanity, Fuller answered without hesitation: "To eliminate poverty housing from the face of the earth. Get rid of shacks!" Currently Fuller heads the Fuller Center for Housing, continuing his quest to end poverty housing and homelessness. Fuller answered "strongly agree" on almost every question about giving. The one area he scored less strongly on was devotion to family. A humanitarian with a huge vision, he is devoted above all to helping the neediest; he responded with "slightly agree" to "I always go out of my way to help my family," and though he condones forgiveness in foreign policy, he admitted that he does not have an easy time forgiving a person who has hurt him.

My point here is that we are all human, even the great givers among us. The scale reflects our philosophies of life, our strengths, and our vulnerabilities.

The scale also reflects changes in our ability to give. Of the youth who participated in our informal summer "giving" program, several started out as high givers and remained high givers. Two others had significant increases in their score in just eight weeks. Brian, a high school student in

California, served as a math tutor to classmates who were struggling with the subject. Brian started out just above the fortieth percentile (a moderate giver) and jumped at eight weeks to a high score in the eightieth percentile (a high giver). In Brian's own words: "I found out how much I like doing this, so I've kept it up and am helping tutor every week for a few hours. I learned how to connect with these kids, and this gave me a sense of what I can do for the world. It's been good for me."

Another teen, Adam, spent his eight weeks helping with yard work for his family and neighbors. He went from a low to a moderate giver in that short time. Volunteering "kept me from wasting my time by playing video games," Adam says. "It was enjoyable and made me happier and gave me a sense of accomplishment, I guess. I continued to help out until the winter."

You may be wondering about me. Of course I took the scale, though as someone who originated it, I'm not sure I'll be dining out on my score as a high giver. (After all, you could say, "Didn't he already know the 'right' answers?") I scored highest on humor and courage. Scale aside, my biggest flaw, as somebody who grew up in New York, is impatience—especially with those in my community. Despite having spent many years in the slower-paced Midwest, I can still race from point A to point B and seem too "busy" to stop and show kindness to individuals in my path, like waiters, cashiers, or the lady who cuts deli meat at the supermarket. I've thought about this small but important way of love a lot since starting IRUL, and I've consciously worked on improving. This morning I got up early and wrote an e-mail to my daughter. Our family was still celebrating her new job. But then, coming in to work, I met a woman outside who was crying because she'd just heard she was *losing* her job. I listened to her story and offered to try to help her find a new job. Two job stories, but one moment I was celebrating with a family member, and another moment: I was offering listening and compassion to a stranger.

Human needs are complicated, and you will find no shortage of opportunities to give. If you become convinced, as I am, of the power of generous behavior to benefit the giver, may you go forward and meet those opportunities. In the giving, you will reap generous rewards.

Three

The Way of Celebration:
Turn Gratitude into Action

My work has filled me with a joy that I can never put into words. When I try to talk about the richness of my life, I'm often moved to tears."

Those are the words of Richard Fratianne, M.D., known to friends and patients as "Dr. Frat," a colleague of mine at Case Western Reserve University and director emeritus of the Comprehensive Burn Care Center at MetroHealth Medical Center in Cleveland. Dr. Frat is in his seventies now and semiretired. When he started the burn unit, it was a single bed draped with a plastic covering in the intensive care unit. Today it's a regional burn center for all of northeast Ohio.

"I was successful in treating patients with life-threatening, serious burns," says Dr. Fratianne. "But they'd leave the hospital badly scarred and go on to live their life in the shadows, with big floppy hats and long sleeves. I couldn't send my patients back into the world without returning a sense of dignity and wholeness to their lives." To do that Dr. Frat literally "loved" his patients back to life, assembling a team of caring doctors, nurses, psychotherapists, and social workers, all of whose aim was to help the patient heal both body and soul. "A spirit of transforming love came to life in our burn unit. The burn victims began to experience gratitude for life once again. They began to celebrate themselves."

"No other work could have brought me so much fulfillment," he says, and tells the story of Lucy, who was four years old when she was nearly burned to death in a fire. She needed twelve surgeries, prosthetic legs, and months of therapy at the Comprehensive Burn Care Center. "Lucy," says Fratianne, "always celebrates life. She comes to our burn camp every year and participates in everything, rides horses, plays tug-of-war, swims like a fish, and if you look at her with pity she gives you a big smile as if to say, 'I'm happy, I'm good, I'm okay, and glad to be alive.' Tomorrow is promised to no one. Every day is precious. This is what my work with burn patients has taught me."

Every day is precious. How shall we celebrate? Celebration is, quite simply, the way we express gratitude. It's gratitude in action. In the words of the psychologist Abraham Maslow, we "appreciate again and again, freshly and naively, the basic goods of life with awe, pleasure, wonder, and even ecstasy." Here are what I consider fundamental truths about celebration and its power:

Celebration wells up from a state of gratitude, a state that has been intensively studied for its health benefits. Within just a few weeks of keeping daily gratitude journals, for instance, individuals across all walks of life, even the chronically ill, find themselves happier, more optimistic, sleeping better, and feeling more connected to others. In addition, new research from the Institute shows that gratitude can help us through extremely difficult situations, such as caring for a loved one who has Alzheimer's. It can also inspire us to profound giving—such as donating organs to save the lives of strangers—according to a new study out from IRUL.

Celebration creates a circle of love. When we rejoice in the presence of others, they feel uplifted. Research has shown that one act of gratitude encourages another, creating a circle of reciprocal love.

Celebration moves us from fear to faith. Studies show that the most grateful individuals have often been through difficult and challenging experiences. Individuals who have overcome adversity in youth are more optimistic and grateful than the average person. Research with hurricane survivors suggests that feeling grateful is one of the predominant emotions people feel in the aftermath of a natural disaster. Interviewing thirteen parents who lived in south Florida at the time of Hurricane Andrew (1992), the researchers discovered that one of their strongest emotions was an overwhelming sense of gratitude for what they had *not* lost. The homes of five of these families had been destroyed, but none of them had lost a loved one.

Celebration shifts us from tired to inspired. "We need to remind ourselves of how good life *really* is," says the psychologist Philip Watkins of Eastern Washington University. Recent research shows that emotions work at lightning speed and often bypass reasoning, activating more ancient parts of the "emotional" brain. By cultivating gratitude, we encourage positive feelings that are almost instantaneous. They are more powerful, in their own way, than positive thoughts.

How Celebration Heals

The poet William Blake wrote:

> *To see a world in a grain of sand*
> *And a heaven in a wild flower,*
> *Hold infinity in the palm of your hand*
> *And eternity in an hour.*

When I read those lines, I think back to the times in my own life when an hour contained all eternity—when I first fell in love with my wife Mitsuko, a dancer and flutist, or the night before I graduated from St. Paul's School, when I went to the chapel alone to meditate. I remember standing before a stupendous bouquet of roses of every hue, flowers that spilled upwards like a living fountain. They had already been arranged for the next day's ceremony. Then I walked into the woods, a chapel carved by nature. I looked up at the Milky Way. "The vastness of the heavens stretches my imagination—stuck on this carousel my little eye can catch one-million-year-old light," wrote the physicist Richard Feynman. And so it was with me that evening. I had already decided that somehow, some way, I would devote my life to the study of love.

We already know a good deal about gratitude because of a few pioneering researchers studying this state.

Robert Emmons of the University of California at Davis, a pioneer in the field of gratitude research and an editor, along with the colleague Michael McCullough, of the Oxford University Press book *The Psychology of Gratitude*, calls gratitude the "forgotten factor" in happiness research. "Religion and philosophy have long embraced gratitude as an indispensable component of health, wholeness, and well-being," says Emmons, "But science has come a bit late to the concept." In fact, gratitude is strongly linked to emotional and physical health. Let's take a brief look at this research.

Gratitude has profound health effects. According to a recent study that Bob did for IRUL on organ donations, the more gratitude a recipient of an organ feels, the faster that person's recovery. The study questioned both organ donors and recipients about their feelings about this "gift of life." There were seventy-four transplant recipients of either a heart, liver, lung, kidney, or pancreas. Those recipients who expressed gratitude—directly or indirectly in journals—felt physically better and functioned at a higher level than those who did not. I consider this big news for the clinical setting, not only for organ recipients but for anybody undergoing a life-saving procedure. Health care could really benefit from more knowledge of the power of gratitude in healing. Bob is studying both donors and recipients to try to learn more about what he calls "transpersonal" spirituality, which is a kind of big-picture gratitude for the universe.

Gratitude begets joy. A 1998 Gallup survey of American teenagers and adults found that 95 percent of respondents felt at least somewhat happy when expressing gratitude, and over half felt extremely happy. People who see themselves as grateful—to others as well as to creation in general—are healthier, more energetic and optimistic, more empathic, and less vulnerable to clinical depression. They make more progress toward important personal goals. This is true even when scientists factor out other contributors like age, health, and income. Grateful people tend to be less materialistic and thus more easily satisfied with what life brings them.

Just five minutes of gratitude can shift the nervous system toward a calm state. A study in 1995 by Dr. Rollin McCraty, director of research for the Institute of Heart Math in Boulder Creek, California, has found that states of appreciation are correlated with a physiological state known as resonance (or parasympathetic dominance)—where heart, breathing, blood pressure, as well as brain rhythm and even the electrical potential of the skin are synchronized. Resonance also emerges during deep relaxation and sleep. In a state of resonance, says McCraty, the entire body is in a more efficient energy state. When we are feeling stressful emotions such as anger, frustration, or anxiety, our heart rhythms become more erratic. When we are in states of appreciation, gratitude, love, and compassion, heart rhythms are coherent and ordered—calming our neurological and endocrine systems.

McCraty measured thirty individuals' brain activity both before and during states when they were actively focusing on appreciation. He found that heart rhythm and alpha coherence significantly increases during periods of appreciation. In another fascinating study, a fifteen-minute focus on appreciation resulted in an immediate and significant increase in levels of an immune antibody called secretory IgA. Secretory IgA is one of the body's primary defenses against invading microbes. After a month of a daily, fifteen-minute practice of appreciation, thirty individuals had a 100 percent increase in a potent beneficial hormone called dehydroepiandrosterone (DHEA), as well as a corresponding 30 percent reduction in the stress hormone cortisol.

Gratitude is correlated with positive social behavior and health. If you feel grateful, you are more likely to nurture, care for, and contribute to the welfare of others. You will be more empathic, forgiving, and helpful. In a study by Jo Ann Tsang sponsored by IRUL, gratitude improved the lives of caregivers—those who were leading very stressed lives by reaching out unselfishly to help loved ones who were ill. Specifically studying Alzheimer's' patients and their caregivers, Tsang found that just writing about gratitude has a significant impact on caregivers' health.

Gratitude can reverberate down the years. In one study of women at midlife, those who when young were the recipients of mentoring by older adults were much more likely to be mentors themselves nearly two decades later—doing others the favor that had long ago been done them. As an old Russian proverb says, "Gratefulness waters old friendships and makes new ones sprout."

One Researcher's Insights

A feeling of deep appreciation for life is born of experience—including the experience of truly looking deeply into others' lives and knowing the immensity of their challenges and triumphs. Thus, to celebrate we must connect deeply with others. If we are lucky enough to do that, we may cultivate joy that is forged from a familiarity with life in its broadest scope. "As a clinical psychologist," says Paul Wink of Wellesley College, "I am always interested in how we are able to truly appreciate another—which requires shedding narcissism and self-centeredness. None of us can get outside of our own body or mind, so we're condemned to understand life through the prism of our own self."

Paul, who at age fifty-two is tall and slender with brown hair and eyes, grew up in communist Poland, and because his father was a diplomat, he traveled through Indonesia, Ethiopia, Pakistan, and Australia. When the Institute commissioned his longitudinal study on giving and health, he got the opportunity to travel around the country and conduct in-depth interviews with ninety individuals who had already been studied and interviewed periodically for their entire lives under the auspices of the Institute of Human Development. By the time Paul met up with these individuals, they were in their sixties and seventies. He met many types of people from many different walks of life and found that each life had its own moments of adversity and heroism. The interviews, which often lasted up to five hours, led to a deep sense of gratitude that Paul says he now feels daily.

"Interviewing all these individuals allowed me to see and take delight in the diversity of the human experience," says Paul. "It is almost like doing missionary work somewhere in a Third World country where you come into contact with people who are in many ways so different—and yet you share humanity in common. When you hear a person's entire life story, you really appreciate the human spirit. All of these people were willing to reveal their story to a stranger again and again, which is a gift. I think they believed their participation might be beneficial to generations to come, because of what we might find. I also feel deep gratitude for the generations of researchers who—like Moses—were never destined to see the promised land. They died before the study could be brought to its completion. After these interviews, I feel as if I inherited many nieces and nephews. I know what these people talked about when they were fourteen and sixteen and eighteen. It is like actively participating in 184 different novels."

In particular, Paul recalls one woman whose second marriage was very happy and who was very close to her children. She had nonetheless suffered hard knocks when her first husband walked out on her and left her with nothing, not even a house. "I was absolutely just stripped of everything," she recalled. "And my brother had died tragically, and then my mother died, and a child of mine had a concussion and was in the hospital. And then came the divorce. But you know, the beautiful part was that I discovered that nobody can take God from you. What a beautiful thing. Ultimately I took the tragedies as a real plus, rather than a minus."

Celebration is a quality to be woven into life itself, through the highs and lows. It is often easy, simple, and natural. I received this lovely example of celebration in an e-mail letter from a woman who subscribes to the Institute's newsletter: "One Sunday, on the way home from an especially inspiring church service, I was engrossed in thinking about Love, and how it can be best described as an overwhelming embrace of all of life. As I pulled out of the parking garage on my way home, the parking lot attendant and I greeted one another. As we were talking I noticed how brilliantly his blue shirt blazed against his darkly mellow Indian skin. I did not hesitate to compliment him on the color of his shirt, and how good it looked on him. You should have seen his reaction to a simple compliment! He was truly flattered and uplifted.

"Continuing on, I stopped at our local farmers' market to buy some figs. An older gentleman next to me was asking the clerk if he could purchase only two figs, rather than an entire basket. While the salesperson was away asking permission from her boss, I simply gave the man two figs from my own basket. His reaction of surprise and pleasure made my day."

This young woman wasn't just offering a compliment or a few figs. She was communicating, through these simple acts, a basic appreciation for another human being. The inspiring church service had shifted her to a state of love where she wanted to celebrate and embrace others. There was no need to search for a special way to do it—the events arose naturally as she drove home that spring Sunday. Celebration flows naturally out of a happy heart.

Lessons from the Frontiers of Research

Celebration is gratitude with a kind of added zing, an ebullience and joy. And so the following insights about gratitude are drawn from the compelling scientific literature with an emphasis on joy and action. We can celebrate in small and big ways, in tiny daily acts as well as in lifelong commitments.

LESSON ONE: SAVOR THE DAY

"The ability to notice, appreciate, and savor life is a crucial determinant of well-being." says Robert Emmons. "And this appreciation can be practiced and cultivated." According to Emmons, we often unwittingly climb onto a "hedonic treadmill"—where we rapidly adapt to good things and begin to take them for granted. Two ancient brain regions—the amygdala and the nucleus accumbens—modulate our anticipation of pleasure and reward, and these centers inevitably cause us to crave *new* pleasure. Consciously focusing on gratitude may help us subvert our own insatiability. So, celebrate—savor the day, the here and now. Here's how:

❧ *Keep a journal.* My personal journal *is* a place: the river, towering trees, and waterfalls in the town of Chagrin Falls, outside Shaker Heights, Ohio, where I live. The charming and mysterious name of the town may come from the Indian word *shagrin*, which means "clear water." For me, Chagrin Falls is precisely that: the place to clear my mind and heart and appreciate life. It is my living journal. I go there to walk by the river and remind myself how lucky I am. As Albert Schweitzer said, "There is within each of us . . . an inner exaltation, which lifts us above dependence upon the gifts of events for our joy." And the philosopher Emile Rousseau recalled a childhood where every day was celebration: "I rose with the sun, and I was happy; I went to walk, and I was happy. . . . I worked in the garden, I gathered the fruits . . . and happiness followed me everywhere . . . it was all within myself; it could not leave me for an instant." Now *that's* a worthy entry in a celebration journal!

This approach is surprisingly powerful. As Emmons points out, just reflecting once a day on your blessings has an immediate impact on your well-being. In three separate studies of undergraduates, Emmons found that regularly focusing on one's blessings increases happiness. Self-guided daily gratitude exercises have a similar effect. Emmons says that he himself was surprised by the strength of his own research findings:

"There was a sustained and reliable increase in people's happiness after just a short time of keeping a gratitude journal," he says. "The idea that you could shift your set point of happiness by a minimal intervention, by just pausing once a day to focus on the things you're really grateful for, was astonishing. We saw as much as a 20 percent increase in positive mood. We even saw it in people with muscular dystrophy or post-polio syndrome, people who have functional limitations every day and are in pain and fatigued. We had them keep a gratitude journal for twenty-one days and found that this simple intervention resulted in greater amounts of high-energy positive moods, a greater sense of feeling connected to others, and better sleep duration and sleep quality."

Even more impressive is the fact that when Emmons went back to this last group six months later, over half said they were continuing to keep a gratitude journal even though the study was long since over. He says, "I suspect they will experience permanent shifts toward greater happiness."

"Gratitude is an approach to life that is available to everyone," says Emmons. "It's a universal human virtue." So keep a journal—a place where you conscioulsy take time to celebrate your life. This can take many forms, from a document stored on your desktop to a beautifully bound vellum diary, a stack of note cards, moments spent daily while on a train or bus, or any other format that suits your fancy. It's important to daily renew your joy and to make the familiar new again.

❧ *Set celebration within ritual.* Rituals are as ancient as we are, and for a good reason. They enshrine and structure meaning. A celebration can be as simple as saying grace, in whatever form grace takes in your world, whether a prayer, a Tibetan mantra, or lines from your favorite poet. Visit a church or other house of worship where chanting, singing, organ music, gospel choirs, or other celebrations through sound take place, and participate. Let the music enter the marrow of your being. Take time each day to read from books of traditional wisdom—pause for a paragraph or a page a day. I often return to the philosophical works of those great thinkers on love who shaped my thinking many years ago: Pitirim Sorokin, founder of the Department of Sociology at Harvard in 1931, who wrote *The Ways and Power of Love* in the twilight of his career. Sorokin emigrated from Russia after being jailed by both the tsar and later Lenin, who sentenced him to death; having experienced the dark side of human nature, Sorokin was so appalled by the bombing of Hiroshima that he founded Harvard's Center for Creative Altruism. He was the first social scientist to suggest that creative works need to be in service of a shared humanity, rather than put to destructive purposes (such as inventing an atomic bomb). It inspires me to reread Sorokin and even recite out loud some of his insights. Here's a favorite: "Love beautifies the whole universe."

LESSON TWO: CELEBRATE OTHER LIVES

By what are we truly blessed? By connection to others. A *Time* magazine poll of over one thousand Americans found that the first four major sources of happiness were all about others:

- For 77 percent, their children were the major source of happiness.
- Friendships were a source of happiness for 76 percent.
- Contributing to the lives of others made 75 percent happy.
- Their relationship with their partner was a major source for 73 percent.

Perhaps you can pause now to reflect on the richness of your connections to others, and not only those who surround you today. We're blessed by connection to those who are no longer with us but stay with us in time and memory. I like to meditate on great figures of history who have shaped my life indirectly—a few favorites are Abraham Lincoln and Thomas Edison. I especially like Lincoln's sense of humor. He wrote this about himself when he was a teen: "Abraham Lincoln/His hand and pen/He will be good but/God knows when." Needless to say, Lincoln was more than good—he is beloved as one of the great American presidents.

Here are a few ways to start celebrating others:

❧ *When you help, let others know it's sincere.* In a very interesting study, Jo Ann Tsang found that people feel significantly more grateful for help when they know the other person has benevolent intentions toward them. They also feel more connected. "It was the philosopher Seneca who said that whenever we feel grateful to somebody we enter into a friendship with them," says Tsang. So take care to let others know you care and that love, not just duty, moves you.

❧ *Celebrate now.* I recently spoke with the psychologist Dale Ironson, Ph.D., who, with his sister, the psychiatrist and psychologist Gail Ironson M.D. Ph.D., of the University of Miami, is studying spiritual transformation in AIDS patients. I asked him what he wanted to celebrate at that very moment, and he did not hesitate to reel off a list: "My nice conversation with you. My many friends, the beautiful day, the delicious food I eat when people in other places are starving, and the incredible age I'm living in with all the fantastic discoveries going on." Keep your celebration list or journal easily available and add to it when you have the time and inclination.

❧ *Make a celebration visit.* This exercise is inspired by one developed by the positive psychologist Martin Seligman, former president of the American Psychological Association and author of the best-seller *Learned Optimism*. Seligman suggests that making a "gratitude visit" will almost instantly boost happiness. Simply writing out a thank-you letter to anyone to whom you feel genuine gratitude (a teacher, friend, parent, or child) and then visiting that person and reading the letter has a remarkable effect, according to Seligman. Even a month later you are measurably happier. Adapting that idea, I suggest a celebration visit. Write out a letter that celebrates the qualities or traits of someone close to you. Describe that person's courage, constancy, loyalty, kindness, intelligence, wit, persistence, caring—all of us have many qualities worth celebrating. Then set aside a special time to read that person your letter and not only thank them but truly celebrate with them the miracle of their life.

You can also make a celebration visit to strangers. "When I began to focus on kindness and gratitude, I went from being a sort of grouchy single woman to being very joyful with lots of friends," says Gail Grant, founder of the Bright Lights program in Palo Alto, California. Bright Lights is a volunteer program in which children under age twelve help senior citizens at a nursing home. "The kids love it," says Grant. "One of the older girls told me that Bright Lights taught her how to help others and to feel good about herself. The children can see they're making a difference to the seniors. They can see the smiles and the light in their eyes." That moment of communion is actually one of celebration, where old and young join together. "Gandhi said, 'Be the change you wish to see,' " says Grant. "Helping others is a critical exercise for the heart. You need to help those who aren't part of your inner circle, and it's good for you as well as the other person."

❧ *Remember those who celebrated you.* In the same spirit, make a mental visit to those who have celebrated you. I keep a list of individuals who mentored or loved me deeply, and who have passed away, on the inside cover of my worn, treasured copy of *The Book of Common Prayer*, which I first got as a child. Right now there are seventeen names in my book. These are people who celebrated and believed in me, and inevitably they did so for others too. There is my classical guitar teacher, Leonid Bolotine, who always embraced me with such warmth; my lifelong philosopher friend Bob Leisey, who helped guide me in big life decisions; my mom, who simply and purely loved me. This list is a kind of celebration in itself, and you may want to glance at it and close your eyes and remember one of the people on it and the warmth and radiance you felt in that person's presence. This exercise is especially helpful when life is difficult—to remember how others have celebrated you.

LESSON THREE: REFRAME YOUR LIFE, REPAIR YOUR MOOD

You can turn to gratitude and celebration during tough times. You don't have to be a "victim" to your present circumstances. Primo Levi writes of this in his book *If This Is a Man*, in which he describes life in the Nazi death camps: "It is lucky that it is not windy today. Strange how, in some way, one always has the impression of being fortunate, how some chance happening, perhaps infinitesimal, stops us crossing the threshold of despair and allows us to live. It is raining, but it is not windy. Or else, it is raining and is also windy: but you know that this evening, it is your turn for the supplement of soup." There is an undertone of terrible irony in those beautiful sentences, and yet they are also a recognition of the resilience of the human spirit and our ability to appreciate even the meanest moments of existence.

Gratitude and celebration offer help. In one study conducted by Philip Watkins and his colleagues, gratitude was strongly linked to a form of emotional intelligence known as mood-repair. "Gratitude may give one a helpful perspective on life that assists in mood-repair following a stressful event," Watkins concluded. Further fascinating evidence of gratitude's power comes from a 2001 study of trauma survivors by the psychologist Russell Kolts of Eastern Washington University. Those who scored high on gratitude had significantly lower symptoms of post-traumatic stress disorder.

In addition, as I mentioned earlier, appreciation offers us the same kind of whole-body resonance we experience in deep relaxation and sleep. In this state, our heart rhythms are coherent and our nervous system is calm. When you're feeling stressed, irritable, or simply blue, try these simple ways of celebrating and shifting your state:

❈ *Go to nature.* You will notice that often in this book I suggest going to nature. It works for me! Sometimes the ancient, primal forms of celebration are the most profound. And the way humans have always celebrated life is to commune with nature. Pause to hear the birds in the tree on the street corner, hike or camp with friends and family, or plan a special ritual celebration in nature, complete with prayers, dancing, drumming, and music. You can even hug a tree, like the hippies did in the 1960s. As the great naturalist John Muir said, "Climb the mountains and get their good tidings./Nature's peace will flow into you as sunshine flows into trees./The winds will blow their own freshness into you . . . /while cares will drop off like autumn leaves." Or, as the poet Walt Whitman said in celebrating a blade of grass: "I believe a leaf of grass is no less than the journey-work of the stars."

❧   *Enjoy the small steps.* As I was writing this chapter, I had a talk with my wonderful editor, Kris Puopolo. She mused about the fact that although she would like every book she acquires to become a best-seller, she has learned to shift her view to celebrate each step along the way. "There is usually a deeply satisfying 'aha!' moment I have when editing a book, when I realize exactly what it needs. There is the starred review, or the beautiful cover." Every project has its own special moments. Celebrate those.

❧   *Appreciate the big picture.* My co-author finds the easiest way for her to celebrate is to remind herself of her place in the universe. For instance, late on a spring day in New York, she says, tubeworms that look like flowers, with hemoglobin glowing bright, deep red at their tips, are swaying on the ocean floor. The moon is nearly full and visible like a pale chalk drawing in the April sky in the late afternoon. Apple trees are blossoming white in Riverside Park. Children are playing in the schoolyard outside her window. Somewhere across the world, a camel is kneeling in the desert heat. Everywhere across the world mothers are nursing their newborns. Schools of fish are slithering past coral at the Great Barrier Reef. The Niagara is pouring a cataract of 150,000 gallons of water per second down nearly 200 feet of dolostone and shale rock, and across the Atlantic a tourist in France is standing before the Mona Lisa at the Louvre, contemplating that mysterious, eternal smile. After a few moments of such contemplation, even on the most stressful day, she concludes that the world is nothing short of miraculous.

Your Celebration Score

It's time to answer the questions on the celebration section of your Love and Longevity Scale. We have divided responses into percentiles, or fifths. These are general guidelines; you may score right near the cutoff between percentiles, so please keep this in mind and use the scale as a friendly tool. Remember:

There are two steps to determining your score on a scale. First, determine which items need to be "reverse-scored" (denoted with the ® symbol). For reverse-scored items, see the chart below for how to score.

If you score a …	… assign yourself a score for that item of:
1	6
2	5
3	4
4	3
5	2
6	1

The second step is to add the scores for individual items *After* the reverse-scored items have been reverse-scored. Take the quiz now, and take it again if you wish after you've finished this book and begun practicing celebration in your daily life.

Using the scale provided, please circle the one number that best reflects your opinion about whether or not each statement below describes you or experiences that you have had. There are no correct answers, so please respond as honestly as possible to each one.

1. I make a point of letting my family members know how much I appreciate them.

    1=strongly disagree   2=disagree   3=slightly disagree   4=slightly agree
    5=agree   6=strongly agree

2. My loved ones would say that I'm quick to thank them when they do something kind for me.

    1=strongly disagree   2=disagree   3=slightly disagree   4=slightly agree
    5=agree   6=strongly agree

3. I call and write my loved ones to thank them for things they have done for me.

    1=strongly disagree   2=disagree   3=slightly disagree   4=slightly agree
    5=agree   6=strongly agree

4. I feel uncomfortable saying "thank you" to my family members.[R]

    1=strongly disagree   2=disagree   3=slightly disagree   4=slightly agree
    5=agree   6=strongly agree

5. Because I have gotten where I am in life pretty much on my own, I don't think I owe my family anything.[R]

    1=strongly disagree   2=disagree   3=slightly disagree   4=slightly agree
    5=agree   6=strongly agree

6. I make it a point to let friends of mine know how much I appreciate them.

    1=strongly disagree   2=disagree   3=slightly disagree   4=slightly agree
    5=agree   6=strongly agree

7. I'm grateful for the things my friends have done for me.

    1=strongly disagree   2=disagree   3=slightly disagree   4=slightly agree
    5=agree   6=strongly agree

8. I would not be where I am in life if it were not for the support of
    my friends.
    1=strongly disagree   2=disagree   3=slightly disagree   4=slightly agree
    5=agree   6=strongly agree

9. When I think about the good things my friends have done for me,
    there doesn't seem to be a lot to be grateful for.[®]
    1=strongly disagree   2=disagree   3=slightly disagree   4=slightly agree
    5=agree   6=strongly agree

10. I feel like I owe my friends nothing when it comes to any of my
    accomplishments in life.[®]
    1=strongly disagree   2=disagree   3=slightly disagree   4=slightly agree
    5=agree   6=strongly agree

11. When I think about it, there are many people in my community
    to whom I should be grateful.
    1=strongly disagree   2=disagree   3=slightly disagree   4=slightly agree
    5=agree   6=strongly agree

12. I try to say "thanks" when I am helped by neighbors or colleagues
    I do not know very well.
    1=strongly disagree   2=disagree   3=slightly disagree   4=slightly agree
    5=agree   6=strongly agree

13. I see many things that people in my community do for which I am
    appreciative.
    1=strongly disagree   2=disagree   3=slightly disagree   4=slightly agree
    5=agree   6=strongly agree

14. The people who live in my community almost never do anything
    that I'm thankful for.[®]
    1=strongly disagree   2=disagree   3=slightly disagree   4=slightly agree
    5=agree   6=strongly agree

15. There's not much going on in my community to feel grateful about.[®]
    1=strongly disagree   2=disagree   3=slightly disagree   4=slightly agree
    5=agree   6=strongly agree

16. I appreciate the people who are working to make this world a better place.
    1=strongly disagree   2=disagree   3=slightly disagree   4=slightly agree
    5=agree   6=strongly agree

17. When I hear about someone who has helped others, I feel appreciative that such people exist in the world.
    1=strongly disagree   2=disagree   3=slightly disagree   4=slightly agree
    5=agree   6=strongly agree

18. I'm thankful to live in a world with people who care about the welfare of others.
    1=strongly disagree   2=disagree   3=slightly disagree   4=slightly agree
    5=agree   6=strongly agree

19. There is not a lot happening in the world to feel grateful about.[®]
    1=strongly disagree   2=disagree   3=slightly disagree   4=slightly agree
    5=agree   6=strongly agree

20. It's hard to feel thankful about good things that are happening in another part of the world.[®]
    1=strongly disagree   2=disagree   3=slightly disagree   4=slightly agree
    5=agree   6=strongly agree

YOUR CELEBRATION SCORE

High Giver (80th percentile)	105 or higher
Giver (60th percentile)	99–104
Moderate Giver (40th percentile)	94–98
Low Giver (20th percentile)	86–97

✿

Four

✿

The Way of Generativity:
Help Others Grow

Forty years ago, Jean Vanier, a philosopher and former Canadian navy commander, invited two disabled men to leave their institutions and live in his home. What began as an informal invitation from the heart has matured into the world-renowned International Federation of L'Arche Communities, a network of five thousand individuals in 126 communities and 31 countries. In these communities the healthy (called "assistants") and disabled live together. Vanier is a devout Catholic, but L'Arche communities welcome all faiths, including atheists. L'Arche—which stands for "the ark"—is a place where, says Vanier, "people, whatever their race, culture, abilities, or disabilities, can find a place and reveal their gifts to the world. You know as I do that we all begin in weakness and end in weakness. We are all broken in some way. The only answer to life is to love each other." As one L'Arche assistant says, "Here there is a very pure love you don't experience in other places in society. Here you learn that innocence is beautiful, that the disabled can be like living prayers."

L'Arche soared to fame after the priest Henri Nouwen, a best-selling author and former Yale and Harvard Divinity School professor, left academia to live at L'Arche and later wrote about his experience. He said that he felt more at home in L'Arche than he had ever felt at Harvard or Yale. The tall, patrician, and gentle Vanier still lives in a L'Arche community of one hundred individuals north of Paris. He has written books, travels the world lecturing and fund-raising, and has created a second foundation, called Faith and Light, for relatives of the disabled. Vanier says that community life with the disabled has taught him what it means to be human: "The whole pain of our world today is the pain of walls," says Vanier. "We've had enough of loneliness, independence, and competition."

I asked Jean to tell me one of his most unforgettable experiences with L'Arche. He replied: "I will never forget Eric, whom I met in a local psychiatric hospital, where he had been abandoned since he was four years old. He was then a blind, deaf young man of sixteen who was unable to walk or speak. I had never met anyone so filled with anguish. Even the nurses and helpers found him too difficult to be with. He came to our L'Arche community in 1978, and I had the privilege of living with him and a few others for a year: dressing him, bathing him, helping him to learn to feed himself. Little by little, he began to discover that he was loved and seen as a person, unique and important. He gradually grew more peaceful. During the evening prayer we had in our little home, he would rest quietly in our arms. And Eric taught us as well. He taught us to be gentle and attentive to his personal needs, he taught us what could help him grow in autonomy. He taught me, especially, to be more human and loving. By the time he died, he had changed, and I too had changed. Eric, above all, made me realize that each person is important no matter what their abilities, disabilities, religion, or culture."

Jean Vanier is a living emblem of the ability to nurture others, what scientists call *generativity*. The term was first coined by the psychologist Erik Erikson and has come to mean selfless giving to others, in particular to future generations. Generativity means nurturing others so that they are better able in turn to manifest their own gifts of love. I call this the way of the nurturer.

In Vanier's life, the single act of providing home and acceptance for two disabled men has now become a way of life for five thousand men and women around the world, many of them youthful volunteers. Just recently, Jean tells me, the mother of one of these young volunteers—a nineteen-year-old named Pauline—came to visit her daughter. "Pauline has only been at L'Arche four months," says Jean, "but her mother tells me her daughter has been transformed. She feels she is giving life to the people around her, that she is loved by them, and that new energies of caring and communion are flowing from her. This work has awakened her heart and what is deepest within her at such a young age: her capacity to give life, joy, and hope to other human beings."

Plant Another's Garden

Generativity is one of the most studied capacities of all time. In this chapter, you'll learn how nurturing others may be the best way to ensure a happy, successful life—from childhood onward. In fact, it turns out that this kind of giving may be a way to combat teen angst. In any case, whatever your age, you'll learn how to find ways to weave generativity into your days . . . and reap the benefits in heart, mind, and body.

The research on this unique human ability is substantial and fascinating. Generativity is best summed up in the words of the Harvard psychiatrist George Vaillant, whose decades-long study of Harvard men and their health distilled this trait as a key component to a fulfilled life. Says Vaillant: "Winter comes to every one of us sooner or later. And every spring, just like clockwork, the garden is reborn. By the time we die the real question is, 'What have we done to leave our garden better prepared for spring—someone else's spring?' "

In essence, generativity is the act of preparing another's garden for spring. It's power in the service of love. It's an act of giving that enables another person to manifest his or her own strengths and gifts through love. It can be as simple as listening and giving support to others—renewing their sense of self and hope. It can be as demanding as raising a child well, or mentoring a student in a difficult and challenging field.

This chapter looks at the startling good news on generativity. Some inspiring findings from the science include:

Generativity protects our mental and physical health across an entire life span. When we nurture others, we nurture ourselves. One of IRUL's most impressive new studies shows that teens who are generative in high school live significantly longer, happier lives than their less giving counterparts. Nurturing others when you're young becomes a lifestyle that is protective of mental and physical well-being for the next fifty years!

Four special pilot studies on teens and giving, sponsored by IRUL, highlight a gender divide in generativity and youth: boys show significant improvements in self-esteem and happiness when they are giving, while girls do not seem to show the same boost. However, if girls are *low* in giving, they suffer low self-esteem, depression, and anxiety. We really need to look hard at how we encourage and reward helping behavior in girls and boys, since it may be that girls are *expected* to be nurturers and are not given the same positive feedback for giving that boys are. These studies are only preliminary, but fascinating.

For older adults, studies show that generativity protects and improves psychological well-being—and delays mortality. Nurturing others helps those suffering from illness too: studies on multiple sclerosis sufferers and those living with HIV/AIDS found that when individuals reach out to help others in the same plight, they feel greater mental well-being and have fewer exacerbations of their illness.

Generativity is linked to leadership and high self-esteem.

Generativity gives us a feeling of power along with *love, rather than* instead of *love.*

Generativity Lasts a Lifetime

As we saw in the last chapter, of all the studies the Institute has funded, one of the most astonishing turns out to be the brainchild of Paul Wink of Wellesley College. Paul got lucky—he was able to mine very rich data from the lives of folks born as long ago as the 1920s. Wink inherited a study that began over sixty years ago and has followed individuals for their entire lives. He studied nearly two hundred individuals who had participated for a lifetime in this study, which was initiated at the University of California at Berkeley in the 1920s. This study was established by the Institute of Human Development to gather data about human development and originally included newborns and children age ten to twelve. Every decade these individuals were interviewed by professional clinicians about everything from family to work, health, leisure, volunteer activities, personal interests and social and political attitudes.

Paul found that generativity in *high school* predicts good physical and mental health in late adulthood, a time interval of over *fifty* years. As Paul sums it up: "This study was a gold mine, like Wagner's ring at the heart of the Niebelungs. I was really surprised by the strength of the findings. The connection for mental health is particularly strong, but the physical health results are also highly significant."

Longitudinal studies like this are richly detailed and give us an unprecedented picture of the power of giving. They truly allow us to see a life unfolding. And this one is particularly rich because 90 percent of the folks stayed in the study. Paul explains: "Clinicians had conducted such in-depth interviews that they had unwittingly gathered a great deal of information about altruism, generativity, and spirituality; they just hadn't analyzed it yet." With funding from the Institute, Paul and a colleague interviewed 180 of the original study participants. It took him three years as he crisscrossed the country and spent up to five hours with each individual. Here are some of the specifics that Paul discovered:

Generativity predicts that we will be successful. It has a positive impact that is not related to social class, IQ, or religiousness. However, teens who are highly generative tend to end up in a higher social class.

Generativity is linked to spirituality. Teens who are generative are moderately or highly religious by early adulthood.

Teens who are generative tend to already have warm family relations. A warm, close family probably models generativity for us when we are young—but those of us who adopt generative behavior on our own or in spite of family problems will also be protected. Even when Paul recomputed his analysis of the data so that family warmth would not be a factor, he found generativity to be a significant predictor of physical and psychological health.

Generative youth will have better health habits in middle age. They are more likely in middle age to have an adequate health plan, less likely to smoke, less likely to drink a lot, and more likely to have physical checkups.

Generativity is linked to social competence. Social competence is the gem at the heart of generativity and is strongly linked to physical and psychological health. Why is social competence a key? In order to give effectively to others, you need to be able to connect to them. This requires social skill, empathy, and self-esteem.

Paul does note a few caveats to this study: the participants, by virtue of the population that was chosen, grew up in San Francisco's East Bay in the 1920s and were mostly white and mainline Protestant, although they were evenly distributed among lower, middle, and upper classes financially. They also came from an era when civic responsibility was expected. Even so, says Paul, "the beauty of this study for me was that it forced me to see and take delight in the diversity of so many different human lives." For Paul, the take-home message of this study is that generativity should be encouraged in our youth and that, for all of us, "good deeds allow us to see the good in our own nature, to develop a certain confidence about ourselves that helps us through difficult times."

The generosity of one teenage girl was striking, says Paul. When asked what she would do if she were given $10,000, she answered that she would use the money to pay her family's medical bills. A teenage boy in the study voluntarily used his money from part-time jobs to help support his parents who were financially strapped. Later, as these individuals matured into adults, they demonstrated the same compassion. After one woman's brother-in-law was killed in a plane crash, she and her husband dissolved all of their savings to help his widow and five children. Even after she herself was divorced and struggling with many personal health problems, she inevitably had one or two of her nephews living with her. This same woman also worked as a teacher of severely troubled children and later in life dedicated herself to environmental causes; she and her second husband maintained a low-profit nature store. And finally, one member of the study, now retired, spent one evening a week with a neighbor suffering from dementia so that the man's wife could have an evening off.

Lessons from the Frontiers of Research

The new studies on generativity sponsored by IRUL, along with the potent and compelling literature on this trait, add up to some lovely insights about how to bring generativity into our lives. We can do this in small and big ways; in tiny daily acts as well as lifelong commitments.

LESSON ONE: BE A KEEPER OF MEANING

We gaze at the night sky and connect star to star, naming constellations and bringing them to life—Aries the ram, Virgo the virgin. We hear wind and rivers rushing and tell stories of nature spirits. Fifteen thousand years ago, we painted horses and mammoths galloping in herds on the walls of caves, working by torchlight—today visitors still marvel over these paintings. We are truly keepers of meaning in "a universe whose amazing spectacle is a moral end in itself," to quote Joseph Conrad.

In the classic book *Man's Search for Meaning*, the Nazi concentration camp survivor Viktor Frankl writes, "Being human always points, and is directed, to something, or someone, other than oneself—be it a meaning to fulfill or another human being to encounter. The more one forgets himself—by giving himself to a cause to serve or another person to love—the more human he is and the more he actualizes himself. . . . self-actualization is possible only as a side-effect of self-transcendence."

I'm from Long Island, and so I fished a lot when I was growing up. In a way, I find, we're like a school of fish deep in the ocean. Every once in a while a fish sees a glimmer of light at the surface of the water and leaps up toward it, and there it is between sea and sky, a whole new world revealed. There's a transcendent quality to our lives, and even though we live in various degrees of darkness, we can leap into light—into meaning.

When we are generative, we create meaning in others' lives. George

Vaillant of Harvard Medical School has discovered this while directing his remarkable, sixty-year investigation of the lives of Harvard men. Vaillant's book *Aging Well* takes an even wider scope, looking at three research projects that followed over eight hundred people from their adolescence through old age: the Harvard men (which began in 1921), inner-city non-delinquent males (1930), and the Terman Women study of gifted females (1911), which was launched by the psychologist Lewis Terman to study intellectually gifted individuals.

Vaillant's discovery: generativity blends the capacities to love and to lead. At first, says Vaillant, generativity manifests as caring for one or a few younger persons in a direct way—such as mentorship or parenthood. Later, generativity expands so that the individual emerges as a keeper of meaning—playing a role in the larger community as a guide to cultural values and traditions. And though we may think of generative folks as self-sacrificing volunteers, it turns out that most successful CEOs are powerfully generative, inspiring leaders. One man in Vaillant's study put it this way: "From twenty to thirty I learned how to get along with my wife. From thirty to forty I learned how to be a success in my job, and at forty to fifty I worried less about myself and more about the children." He went on to spend the rest of his life as the dean of a small college. For him, says Vaillant, there was little distinction between his generativity and his success at loving relationships.

Generativity is available to anybody: one inner-city man in Vaillant's study named Bill grew up poor, lost his mother when he was sixteen, and had a father on disability. Bill's IQ was only about 82. His early life certainly did not look like a model for generativity, yet he married well and happily, worked as a carpenter for the Massachusetts Department of Public Works, and became a union steward who was highly respected by senior management, as well as an attentive dad who liked to take his sons fishing. He described his wife as "everything you want in a woman," and in an interview his wife said, "Bill is my best friend." Together they donated time to a candidate for mayor, and Bill was active in an umbrella organization for charitable clubs in Boston. When Bill spoke of his life, he often said how grateful he was to those who'd helped him—a common finding among generative folks. They tend to feel gratitude for what they have rather than resentment at the challenges they've faced.

Nurturing others brings meaning and a kind of benevolent power to our lives. Columbia University psychologist Eva Midlarsky, author with Eva Kahana of *Altruism in Later Life*, suggests five reasons:

1. We gain a greater sense of the meaning of our life.
2. We can cope with our own stress by shifting our focus to others.
3. We feel socially integrated and connected.
4. We feel more competent and effective.
5. Nurturing others may lead to a more active lifestyle.

There's also the simple fact that helping others makes us feel good: "When you open your heart to other people and care about them, it changes the way you look at the world and you're happier," says the behavioral scientist Carolyn Schwartz, who studied over two thousand Presbyterians and found that improved mental health was more closely linked to giving help than receiving it. "This was a robust finding," says Schwartz, whose study was published in *Psychosomatic Medicine* in 2003. "Giving had a really substantial mental health benefit."

Providing meaning is one powerful way that generativity is likely to buffer our health. Midlarsky and Kahana interviewed eighty-five individuals who had rescued one or more Jews during the Holocaust and another seventy-three bystanders who had lived in Nazi-occupied Europe but did not participate in the rescue of any Jews. The rescuers scored significantly higher than the bystanders on social responsibility, empathy, risk-taking, and autonomy. Rescuers also reported *more* satisfaction with life and higher levels of joy in family and friendships—even though the rescuers were not healthier or wealthier than the bystanders. The rescuers were likely to feel a deep inner contentment with their lives because they had lived life in accord with their values.

So how do you bring meaning to the lives of others? Here are some simple exercises you can begin with right now.

❧ *Write down your life goals and passions.* When you review them, look to see whether at least two or three are purely generative (such as raising happy, healthy kids, mentoring colleagues at work, or being active in helping activities as a volunteer). If there are no generative activities high on your list, think of a few that would appeal to you and add them.

❧ *Learn how to save somebody's life.* Take a course in CPR, learn the Heimlich maneuver, or take training as a paramedic or a lifeguard. There is no more powerful act than snatching someone from the jaws of death! In Elizabeth Midlarsky and Eva Kahana's 1994 study of folks paying for a CPR course, several commented that "any amount of money" was worth learning how to help people in life-and-death emergencies.

❧ *Use your skills to empower others.* Become a Big Brother or Sister to an underprivileged child. Teach immigrants to read or speak English. Volunteer for a help hotline of any kind.

❧ *Start where you are, at this moment.* Whatever you are doing, whether in school, at home or work, think about what you might do for the person who is closest to you, physically or emotionally. That could be your colleague, a stranger on the bus, or a family member. Offer a smile and a warm comment to a stranger. Help a colleague refine her skill at a task. Give a compliment to a family member about something essential to his being ("I was thinking about how good a listener you are," or, "I was just appreciating how skilled you are at juggling all your responsibilities").

LESSON TWO: VOLUNTEER

A truly remarkable study emerged from England in 2004 from researchers at the University of Essex: they found that neighborhoods with the highest levels of volunteerism had less crime, better schools, and happier, healthier residents. This was true of every place studied, from the inner city to the rural village. The researchers looked at 101 localities, mailing questionnaires to nine thousand individuals and interviewing three thousand in depth.

According to Doug Oman of the University of California at Berkeley, "Volunteering is associated with substantial reductions in mortality." Volunteers not only live longer but are healthier, says Oman. One thirty-year study of 427 women in upstate New York who were both wives and mothers found that those who did any kind of volunteering had better physical functioning thirty years later. Another 2003 study of over 1,500 adults from 1986 to 1994 found that volunteering predicted significantly less functional disability. A very important point highlighted in studies both here and in Europe, says Oman, is that folks who also have other social connections and support benefit the most from volunteering. "No wonder," says Oman, "that altruism and love have been celebrated down the ages."

Here are some creative ways you can volunteer:

❧ *Create a network of giving.* Find one person you know who seems a bit unhappy or isolated, and invite him or her to come with you and help somebody else in a bit of trouble. Participate together in a helping activity. Not only will you be giving to others, but you will help this person light up his or her own heart.

❧ *Give what you need.* I've discovered a beautiful paradox: giving others what you yourself need can be potent medicine for your own life. Giving is nondualistic—there is no contradiction between being generous and receiving benefits and pleasure from that generosity. Giving *is* receiving. In particular, giving someone what you yourself are longing for brings unexpected rewards, among them a powerful feeling of connection with others like yourself.

Some intriguing studies show that even serious physical illnesses can be affected when one helps others suffering the same condition. In a highly publicized two-year study by Carolyn Schwartz, published in the journal *Social Science and Medicine*, 132 patients who were ill with multiple sclerosis were offered either eight weekly meetings in which they were taught coping skills or monthly phone calls in which someone else with MS listened and gave them support. The surprise finding in the study turned out to be the five MS sufferers who were trained by Schwartz to offer compassionate listening and support over the phone. "I met with these five people monthly," recalls Schwartz. "By the end of two years, this group of five people were very good at listening compassionately to others."

When Schwartz applied scientifically rigorous data analysis to the total group of 137, she found that *giving* support improved health more than receiving it. Those five MS sufferers felt a dramatic change in how they viewed themselves and life. Depression, self-confidence, and self-esteem improved markedly among these givers. Love, in the form of generativity, was vitalizing for the spirit. "These people had undergone a spiritual transformation," says Schwartz, "that gave them a refreshed view of who they were."

Similarly impressive findings come from Gale Ironson of the University of Miami, who studied seventy-nine long-term survivors of AIDS—folks who had survived more than twice as long as expected after getting their first serious AIDS symptom. The survivor group was significantly more likely to have volunteered—especially in helping others with HIV. These volunteers suffered less depression, anxiety, and perceived stress. In a second study, Ironson found similar, astonishing results: she followed 177 individuals diagnosed with HIV who had never had a serious, AIDS-defining symptom. She monitored their viral loads and immune function along with their emotional and physical well-being. Helping care for others and scoring high on measures of altruism significantly slowed increases in their viral loads over the next two years. Ironson concludes: "Altruism is such a potentially powerful positive force that considerable effort should be directed at understanding it better."

These studies are small but extremely important, because they help answer the perennial question: which came first, the generosity or the well-being? Here we have people who were already ill, and yet giving bolstered their emotional and physical well-being. This is a very provocative/finding. We can see it in the story of Vic Leanza, a blind man whose life changed when he learned to sail.

A visually impaired student at the University of Notre Dame, Leanza was walking by one of the two campus lakes when a small, muscle-bound man in a swimsuit noticed him and suggested they meet over by the boathouse. The man, who turned out to be a priest in charge of weight-lifting at the student athletic center, unlocked the doors at the top of a ramp leading down to the boathouse, and together they carried a boat into the water. "That priest taught me how to sail. I didn't steer the boat, of course, but I handled the lines, and it was a big thrill to be on an intercollegiate team with my disability. He saw an ability in me that I didn't yet see in myself."

If that is not the essence of generativity, what is? But generativity rarely stops at the receiver, for the receiver—expanded by the gift of love from another—wants to pass that gift on, and that's what Vic Leanza did. He soon married, and even though he only had 10 percent vision at that point, he went on sailing, in spite of several surgeries for corneal transplants that failed. "I was totally blind by the time I was in my early thirties," says Vic, "and I was still working on my doctorate in psychology. It took me ten years to get it, because of all the surgeries and the fact that I was also work-ing. But I kept at it and built a private practice, and I've gotten many refer-rals for folks with disabilities." At the same time, Leanza bought sailboats and began teaching sighted friends, as well as his two children, to sail. He became commodore of the Cleveland Sight Center Sailing Program, which has two sailboats and eighty participants, half of them sighted and half vi-sually imparied. "Two teams go out each evening during the week from May through October," says Leanza, "and the sighted gain as much as the blind folks. I named one of the boats *Nexus*, which is Latin for 'connection between people.' Onboard a sailboat you're having a nexus experience, you're all working together, and within a few weeks everybody is learning about how you can sail without sight. We have people come in their six-ties, seventies, even eighties, who are losing their vision and have never sailed before, and they learn what a knot is and a nautical mile and a jib and forestay, and they get excited and ask questions and want to learn more. Sighted people will report over and over that *they* learn from the blind. They might say, 'Barbara just puts me to shame because I complain that my cell-phone battery went out and Barbara is steering the darn sail-boat and she's blind and has a full-time job and two kids.' Or a blind person will say, 'I hear a seagull over there at six o'clock to the boat,' and the sighted crew will look back, and there's a seagull, and they marvel at what they didn't even notice!" In the end, says Leanza, "I give something with-out losing anything. That's what teaching is all about."

Take a moment now to ask yourself, "What in life do I desire?" A greater sense of play or whimsy? To improve skills in a certain area at work? A vacation day? A wonderful home-cooked meal? A card from someone you love letting you know they appreciate you? A surprise gift? Whatever it is that you'd like to receive, try giving it. You'll be surprised at how much joy it brings, and of course, if you regularly give what you wish for, you're likely to be the recipient of others' generosity in turn.

❧   *Start small, grow big.* It began with a $4.99 buffet lunch in March 2002. Cass Forkin, founder and executive director of the Twilight Wish Foundation, was eating in a diner with her daughter and noticed a group of elderly women counting out change to pay for their lunch. On a whim, she called the wait-ress over, gave her a twenty-dollar bill, and said, "Tell them that their lunch is paid for." "It seemed like a very small thing to do," recalls Forkin, "but one of the women came over and hugged me with great emotion and said, 'I didn't know there were people like you in the world anymore.'"

A few years later, inspired by that afternoon, Forkin—who has an MBA in health care administration—started the Twilight Wish Foundation, a nonprofit charitable organization that gives the elderly gifts they cannot afford themselves. It may be as simple as a baseball game, a special wheelchair, a new blanket, a balloon ride, or a tombstone for a relative. In fact, the first wish her foundation granted was a tombstone for the late son of an eighty-two-year-old woman, Margaret, in a nursing home. "It took about two months because it was winter, and the stone had to be made and set. When the time came, we threw a big party and brought Margaret from the nursing home with all of her friends, family, her Baptist preacher, and folks from the Twilight Wish Foundation. Then we went to eat a big Italian meal, where she had two pieces of cheesecake." Since that time the Twilight Wish Foundation has granted many thousands of wishes and now has nearly seven hundred individuals in every single state who want to set up chapters. "We sent a man with only six weeks to live on a barge down the Mississippi," says Forkin. "We brought a couple in their nineties, both in a nursing home, to an outdoor market they always used to go to, and the husband, Raymond, got to order chicken pot pie one last time. A hundred-year-old lady got to ride a Harley on her birthday. My goal is to make people happy, and I've found it's never too late to make a difference. And they'll say things to me like, 'This is the highlight of my life. This is the best gift I've ever received. It's like Christmas.'" For Forkin, "the face of a senior citizen when they're receiving their gift is precious. And in the end, it isn't really about the wish. It's about the recognition. It's their realization that you care and that they matter."

And it all began with a lunch that cost less than twenty bucks. I don't think we stop to think that a person's entire perspective can be shifted and literally lifted into joy by a tiny act of giving. When I remind myself to focus on small acts of generosity, I always marvel at the effect—how even offering an especially warm, tender smile to a neighbor or stranger can momentarily buoy them up. Cass Forkin herself was astonished that by buying lunch for a few ladies, she reaffirmed their faith in humanity. We all can spare a lunch for a stranger or an extra ticket to a baseball game for an older neighbor, especially if we realize that such actions are powerful symbols that resonate deeply in another's life.

Start small. Identify a few things around you that others need help with. Paul Newman started small. He grew up a few blocks from my home in Shaker Heights and sold lemonade on the corner. Now he sells lemonade all over the world, and most of the profits go to help children. The key here is to do something small with a big heart and stick with it.

❧ *Turn giving into a pleasure.* I was happy, though not surprised, when scientific findings started rolling in showing that we're hardwired to feel good when we do good. These new findings reinforce one of my cherished philosophical tenets: giving need not be a sacrifice. You can make it a pleasure. After all, your genes are already on your side.

New research shows that nurturing others may feel good because it is rewarded by spikes in dopamine. A 2005 study in the journal *Molecular Psychiatry* found that a common variation of a gene that regulates the neurotransmitter dopamine was highly linked to altruistic behavior. Dopamine is the chemical linked to craving, pleasure, and reward. The researchers looked at 354 families with more than one child and found that our most common genetic subtype of dopamine—known as the D4.4—is significantly linked to generous, giving behavior. Even the littlest tot trying to comfort his baby sister or brother may be doing so in part because innumerable little dopamine-loving neurons are lighting up his brain with bliss. If so, nature has wisely ensured that generativity provides its own intrinsic rewards. Science recognized this years ago when researchers coined the term "helper's high."

I've thought a lot about this since these studies came in. In particular, I've turned to the evolutionist (and my friend) David Sloan Wilson, author of *Darwin's Cathedral.* David is the brilliant thinker who resurrected Charles Darwin's idea of group selection to explain why we give and why we enjoy giving. He has pointed out that groups whose members are giving actually survive and flourish. Imagine a world, says David, that ranges from the most pristine giving to the most wanton selfishness. Winners survive and reproduce and truly "inherit" the earth, while losers pass out of existence. So who are the winners and losers? You'd think givers would lose in such a world, because they would constantly be taken advantage of. But givers thrive—as long as they interact with other givers. They band together in generous, caring groups and thrive. Over time, David suggests, evolution has slowly selected giving as a profoundly healthy trait in our very social species. "A woman who helps disaster victims is obviously increasing *their* health," says David. "The striking result is that she also seems to be increasing *her* health."

❧   *Savor the joys of giving.* Nature has ensured that we thrive—by making us feel good when we give. How can you integrate that insight into your life? One way is to really enjoy the joys of giving. Each time you give, pause and let yourself feel good. Let joy fill you from your toes to your fingertips.

❧   *Appreciate others' responses.* Take notice of or even write down how the people you helped expressed their appreciation and the ways in which it made you feel good.

❧   *Get together.* Meet with your network of helpers from time to time to simply celebrate love and life. Talk about the people you've helped. Share your pleasure in having found your own "band" of givers.

❧   *Be a mentor.* The turning point in a young person's life is often the influence of a caring adult who inspires them. In my case, it was my guitar teacher, Leonid Bolotine—a musician himself who always greeted me as "sonny boy" and enveloped me in warmth and enthusiasm. I could hardly wait each week to get off the train from Long Island and play for him.

Jes Ward, director of the Colorado branch of PeaceJam, knows first-hand how adults can transform youth. PeaceJam is an international foundation that gathers Nobel Peace Prize Laureates like the Dalai Lama and Archbishop Desmond Tutu to work personally with youth to pass on the spirit, skills, and wisdom they embody. Ward encountered PeaceJam as a teen, and it transformed her life.

Ward had a difficult childhood. Her mother was alcoholic and often was unable to bring her to school or find money for food. Ward often stole food from grocery stores to feed her five younger siblings. At age twelve, she moved in with her grandmother, and over the next eight months each of her siblings joined her. Ward calls her grandmother her private hero.

In high school Ward went to a PeaceJam meeting, where, she recalls, "the room was packed wall to wall with kids on the floor, desks, tables. They were talking about the Dalai Lama. I had no idea who he was. At the next meeting they were talking about apartheid in South Africa and Desmond Tutu. I'd never heard of him either. We began to study these people who every day get up and try to make a difference in the world. Our club became a chapter of Amnesty International. We'd make peanut butter and jelly sandwiches for the shelter, lead awareness campaigns, and engage in local and international activities. I couldn't do anything to help my mom, but in PeaceJam I could help other people. And once you start helping others, you start helping yourself."

In 1997 Ward met her hero, Desmond Tutu: "It was the most transformational event of my life. Four hundred teenagers were packed into this tiny room, and his stage was only five inches wide. He is a small guy with an extraordinary, booming voice. One thing he said stuck with me forever: every movement that has created positive change has been started and carried through by young people."

Now, says Ward, there are eighty-six PeaceJam groups in Colorado alone. "You see students walk into their first meeting like I did, and this switch is flipped. Something happens when you are told that you can change the world and that you hold the future in your hands. When adults say, 'It's time for *you* to start taking responsibility,' you realize you are a full participant in the world, and that's really an amazing feeling."

Where kids are concerned, there is no substitute for inspiring, loving mentors. Patty Anglin, a child of missionary parents in Congo, Africa, is cofounder of the orphanage and referral center called Acres of Hope, as well as chairman of Children's Health Alliance of Wisconsin and regional coordinator for Adopt America Network. Patty and her second husband, Harold Anglin, already had a family of seven children when they began to foster special-needs infants and, later, abused children—some of whom they were able to adopt. One day, while visiting her sister in Wisconsin, Patty noticed a two-hundred-acre farm and thought, *This will be our farm, where we can raise all these children, and we'll call it Acres of Hope.* Though the farm was not for sale, Patty told the farmer of her mission and inspired him to sell it to her, and not long after, Acres of Hope was born and the

Anglins had eight more special-needs children. One was Levi, a baby left in a Dumpster by his drunken mother and suffering from fetal alcohol syndrome; in fact, the alcohol content in his blood was so high that it saved his life by preventing him from freezing. Another was Zachary, a Nigerian baby whose father wished to kill him because he was retarded and deformed—and in his culture this was regarded as an evil omen. Patty Anglin recalls the moment she heard about Zachary: an adoption agency called her to tell her about the infant who was deaf in one ear, had no arms or legs, and had a shriveled kidney. "That's my son," Patty heard herself saying. "That's my African angel that's just come home." Zachary has since received prosthetic legs. Another adopted child, Serina, was born addicted to crack cocaine, at only one pound and three ounces, and with a severe brain infection that had destroyed 70 percent of her brain. "For the first two years of her life she had 150 seizures a day and did not communicate at all," says Patty. "I carried her everywhere and slept with her. Doctors said she'd be a complete vegetable. At two years, she made her first eye contact with us. She's actually very gifted. She can listen to music and sit down and play it."

❧ *Teach others.* There are many ways to pass along skills and wisdom. Take a moment to write down what you consider your top five skills (are you a genius hedge fund trader? can you put together a lovely meal at the last minute?) and then your best personality traits (are you inspiring? charismatic? gentle? energetic and exciting?). Finally, make a short list of truisms and other wisdom you have gleaned from life (it's better to be happy than right all the time; discipline and patience are eventually rewarded; tough times never last but tough people do). Now think of opportunities, formal and informal, to share those skills, traits, and insights with others. It can be as simple as teaching the neighborhood kids or your own children and grandchildren how to do something. My grandfather used to teach the neighborhood children to whittle wood.

LESSON THREE: TEENS WHO HELP OTHERS DO BETTER IN LIFE, PERIOD

After I gave a talk on generosity at my former high school, one student wrote me: "A candle loses nothing of its light by lighting another candle.

We are the candles. By lighting the heart of someone else, we allow our own hearts to be lit."

Our youth—my kids, your kids, the light of our lives and, of course, the future of our world—are trying to make their way in the complex and challenging terrain of this multicultural global society, and they need help. New science from IRUL, coming from scientists as esteemed as David Sloan Wilson, Peter Benson, Paul Wink, Carolyn Schwartz, and Margaret Beale Spencer, suggests that one of the best ways we can help our kids is to encourage their own generosity. As Paul Wink's study so powerfully shows, if you start giving young, you protect your mental and physical well-being for a lifetime.

In 2005 the American College Health Association surveyed more than forty-seven thousand students from seventy-four universities and found that 45 percent reported feeling so depressed at times that it was difficult to function. One out of ten students said they'd seriously considered suicide in the past year. That is horrifying to know. But it is not inevitable.

Teens who actively volunteer do better in life: they have higher grades in school, use drugs and alcohol less often, have lower pregnancy rates, and are likely to continue volunteering for the rest of their lives. The impact is strongest when kids are inspired to volunteer on their own, but even when they are required by school-based programs to do so, the positive impact is significant, according to Catholic University of America's James Youniss.

Let's look at some of the older research before we get to the powerful new research funded by IRUL. In one fascinating ten-year study by Zipora Magen of Tel Aviv University, youth who volunteered to help others in need had more intensely happy moments. In fact, teens who were actively involved in helping others reported almost twice the capacity for exhilarating experiences and events. Self-fulfillment and commitment to the well-being of others are inseparable, Magen concluded.

Teens who volunteer make healthier life choices. A 2004 study of nearly 31,000 Vermont teens found that volunteerism was closely linked to avoidance of risky behaviors. According to the Harvard psychologist Dan Kindlon, who studied 654 teens as well as 1,078 parents of teens, simple tasks like doing chores for a weekly allowance helped teach teens to be other-centered. This is particularly important for youth suffering from what Kindlon nicknames "affluenza"—a malaise of discontent that may stem in part from well-meaning but overindulgent, financially comfortable parents.

How do we help our kids? We need to be present and supportive. Dr. Arthur Janov, author of *Biology of Love*, puts it this way. "Kiss that brain into maturity." We matter to our kids—immensely. The Search Institute in Minneapolis, renowned for its many decades of research on over two million adolescents, found that the strongest predictive factor for helpful behavior in teens was the presence of supportive adults.

Giving *can* be cultivated, right from the start of your child's life, according to new research. The Child Development Project, a famous school-based program of the 1980s promoting caring behavior, taught teachers techniques to guide kindergarten through fourth-grade children in caring, giving behavior. Even when followed up years later, students who had reached the eighth-grade level had higher scores on moral reasoning, conflict resolution, and caring, sharing behavior. The Child Development Project has been resurrected more recently in six schools over a three-year period—and students gained in personal, social, and ethical values and had significantly lower levels of substance abuse and problem behaviors. A caring teacher, like a caring parent, can make a big difference to a kid.

LESSON FOUR: GIRLS AND BOYS NEED A DIFFERENT APPROACH

As the father of both a girl and a boy, there's no doubt in my mind that there are innate gender differences, although of course all of us are individual. Yet I was surprised, even taken aback, when three of four IRUL studies I funded on youth and volunteering turned up a clear gender divide. These pilot studies hint that there is a genuine difference in the impact of giving on boys and girls. Overall, girls give more than boys do. And yet they may not benefit as much from that giving. In fact, they suffer depression and anxiety when they *don't* give. Boys, however, clearly benefit from extra giving and helpfulness: it increases their confidence and self-esteem.

Now, these are only preliminary studies, so they raise as many questions for future directions in research as they answer. But they are notable because they deal with such different groups of young folks, and because the researchers were working independently. These studies have influenced my thinking on how we might encourage our kids to be more generous.

First, helping others helps boys, and *not* helping others hurts girls, according to the Search Institute. They looked at 931 young folks and found that boys benefit markedly from feelings of love and altruism. In contrast, girls seem to start out ahead of boys, with higher levels of altruism and helping—and yet they don't get the same marked benefits.

Twice as many girls were high on actual helping actions, compared to boys. For girls, if their altruistic feelings *or* behaviors *decreased*, their depression and anxiety dramatically *increased*. And girls who began the year low in a giving disposition were already higher on depression.

Second, in underprivileged families, girls don't get a spike in well-being from helping unless they have supportive, appreciative fathers who value their help, according to Margaret Beale Spencer of the University of Pennsylvania's Center for Health Achievement, Neighborhood Growth, and Ethnic Studies (CHANGES). Margaret found that inner-city, underprivileged junior high boys had significantly lower emotional distress if their helping behavior was high. But girls didn't automatically get the same benefits. "With kids from poor families, helping behaviors usually occur in the home and not out in the world," says Margaret, "and girls have to fill gaps in family life. When boys help the family, this may be perceived as a special contribution and be rewarded." Margaret studied seven hundred students between the ages of nine and sixteen, most of them African American and Latino.

Third, Carolyn Schwartz found that girls benefit most from the connectedness they feel when helping, while boys benefit from task-oriented helping—and yet even so, girls don't get the same marked benefits as boys. Carolyn is with DeltaQuest Foundation and the University of Massachusetts Medical School. She and her associates Penelope Keyl and Jack Marcum looked at 457 teens affiliated with American Presbyterian churches.

The aspect of girls' well-being that was most deeply affected by altruism was their sense of connection with others. It seems like the interventions we design to guide our children may need to be different depending on gender. Says Carolyn, "Boys' play interactions are generally more emotion-neutral and task-oriented. Boys may play soccer or baseball or construct buildings with Legos. Their focus is on an object that is outside of themselves or their own identity. In contrast, when girls play, they might focus on play-acting different relationships between themselves. For example, they might say things like, 'You are the mommy and I am the baby,' or, 'We are both princesses.' Girls' relationships are more complex even at young ages, where conflicts arise around who is 'best friends' with whom, whereas boys might have conflict around sharing a basketball. It may sound a bit sexist, but I think a program for boys might focus on encouraging them to help around the home and teaching them good-citizens skills and habits. For girls, developing a broader attitude of helping, such as seeing themselves as agents of goodness and kindness in the world, will probably enhance their well-being. We want both boys and girls to enter adulthood well equipped to deal with the ups and downs of life."

And finally, girls generally tend to help more than boys, according to an IRUL study from the brilliant David Sloan Wilson. David mined data from research by the renowned psychologist Mihaly Csikszentmihalyi and the sociologist Barbara Schneider. This study had originally followed over one thousand students from thirty-three schools for five years. David looked at seventeen of the four hundred questionnaire items that were linked to what we call pro-social behavior. He found that girls were far more "high-pro" than boys. He also found that high-pro teens seemed to thrive as individuals—as long as they were in the right "niche" for altruism. That niche was a stable, nurturing environment. In this environment, says David, high-pro, giving teens were the very picture of health "at both the societal and individual levels."

So what can we do for boys and girls that will reward and encourage generativity? Here are a few ideas:

❧ *Praise girls*. If these pilot studies are hinting at a deeper truth, we need to nurture girls by praising, appreciating, and encouraging their innate kindness. We want to inspire the confidence and self-esteem that arise from their natural helpfulness. Saying something like, "You're the kind of person who likes to help others whenever you can—you're very nice and kind," is highly reinforcing, and it will help a child become generally help-ful rather than repeating a specific action that was praised.

❧ *Encourage boys.* At the same time, we need to encourage boys to en-gage in more concrete giving behavior—like family chores—because goal-oriented tasks come naturally to boys and we know such behavior will increase their sense of efficacy and purpose, and thus their well-being. Say-ing something like, "You did a great job helping us renovate the recreation room," may be just the ticket for boys.

❧ *Inspire girls and boys through movies and literature.* For both girls and boys, learning the value of giving is important. The psychologists Paul Vitz and Philip Scala suggest watching inspiring movies—such as *It's a Wonder-ful Life*, *To Sir with Love*, *An Officer and a Gentleman*, *Brian's Song*, and *The Miracle Worker*—and reading inspiring books with them such as biogra-phies like Tracy Kidder's *Mountains Beyond Mountains*, about the great physician-altruist Paul Farmer; Patty Anglin's *Acres of Hope: The Miracu-lous Story of One Family's Gift of Love to Children Without Hope*; Millard Fuller's *More Than Houses: How Habitat for Humanity Is Transforming Lives and Neighborhoods*; or Christina Noble's *Bridge Across My Sorrows*.

❧ *Talk it out with your kids.* Let your children talk about how those movies and books made them feel. Then ask your kids to try performing one giving act a day—washing dishes for a sister or brother, offering an older person a seat on the bus, shoveling snow for a neighbor. In Vitz's re-search, youth reported these simple acts in a diary.

❧ *Work with parents and teachers to inspire youth.* At school, parents, teachers, and children can raise money for a charity or help senior citizens at a nursing home. Work with other parents and teachers to set aside a day every month for community when students, faculty, and staff may spend the day helping a group in need. Ask youth to present their thoughts and feelings about this day at an open-mike session.

LESSON FIVE: LIVE LONG AND VOLUNTEER—
GIVING ENERGIZES THE ELDERLY

If you're an older adult, I have one recommendation: volunteer! Volunteering lengthens life—*and* improves the quality of life. Volunteering is going to be increasingly important for Americans, says Adam Hirschfelder, since we're facing an unprecedented demographic shift. Seventy-seven million babies were born during the "boom years" of 1946 to 1964. Now, as older adults, these individuals can have a huge transformative impact on society, says Hirschfelder, since adults over fifty-five give "a staggering total of five billion hours in volunteer time every year." Not only can older individuals help society, but they will benefit themselves by giving this help.

The remarkable fact is that giving, even in later years, can delay death. In one 2005 study conducted by Alex Harris and Carl Thoresen of Stanford University, frequent volunteering was strongly linked with later mortality in more than 7,500 Americans over age seventy who lived in communities for the elderly. Called the Longitudinal Study of Aging (LSOA), the study followed these older individuals for six years. Volunteering was a powerful protector of mental and physical health, and frequent volunteers were protected the most. A 1992 survey of 3,617 older folks by Neal Krause of the University of Michigan found that helping others lowers depression. Krause also found that, for older men, ten years of volunteering slashes death rates significantly.

Just as striking is the earlier, meticulous work of Doug Oman. Oman and his colleagues looked at 2,025 older California residents and found that those who volunteered regularly had a 44 percent reduction in mortality—and those who volunteered for two or more organizations had an astonishing 63 percent lower mortality than nonvolunteers. Says Oman: "Volunteering had a larger effect than physical mobility, exercising four times a week, and weekly attendance at religious services." That's powerful.

"Many folks say with age they finally have the time to be generous," says Elizabeth Midlarsky, a psychologist at Columbia University. With her colleague Eva Kahana, she studied four hundred older adults. Over half found helping others to be especially rewarding. "One eighty-eight-year-old said, 'Even though there are things I can no longer do, I can still bring a smile to my neighbor's face.' "

You can make helping others a cherished habit. The psychologist Linda Fried of the Johns Hopkins School of Medicine evaluated a program for older, mostly African American female volunteers at the Experience Corps in Baltimore, Maryland. There were seventy active volunteers. The active volunteers helped schoolchildren in four different programs, and when they were evaluated as long as eight months later, their physical activity, strength, and cognitive activity were all *significantly* increased. They found the volunteering so pleasurable that 80 percent wanted to keep on volunteering the following year.

Finally, Stephanie L. Brown, a researcher at the Institute for Social Research at the University of Michigan, recently reported on a group of 423 elderly couples followed for five years. Those who reported helping others—even if it was just giving emotional support to a spouse—were only about half as likely to die as those who did not. And giving emotional support to one's spouse, on its own, reduced the risk of dying by 30 percent.

Let me pause here to mention an important caveat: helping excessively can be stressful and overwhelming. I know that's obvious, but studies *do* show that large amounts of volunteering can actually increase the risk of mortality. A study from the *Journal of Gerontology* in 1999 found that for adults over sixty-five, the volunteering impact was the strongest when volunteering was limited to about forty hours a year or less.

※ *Pass the torch.* As an older adult, you are a distillation of your life's wisdom and skill. Recognize your own value, and take some of your newfound free time to help others. Help schoolchildren or neighbors, family or friends.

※ *Encourage older relatives to help others.* If you have older relatives who are feeling a bit isolated or depressed, encourage them to volunteer. Perhaps you will need to jump-start the process by joining a group with them. Once they discover the joys of giving, they'll be flying on their own.

Love begets love. In the end, as George Vaillant says, love nurtures all life: "God is love, or if you prefer, love is God. After all, light serves us equally well if we conceive it as waves or as particles. As Shakespeare's Romeo put it: 'The more I give to thee, the more I have, for both are infinite.' "

Your Generativity Score

It's time to answer the questions on the generativity section of your Love and Longevity Scale. We have divided responses into percentiles, or fifths. These are general guidelines, and you may score right near the cutoff between percentiles, so please keep this in mind and use the scale as a friendly tool. Remember:

There are two steps to determining your score on a scale. First, determine which items need to be "reverse-scored" (denoted with the ® symbol). For reverse-scored items, see the chart below for how to score.

If you score a . . .	. . . assign yourself a score for that item of:
1	6
2	5
3	4
4	3
5	2
6	1

The second step is to add the scores for individual items *after* the reverse-scored items have been reverse-scored. Take the quiz now, and take it again if you wish after you've finished this book and begun practicing the art of generativity in your daily life.

Using the scale provided, please circle the one number that best reflects your opinion about whether or not each statement below describes you or experiences that you have had. There are no correct answers, so please respond as honestly as possible to each one.

1. When people in my family say they need something, I instantly think of ways I could help.
   1=strongly disagree   2=disagree   3=slightly disagree   4=slightly agree
   5=agree   6=strongly agree

2. I always go out of my way to help members of my family.
   1=strongly disagree   2=disagree   3=slightly disagree   4=slightly agree
   5=agree   6=strongly agree

3. It's not that personally important for me to be helpful to members of my family.®
   1=strongly disagree   2=disagree   3=slightly disagree   4=slightly agree
   5=agree   6=strongly agree

4. I'm not really good at figuring out ways to help members of my family.®
   1=strongly disagree   2=disagree   3=slightly disagree   4=slightly agree
   5=agree   6=strongly agree

5. It's not that rewarding to offer my time to help members of my family.®
   1=strongly disagree   2=disagree   3=slightly disagree   4=slightly agree
   5=agree   6=strongly agree

6. I would donate bone marrow or a kidney if a friend needed it.
   1=strongly disagree   2=disagree   3=slightly disagree   4=slightly agree
   5=agree   6=strongly agree

7. It's personally important for me to be helpful to friends.
   1=strongly disagree   2=disagree   3=slightly disagree   4=slightly agree
   5=agree   6=strongly agree

8. I always go out of my way to help a friend.
   1=strongly disagree   2=disagree   3=slightly disagree   4=slightly agree
   5=agree   6=strongly agree

9. If a friend needed money, I would probably not loan it to them,
   even if I had it.[®]
   1=strongly disagree   2=disagree   3=slightly disagree   4=slightly agree
   5=agree   6=strongly agree

10. I'm not really good at figuring out ways to help friends.[®]
    1=strongly disagree   2=disagree   3=slightly disagree   4=slightly agree
    5=agree   6=strongly agree

11. I take pleasure in doing favors for people in my neighborhood or
    at work.
    1=strongly disagree   2=disagree   3=slightly disagree   4=slightly agree
    5=agree   6=strongly agree

12. If a neighbor or coworker needs help, I offer it.
    1=strongly disagree   2=disagree   3=slightly disagree   4=slightly agree
    5=agree   6=strongly agree

13. It's important for me to be helpful to neighbors or coworkers in
    some way.
    1=strongly disagree   2=disagree   3=slightly disagree   4=slightly agree
    5=agree   6=strongly agree

14. I seldom go out of my way to help a neighbor or coworker.[®]
    1=strongly disagree   2=disagree   3=slightly disagree   4=slightly agree
    5=agree   6=strongly agree

15. I don't find it very rewarding to offer my time to help neighbors or
    coworkers.[®]
    1=strongly disagree   2=disagree   3=slightly disagree   4=slightly agree
    5=agree   6=strongly agree

16. Many of my efforts are motivated by my desire to help humanity in some way.

    1=strongly disagree   2=disagree   3=slightly disagree   4=slightly agree
    5=agree   6=strongly agree

17. I try to donate blood regularly.

    1=strongly disagree   2=disagree   3=slightly disagree   4=slightly agree
    5=agree   6=strongly agree

18. I think it's important for me to try to leave this world better than I found it.

    1=strongly disagree   2=disagree   3=slightly disagree   4=slightly agree
    5=agree   6=strongly agree

19. Donating money to charity is not, and probably never will be, a priority for me.®

    1=strongly disagree   2=disagree   3=slightly disagree   4=slightly agree
    5=agree   6=strongly agree

20. It's not that rewarding to give things away to people I don't know.®

    1=strongly disagree   2=disagree   3=slightly disagree   4=slightly agree
    5=agree   6=strongly agree

Your Generativity Score

High Giver (80th percentile)	100 or higher
Giver (60th percentile)	93–99
Moderate Giver (40th percentile)	87–92
Low Giver (20th percentile)	77–86

Five

The Way of Forgiveness:
Set Yourself Free

I am a mum to every street child in Vietnam. The orphan children are
called *bui doi*, meaning 'the dust of life.' I taught them to be proud of this
name. When I walk the streets of Ho Chi Minh City, children will give
me a thumbs-up and say, 'Hey, Mama Tina. *Bui doi* Number One.' "

Those are the words of Dublin-born Christina Noble, whose Christina
Noble Children's Foundation in Vietnam and Mongolia has won her
international awards, accolades, and honorary degrees. The remarkable
Christina went to Vietnam when she was forty years old and, against improbable odds, convinced the Ministry of Labor in Hanoi to give her
official permission to work with street children; she then raised money for a
foundation that offers medical care, nutritional rehabilitation, education,
and vocational training for homeless children. She imported incubators,
cots, and medicines. She built a hospital, schools, and a shelter. Her foundation has helped more than 200,000 destitute children in both Vietnam
and Mongolia.

Why did she do this? Because of her own brutal childhood. Instead of losing herself in bitterness and rage, Noble chose to forgive as much of the past as she could and to alchemize her pain into good works. "If you don't forgive, you won't grow," says Noble. "You won't love yourself or anyone else. I have a big spirit, and if my spirit goes comatose, then it's over for me as a human being. I had to forgive to keep my spirit alive."

Born in a "God-struck, beer-soaked slum in southwest Dublin," Christina was the oldest of eight children, all of whom crowded together in the living room each night to sleep. Her father was a physically abusive alcoholic. Her mother suffered from a damaged heart valve. When her mother died, the eight children were separated into different institutions in Ireland. Some years later Christina was released from an institution with five Irish pounds. Her father picked her up at the train station, took the five pounds, and said he was going to get change for the bus. "He went into a pub and disappeared out the back door, and I did not see him again. I went to live in the park. I was sixteen."

While living in the park, Noble was gang-raped. "I was bleeding badly and had to cover myself up with dirt and scraps of paper. I remember shouting to God, 'Why did you take my mother? Why do I have to suffer this way?' That rape resulted in a child being born, and the child was taken from me against my will. The experiences of loss never seemed to stop. I use the word *nothingness* to describe my life back then. I was a nothingness, and nothingness doesn't feel it really exists as a human being. I created a fantasy world with a mommy, daddy, and a house with yellow lights, books, chairs, and friends."

At eighteen, Noble moved to England, married, and had three children. "I knew that if I did not forgive, I would carry pure hatred inside and would not be able to love anybody." The first step in forgiveness required simply being heard. "I had a very good doctor who listened to me without judging. I also went to a highly qualified psychotherapist for seven years. It wasn't easy to share my pain, but I did it."

The second key to forgiveness was action: dedicating her life to helping other street children. "When I began, people said what I wanted to achieve was impossible. 'You are only one person,' they said. But when I was a child, I needed only one person."

A third, profound step was writing her 1994 autobiography, *Bridge*

Across My Sorrows. "I must have written that book fifty times in my mind," she says. "I feel very lucky, in a way, that I was strong enough to face all this head on and feel so much determination and love. I'm especially grateful that I never once thought about hurting other people. I could have hated the world and tried to destroy others. But I never did. I was born able to forgive."

Every time Christina Noble helps an orphan child in Vietnam or Mongolia, she helps the little girl inside herself—that orphaned "nothingness" of long ago. That is a daily form of forgiveness. If Christina's father were alive today, she says, she would tell him: "I remember all the beauty. I remember sitting on your lap when you played the song 'Danny Boy.' I remember our long walks down to the river. I also remember when you left me at the door of the pub and never came back. Do you know how long I waited for you to come back?" She adds, "It's important to remember the good and just as important not to be in denial about the bad. I live with the consequences of a terrible early life. I also know that love is an incredible gift, and to share it is even more beautiful, and I just adore children. They make me laugh. They give me back so much."

No wonder the Irish pop star Sinead O'Connor joined the musician and songwriter Luka Bloom to sing the song he'd written and dedicated to Christina Noble, "Love Is a Place I Dream Of." The simple refrain is: "Someday I will cross the world for you/No matter how far/just to be there."

Forgiveness: Let Go and Live

Forgiveness is love that can *only* emerge when the giver has first suffered harm. It frees the giver from bondage to a bitterness that could easily darken his or her view of life. Without forgiveness, retribution would haunt our lives. How long would any one of us last?

There is power and joy in letting go. There have been at least a hundred apologies made by politicians and religious leaders to nations and groups around the world for harm done to them, including racism, slavery, genocide, and concentration camps, according to the psychologist Samuel Oliner of Humboldt State University in northern California. African

Americans in Alabama accepted Governor George Wallace's apology for his racist acts during his 1982 reelection campaign and voted for him in large numbers. During the summer of 2003, Sam interviewed members of three Kentucky religious communities that had apologized to African Americans for participating in slavery and had established scholarships for minorities. Slaves had cleared land and built churches in the early 1800s, and at that time nuns joined convents with slaves as dowries. The first apology took place at a church in Bardstown, Kentucky, in 2001, and was attended by about four hundred individuals. "They rejoiced in the power of apology," Sam told me, "noting that all their ancestors, black and white, were 'crying tears of joy in heaven.' "

"The verb used in the Hebrew Bible for forgiveness is *shuv*," Sam notes. "It means to turn or to return, and suggests that we have the power to turn from evil to good." Sam's own life story, which is told later in this chapter, is a remarkable example of forgiveness: he was only seven when his entire family was slaughtered in the Holocaust.

And yet, as every one of us knows, forgiveness is a challenging form of love. When we've been harmed—and sometimes deeply so—it can feel nearly impossible to let go of outrage, anger, and grief. Vengefulness is enticing; there is almost a lust to eradicate those who have transgressed against us. Grudge matches are notorious between families, clans, and countries. This natural tendency is seductive, but we end up reliving the original harm a thousand times over.

"Most of us have been deeply hurt, and we need ways to deal with that hurt," says Robert Enright, professor of human development at the University of Wisconsin at Madison. "Sometimes, when life pushes us to the brink, there's little else we can do than to be merciful."

For me, forgiveness is often a family affair. With immediate family, it is impossible to rely on the witticism, "Out of sight, out of mind." You see your family every day. In my marriage, which I consider very good, there have been times of serious conflict. My wife sees me as a blend of all that's good and bad about the American male. My penchant for waking up at 5:00 A.M. and disappearing to the office until the evening, or working on academic papers until midnight, required a lot of adjustment and some forgiveness on my wife's part. The Japanese symbol for the word *busy* is a heart with a line crossed through it—in essence, no heart. There's no doubt that sometimes I was too driven and offered too little heart. One snowy evening we were heading off to the Ponderosa for dinner; the snow was so heavy that I changed my mind and turned in to Burger King. My wife uttered a phrase in Japanese that I was certain I'd misunderstood. "Mitsuko," I asked, "did you just call me a decayed man?" She answered me calmly, "Yes, because in Japan no real man changes his mind!" Suddenly I understood those many John Wayne movies in which Japanese soldiers keep running into machine-gun fire instead of veering to the left or right or running for cover. They are worried that their wives will think them "decayed." I offer this only as a small, humorous insight into my own multicultural marriage, which has forced both Mitsuko and me to grow tremendously.

We all succumb to failures of every variety. We are prodigals traveling home, hoping to be welcomed with open arms and forgiven. "It is easier to forgive if we really and truly face the fact that, were we in another's shoes, we might also make mistakes that seem horrendous in retrospect. We need to recognize our shared humanity," said one forgiveness researcher in a private conversation after the birth of her first baby. She admitted that she was so sleep-deprived that she sometimes had the impulse to hurl her adored baby against the wall. "My little tiny daughter would be crying in the middle of the night, and sometimes I felt I just couldn't cope," this researcher confessed. "And of course I understood that if I gave in to my impulse, I'd not only kill her, I'd cause unthinkable torment to my husband and her grandparents and I'd go to prison forever. Even so, I remember realizing that if I were a single mom in the ghetto, with an alcohol problem and suffering from depression, perhaps I could have reached a turning point where I gave in to that impulse. I was lucky because I had good self-control, a wonderful job, great parents, and a loving husband. I had so many advantages."

By forgiving, we restore our own faith in the essential goodness of life. And yet, the way we choose to do so is always individual. As you read this chapter, consider that you will craft your own quilt of forgiveness in a way that feels right to you, and it will vary from situation to situation. Your goal is to move past the natural tendency to seek revenge. It may be that you heal a broken relationship and find yourself with a new understanding of another's humanity, or you let go without ever telling the other person about your own journey to greater peace. It may be that you *offer* an apology.

In the last decade there has been a literal explosion of scientific and popular interest in forgiveness, and there is now tantalizing evidence of the power of forgiveness to enhance mental and physical health. Before 1985, there were a mere handful of peer-reviewed studies on forgiveness. Today there are more than 1,400. Psychologists studying forgiveness have now outlined how forgiveness develops, what its benefits might be, and how to create effective forgiveness interventions. Here are some highlights of IRUL-funded and other research on forgiveness:

Forgiving others improves health more than being forgiven. According to a 2003 study by Neal Krause, a research professor at the Institute of Gerontology at the University of Michigan, forgiving others unconditionally is linked to well-being even more strongly than forgiving others who have earned it through contrition and apology.

Forgiveness alleviates depression—even in war-torn areas. Robert Enright is teaching forgiveness in schools in violent areas like Belfast and Jerusalem, as well as an impoverished inner-city neighborhood in Milwaukee, Wisconsin. One powerful way he leads them to forgiveness is by emphasizing the inherent worth of all beings. For instance, he shares the Dr. Seuss book *Horton Hears a Who*, which contains the line "A person is a person, no matter how small." "We go to Belfast," says Enright, "because they've had eight hundred years of conflict, and we go into the poorest neighborhoods. In one school of two hundred twelve children, a hundred were being treated for anxiety and depressive disorders. Those children who learned forgiveness went from clinical depression to being non-depressed."

Forgiveness boosts mood and reduces anger. One study from the University of Wisconsin at Madison found that adolescents with higher-than-average levels of anger benefited powerfully from a twelve-week forgiveness program. Anger as a trait and state was reduced. Even more impressively, a follow-up nine months later showed that these changes had lasted. Another study of teenage girls in Korea who were victims of bullying by peers and then became bullies themselves found similar healing results from a twelve-week forgiveness program. People who score high on forgiveness as a personality trait are less likely to be depressed, anxious, and hostile. Combat veterans suffering from PTSD suffer less depression and fewer symptoms of trauma if they are able to forgive themselves and others. When people are in a more forgiving state than usual, they report higher levels of satisfaction with life, fewer illness-related symptoms, and a better mood.

Forgiveness lowers stress hormones. A 2005 study by Marina Butovskaya and her colleagues at the Institute of Ethnology and Anthropology in Moscow, Russia, found that reconciliation and peacemaking lowered stress hormones in boys ages seven to eleven. Another study from Robert Enright found that learning forgiveness improved blood flow to the heart for veterans who were cardiac patients.

Forgiveness preserves close relationships. New research shows that the degree to which romantic partners report having forgiven each other is linked to their mutual satisfaction and commitment.

Lessons from the Frontiers of Research

Forgiveness replaces pain with peace. However, forgiveness is not a simple act or a onetime gesture; nor is it a pardon in some official sense. It is an approach to life, a work in progress. It is perfectly human for anger and pain to catch us off guard even after we have done our best to forgive someone. The literature on forgiveness is deep and finely layered. This hugely important human act and the exact ways in which we carry it out are deeply shaped by our individual experience. And so, as you read the following suggestions and insights taken from the substantial research on forgiveness, I hope that you will find a way to express this form of love that suits you and that you can live with comfortably over a lifetime.

LESSON ONE: FIND OUT WHAT
FORGIVENESS REALLY MEANS

The greatest barrier to forgiveness is that we so often misunderstand the meaning of the word. "I've found that literally one hundred percent of the problems that people have with forgiveness are based on a misunderstanding of the concept," says Robert Enright. Forgiveness researchers come in all stripes and colors, with all types of backgrounds and worldviews, but they universally agree that forgiveness is *not*:

- Forgetting
- Condoning
- Excusing
- Trusting without reason
- Forgoing legal or financial reparation
- Reconciling if it would in any way endanger the victim's safety or health
- Forgoing justice—which in itself requires courage, an important expression of love

"One of the most common and mistaken arguments against forgiveness," says the research psychologist Charlotte Witvliet of Hope College in Michigan, "is that when you forgive someone, you are showing them they can have their way. Why, people ask, should they give an offender such power? But forgiveness is not about giving away power. If you're really good at forgiveness, a deeper excavation has to happen, and it requires courage as well as empathy."

Witvliet conceives of forgiveness as "a powerful act, definitely not flimsy or sappy. In order to forgive you must first tell the true story of exactly what happened, grieve it fully, and *then* turn away from grudges, bitterness, and the kind of ruminating that amplifies the story and gives it too much replay time. It's simply too easy to summarize someone in terms of their worst behavior. They may have profoundly messed up and yet even so have wonderful qualities." And what you wish for the other person isn't by any means that they live a happy-go-lucky life. You may wish, says

Witvliet, that they will undergo an awakening, a kind of reckoning with their dark side that will allow them to grow into a better person.

The empathy and courage required for forgiveness enhance our sense of well-being and control, according to a study Witvliet did of seventy-one students. "We asked them to think of someone who had hurt them deeply," she explains. "And we asked them to respond internally in forgiving or unforgiving ways." The emotions of forgiveness and unforgiveness produced marked short-term changes in the students' physiological states, says Witvliet. "Unforgiving imagery consistently prompts more negative, aroused self-reports and physiological stress responses. Ruminating about negative situations is linked to depression, anxiety disorders, and anger. Ruminating sustains the desire for revenge, and re-creates the physiological stress of the original harm. It also reinforces the victim role, which is linked with passivity and failure. Forgiving responses *calm* the mind and body."

The take-home message? Reliving hurt makes you feel helpless. Empathy, in turn, offers a greater feeling of control. You feel the most control when you imagine ways of granting forgiveness.

Here's the true story of one prominent forgiveness researcher who wishes to remain anonymous. This story shows so clearly the struggle toward forgiveness:

"I lost my father at age twenty in a car accident," she recalls. "The man driving was speeding and fishtailing rapidly, using the right turn lane as a passing lane, and disregarding all the traffic signs. At one point he apparently gunned the motor to try to get around a semi, and the semi crossed the center line of the road and peeled open my father's car to the point where the largest piece of him left was three inches. His body was utterly decimated. This was right around the corner from our house," she recalls. "And the person who caused that accident got out of his car unhurt and complained that the paint job on his vehicle had just been ruined. He had prior infractions on his record but was only sentenced to forty hours of community service. Now, let me ask you, if you love your father profoundly, don't you think his life is worth more than forty hours? There's no way to describe how that event changed my life. I rehashed it, I relived it, I reread the depositions, I felt like every cell in my body had been ripped to shreds, and I had to figure out how to piece this in with the narrative of my life and how not to go find an Uzi and blow this man away. And I had already written a paper on forgiveness in college. Now I was faced with the real challenge. How could I forgive in these circumstances? Especially since the way my dad was killed seemed to play a role in my mom's subsequent development of cancer. By the age of twenty-eight, I'd lost both my parents."

She pauses and says, "I'm a Christian. It's clear this man needs grace. So what do I wish for this man now? I remind myself of his humanity and try to find a way to genuinely wish him some kind of good. I wish that he cared more about human life than his car. I desperately hope and pray that he grows and matures. Now, that doesn't mean I am no longer angry and hurt. I understand that forgiveness is a process."

"There are no hard and fast rules for forgiveness," says Robert Enright. There *is*, however, a simple and elegant definition of forgiveness. According to research by the psychologists Michael McCullough and Giacomo Bono of the University of Miami, *forgiveness is the other side of gratitude.* "In the simplest terms, gratitude is a positive response to benefits," says Bono, "while forgiveness is a positive response to harm."

I find that insight both simple and profound. What is a positive response to harm? It varies with each one of us. For Christina Noble, it was creating a foundation. For descendents of slaves in Kentucky, it was accepting a public apology. Here are ways to find your own path to forgiveness:

❧ *Practice the four stages of forgiveness proposed by Robert Enright:*

1. *Uncovering.* You examine the hurt and feel and acknowledge fully what it has done to your life.
2. *Deciding.* You think about what forgiveness is and is not, and what it would mean to you to forgive a particular person who has harmed you. This phase may take some time, and you may want to write in a journal about how you want to forgive this person and what expression that forgiveness might take.
3. *Understanding.* This is a time when you try to understand the person who hurt you, what motivated that person, what his or her stressors were at the time, and what about that person is good as well as bad. Try to see your shared humanity with the person who hurt you and you may feel more warmly toward him or her and begin to forgive.

In some cases, you may even be able to ask that person questions that help enhance your understanding.

4. *Deepening.* During this phase, you may see redemptive meaning in your experience. You may be able to apply your process of being hurt and forgiving to others, offering them compassion. You may think about others you yourself have hurt and offer apology. You see life as richer for the whole experience of moving beyond hurt.

❧ *Think about an incident that hurt you. Write down a definition of forgiveness that* you *feel comfortable with*—whether it be reconciling, reframing silently, trying to see the offender's complexity and humanity, asking for an apology or reparation, reframing other positive events as more important, or letting go and seeking inner peace.

Expressions of forgiveness vary widely according to circumstance and temperament. Forgiveness may open the door to reconciliation, but it depends on both individuals. Reconciliation is usually inappropriate if it puts you in harm's way or if it is reached so easily that the other person does not feel personally responsible for their actions.

LESSON TWO: LEARN THE LIMITS OF A GRUDGE

There is a certain evolutionary value to holding a grudge. Getting angry when somebody has hurt you is natural and self-protective. According to the psychologist Kenneth Pargament, professor of psychology at Bowling Green State University, our first response to harm is to protect ourselves, seek safety, and find ways to conserve our well-being. Anger, fear, hurt, and resentment are actually emotional coping techniques that help us do just that. Anger is a source of energy and power. It counteracts the feelings of loss of control that come with being harmed by another. Fear helps protect us from further harmful encounters. Hurt is actually a source of comfort, since it reminds us that we deserve better. Rumination can actually energize us, because it reminds us continually that something important to us has been threatened and needs to be restored. It may be a very old adaptation to group living: rumination can spur people to search for and restore their safety and status. Even resentment can be useful, since expressing it helps remind others of our difficulties.

We've all experienced these feelings, and at first they do indeed help us cope. It's only over time that they begin to erode our sense of well-being. As Pargament points out, chronic anger can reinforce a feeling of power-lessness; chronic fear can remind us that terrible things could happen again; and with resentment and hurt comes an underlying feeling of shame and being a victim.

The more severe the harm, the more difficult it is to forgive. Every for-giveness researcher acknowledges this. "If there is very severe harm and no apology and you have no close relationship with the other person, it's really hard to forgive," admits Julie Exline. "Sometimes there are devastat-ing consequences to an event, and you may wake up every morning of your life and be reminded of what happened. The pain might continue indefi-nitely and require healing and coping. It's also especially hard to forgive when somebody you love has been hurt, especially your own child. But if you continue to hate the guts of the person who hurt you or someone you love, you are ultimately hurting yourself. Even if you fear that person, even if you suffer great loss, it is important not to be trapped in a cycle of hatred and bitterness."

Here's a small example from my own life. A colleague I'd written many papers with stole five pages of an article I wrote and presented it as his own work at a conference that he did not know I was attending. I was in the au-dience listening to him read my work as his. Afterwards I confronted him in the hallway loud and clear, with many of our peers around us. I even lost my temper a bit. But three months later we had a talk, and I said, "I know you're remorseful. It's water under the bridge. I don't think I can work with you again, but if you sit next to me at a meeting I'll be happy to offer you a cup of coffee." That was my way of saying that I'd forgiven him even though I was unlikely to trust him enough to work with him again.

Here are some ways to think about the limits of holding multiple chronic grudges:

❧ *Start counting people* (from family to friends, colleagues, and neigh-bors) against whom you bear a grudge or resentment, even relatively small

ones. Imagine putting a potato into a sack for every slight or hurt you have
not forgiven. Now, imagine that for a week you have to carry that sack
around everywhere you go—to the bathroom in the morning, in the car or
on the train to work, at your desk, at meetings, during mealtime, and in
bed at night. Have a good laugh at the amusing image. Don't you feel ex-
hausted just contemplating that huge sack of potatoes?

❧   *Engage in metaphorical forgiveness exercises.* Imagine taking a big
marker and writing GRUDGE across your palm. Let the ink dry and then
try to wash it off with soap and water. What happens? It becomes lighter,
but it's still there. Forgiveness is a process. With practice, your burden becomes lighter each time you "wash" it away.

LESSON THREE: FIRST FORGIVE YOURSELF

The greatest challenge in life is forgiving *ourselves*—and it's actually harder
than forgiving others. The theologian Paul Tillich, a Protestant giant of
the twentieth century, focuses entirely on the challenge of self-acceptance
in his classic *The Courage to Be.* Tillich believes we can achieve full self-
acceptance only by deeply recognizing that we are loved by God despite
the wrong we've done or the good we've failed to do. That is why so many
spiritual traditions conceive of an overriding presence in the universe that
unconditionally loves and forgives. The gap between what we feel goodness requires and what our lives really are will never be wholly closed. In
other words, we all need to be forgiven.

Forgiveness plays a central role in Jewish, Christian, Islamic, Confu-
cian, Buddhist, and Hindu thought. One reason, says Dr. Richard Mollica,
director of the Harvard Program in Refugee Trauma at Massachusetts General Hospital, is that forgiveness is quite difficult in its own way—and we
may feel we need the assistance of a more transcendent force, which we see
as divine. As Mollica puts it eloquently: "One of the great lines in history is
'Father, forgive them, they know not what they do,' which Jesus speaks as
he is dying on the cross. Crucifixion is one of the most painful, disturbing
ways you can end someone's life, and that's why the Romans used that
technique. When I shared the Christ story with Cambodians who'd been
through genocide, they were very moved. So when Christ says, 'Father,

forgive them,' what's really being said is that it sometimes takes God to achieve the most profound depths of forgiveness."

❧ *Think back to other times.* Can you recall an incident in which you hoped to be forgiven for something or in which you were forgiven? What did it—or would it—feel like to be forgiven? Bask in the good feelings.

❧ *Envision someone who loves you.* Imagine yourself from their perspective. Would they judge you as harshly as you sometimes judge yourself?

❧ *Ask a higher power.* If you believe in a personal God, ask for forgiveness.

❧ *Look to nature.* (You've heard that from me before!) If you are atheist or agnostic, this is the equivalent of looking to a god for forgiveness. Instead, look to nature, where evolution is a history of many mistakes with occasional spectacular successes. Allow yourself the luxury of making mistakes just like every living organism does.

❧ *Practice the Buddhist meditation called Tonglen.* Tonglen is part of the Lojong teachings. It's a breathing practice designed to elicit compassion and healing for both yourself and another person. While breathing in, you visualize "taking in" the suffering of a particular person, and while breathing out, you release to that person something positive like relief, peace, love, or healing. By focusing on the pain of others, Tonglen brings a sense of compassion for the flawed beings that we all are.

❧ *Accept resistance until it melts away.* If you feel resistance, anger, or fear when you try to breathe in someone's pain, then breathe in those feelings of resistance and breathe out the healing of that resistance to yourself and all others in the world who feel the same way. Tonglen meditation is about a fearless love that transforms pain into healing energy. You can also visualize your true, wise, and radiant self facing the ordinary you and doing the breathing. This will allow self-forgiveness and self-healing.

LESSON FOUR: SEE FORGIVENESS
AS GOOD MEDICINE

In April 2006, the story of a little girl with a powerful capacity to forgive caught my attention. Five-year-old Kai Leigh Harriott of Massachusetts publicly forgave the man whose bullet had paralyzed her when she was only two. In court, this beautiful African American child with strangely luminous, soulful eyes said clearly to Anthony Warren, "What you done to me was wrong . . . but I forgive you." Three years earlier, Kai Leigh had been sitting on the porch with her older sister when Warren, who had argued with some folks who lived on the first floor, shot three times at the house. He wanted to shoot the person he'd fought with, but hit Kai instead. The bullet shattered her spine. In an article in the *Boston Globe*, reporter Megan Tench noted that when another reporter asked Kai why she forgave Warren, "she shyly but clearly said, 'I wanted him to tell the world the truth. I know he didn't mean to do it.' " The article went on to quote others in the Boston area who disagreed with Kai: "He took her life; now she can't walk forever. Someone should take his life," one man was quoted. But Kai's mother, Tonya David, was inspired by her daughter: "Television footage . . . showed David hugging Warren, twenty-nine, after he apologized for shooting her daughter and just before he was sentenced to thirteen to fifteen years in state prison. She only intended to shake his hand, she said, but he surprised her when he pulled her in for an embrace. Inspired by her daughter's strength, David said she couldn't let the man go."

We each have our own perspective on how much forgiveness should be granted in this kind of tragedy, but it's clear that Kai's strength and compassion freed both her mother and the man who shot her to experience love rather than hate.

Forgiveness reduces the powerful mixture of anger, hatred, and fear that comes with seeing yourself as the victim of another. Chronic anger has well-documented and harmful effects on the cardiovascular and immune systems.

People who score high on forgiveness as a personality trait are less likely to be depressed, anxious, hostile, narcissistic, or exploitative and are also less likely to become dependent on drugs or nicotine. They are more likely to be empathic. Combat veterans suffering from PTSD experience less depression and fewer symptoms of trauma if they are able to forgive themselves and others. "High forgivers" (those who score high on forgiveness as a trait) show less reactivity in blood pressure and arterial pressure when asked about conflict with a parent or caregiver. In contrast, those who score low in forgiveness show high reactivity and poor recovery. In studies in which people were encouraged to forgive, there was increased self-esteem and hope. A few studies have shown that these benefits may last as long as a year.

In one study of thirty divorced or permanently separated mothers with young children, those who had forgiven their ex-husbands reported a greater sense of self-acceptance and purpose and lower levels of anxiety and depression. Peace, hope, ease, connection and renewed faith were the positive states they reported. One 2001 study found that the impact of forgiveness was truly global: from age eighteen onward, the extent to which people reported the tendency to be forgiving strongly buffered them against psychological stress. Even forgiving God is linked to mental health—in one study of two hundred undergraduates, difficulty forgiving God predicted an anxious and depressed mood.

Just deciding to forgive someone doesn't work very well, according to studies. Far more effective is the process of invoking love, compassion, and empathy and practicing forgiveness exercises. These are surprisingly powerful, even in difficult situations. A one-on-one forgiveness intervention conducted by Robert Enright was highly effective in helping women who had been molested increase their hope and decrease their anxiety and depression. After intervention, emotional health in a group of such women was just as good as or better than that of women who had not been molested. Even more remarkably, these improvements remained at follow-up one year later. Says Robert Enright, "All of the incest survivors asked us, 'Are you sure you want me in the study? I will not forgive this person,' and we said, 'Yes, we want you in the study.' Then they said, 'Well, my motivation for being here is to make myself better.' And they felt transformed by the process to the point where they were better able to forgive the perpetrator. Knowing you've been hurt, knowing how much anger has compromised your life, you need to do the hard work of thinking and feeling and behaving in a forgiving way. It means seeing the inherent worth of another human being. It means watching your own release from an emotional prison occurring before your eyes."

That release lasts, according to research. A forgiveness intervention with men whose partners had decided to have an abortion showed the same decrease in grief, anger, and anxiety. At follow-up three months later, the benefits remained. Self-help and informal religious groups also help people forgive. Sixty-one percent of 1,400 Americans who participated in small, informal religious or self-help groups found themselves more able to forgive—and, in turn, more successful in overcoming addiction, guilt, and discouragement.

❧ *Consider—deeply—the other person*. Setting aside your own hurt for now, ask yourself about the person who hurt you. What was it like for that person growing up? Did he or she have a difficult childhood? At the time this person hurt you, was he or she struggling with life issues or conflicts? Can you see this person as a member of the tribe of humanity? How about as a member of your community? Is this person worthy of compassion in any way? Does this person suffer and also need healing?

❧ *Expand even the briefest moments of empathy*. When you think of the person who hurt you, are you able to feel empathy or positive emotions for him or her, even if these emotions slip by quickly? If so, would you be willing to indulge those emotions for a few minutes a day and see whether this brings you a greater feeling of peace and wholeness?

❧ *Regard, once again, the benefits of forgiveness*. Reflect on all the benefits of forgiveness highlighted in this chapter. Think about the emotional relief you will give yourself if and when you decide to forgive the deepest hurts of your life. Remember that it's really difficult to hold inside yourself two opposing emotions at the same time, so that when you are in a forgiving state, you are unlikely to also be in a vengeful state. Understand forgiveness as a form of enlightened self-interest, a gift that you give yourself by learning whatever good lessons you can from an event.

LESSON FIVE: CHOOSE TO PRESERVE

As we age and our values begin to shift, we actually become more forgiving. Forgiving others is uniquely and positively associated with life satisfaction after age forty-five. Research shows that young children are the least willing to forgive; for younger adults, forgiveness is usually triggered by encouragement from family, by the passing of the consequences of the harm, or simply by a good mood. One study of children found that those who imagined "getting back" at friends in imaginary scenarios had fewer best friends and were less accepted by their peers. When we're young, time seems open-ended and life goals loom large. For older adults, as the end of life becomes a more palpable reality, life's concerns shift to meaning, purpose, and loving others. About eight out of ten older adults are more invested in relationships than in competition or achievement. Health and well-being are more dependent on these strong ties as we age, and forgiveness therefore becomes more important. As Giacomo Bono puts it, "Unforgiveness is more costly for older individuals. As we age, we lose the perverse luxury of simply terminating relationships that are troubled and moving on to begin new ones."

LESSON SIX: SHIFT YOUR PERSPECTIVE

As a twelve-year-old boy, Samuel Oliner, of Humboldt State University in California, escaped to the roof of his ghetto home while his family and neighbors were slaughtered by Nazis. "The next day, in a state of trance, I sneaked out of the ghetto," he recalls, "and met a peasant who said to me, 'Those poor damned Jews were slaughtered,' and I had to pretend surprise." Taken in by a Polish peasant woman named Balwina, who taught him the catechism, renamed him Jusek, and sent him out to masquerade as a Polish boy, Sam became a stable boy for a Nazi sympathizer who had taken over a house formerly belonging to exterminated Jews. For two and a half years, he slept in a barn and herded cows. Oliner eventually emigrated to America, where he married and obtained his Ph.D. in psychology. But he was a haunted man. "I was a little on the violent side," he says. "I had to go to therapy and marriage counseling. I suffered from nightmares. I was not very considerate. I felt that anything you can tell me, I've already experienced.

Any evil that you've seen—well, I've seen my family murdered. An igno-rant guy from the South once started talking about Jews, and I got so angry I threw him down the stairs. But when he learned about my history, he ac-tually became my friend."

If forgiveness is a positive response to harm, Oliner's chance to deeply forgive his history did not arrive until he was forty-eight years old. It was then that he began research on the rescuers of the Holocaust—non-Jews who risked their lives to save and shelter Jews, often strangers. Oliner is co-author with his wife of one of the most highly regarded studies to come out of Holocaust literature, an in-depth look at seven hundred rescuers. He found that rescuers are naturally empathic, are easily moved by the pain of others, and have a strong sense of personal and social responsibility. Above all, rescuers are imbued with a quality called "extensivity"—the ability to extend their caring beyond the intimates of their in-group. "It's the essence of the altruistic personality," says Oliner.

Sam Oliner, like all of us, needed proof that humanity has not totally lost its soul. "The project made me feel much better," he says. "I'm grateful for the people who cared. It's because of these people that I'm here." Ac-cording to Morton Hunt, author of *The Compassionate Beast*, "Oliner's inti-mates say that his research healed him. As [one] Rabbi put it, 'He found the spark of decency in human beings.' " Sam recalls being at a colleague's home in Berlin. "He said with tears in his eyes, 'Sam, if we live a thousand years we'll never overcome the guilt of what we've done to your people.' I too was moved to tears. I told him it was not his fault. To forgive is very im-portant because it's self-liberating. You unburden yourself of your own anger and desire for vengeance."

❧ *Shift to gratitude.* If you find yourself ruminating over a hurt and are not ready to forgive, shift to gratitude. Think about all that is good in your life and all that you appreciate. Remember, forgiveness is a positive re-sponse to harm. By focusing on the good, you move anger and hurt to the periphery. As the new-age cliché so correctly puts it, energy flows where at-tention goes.

LESSON SEVEN: FORGIVENESS IS A PROCESS

The marriage and family therapist Shari Delisle, Ph.D., is founder and executive director of Kids' Turn, in San Diego—an organization that helps bring peace to warring parents who are fighting over custody of their kids during and after a divorce. Delisle herself went through what she calls a "nightmarish divorce" when she was thirty-one with four children. "I made so many terrible mistakes, and so did my children's father, with the result that our kids suffered terribly. That fuels my passion and compassion for other parents." Some of the parents she helps have been fighting about custody for as long as ten or fifteen years, and they rate their conflict between a 7 and a 10—10 being the highest possible level. Even so, says Delisle, "I've seen miracles. I've seen parents start to look at things very differently, so that by the time we're done working together they're sitting together with their kids, smiling and talking with one another. People can really transform their relationships if they try."

The exercises that Delisle has developed for parents will work well in any situation where there is hurt and betrayal that escalates into perpetual conflict and an overriding desire to win at all costs. It can even work in long-standing difficult situations.

❧ *Embrace the concept of "higher ground,"* which above all is based on kindness even in the face of extreme negativity and hostility. Says Delisle, "I've worked in locked psychiatric units, and with kids in gangs, and with parents, and what all these folks taught me is that kindness is enormously powerful. It's difficult for people to withstand kindness, difficult for them to hang on to their hardness, when you are being kind." Respect, kindness, and compassion are the best strategies any of us have to pave the way toward forgiveness—and even reconciliation—in difficult circumstances.

❧ *Work with a "surrogate" at first.* If your relationship with someone is extremely difficult, ask a trusted friend or family member to substitute as a proxy for that person. Now have a discussion with that proxy person in which you truly express to them how hurt and angry you feel, and in which you are truly listened to. Also write out your feelings in a journal. Let yourself be listened to, and listen to yourself. This is excavation—the first step in forgiveness.

❧   *Let the surrogate stand in.* Now have that proxy person play the role of the person you are having conflict with. (Coach your proxy ahead of time about the hostile, negative, undermining attitudes and statements you feel are coming from that difficult person.) In turn, practice the skill of taking the "higher ground": respond with grace and forbearance and kindness.

❧   *Tell the surrogate exactly how you feel.* With your proxy person, let yourself feel the fear and hurt that come from being treated badly—rather than responding with anger, which is a mask to cover up those feelings of vulnerability. Experience your own vulnerability. "If we can talk to each other about our fears and hurts," says Delisle, "the anger melts away. Then we can relate to each other on a meaningful level."

❧   *Keep practicing.* Recognize that compassion and forgiveness can be exquisitely difficult and that they are skills that require repeated practice. "You start doing it, but you have to keep doing it," says Delisle. "If somebody cuts me off in traffic, my initial reaction is a hostile response, but then I quickly shift it consciously to, 'It's okay.' "

❧   *Be aware that perspective changes over time.* Think about an event that hurt you in the past and that you thought you could never forgive—a betrayal by a friend, the breakup of a relationship, a humiliation at work. Over time, have you come to see that event in a different perspective? Perhaps your life now has an entirely different focus, and you can accept that event as part of the fabric of your experiences, as a contribution to what makes you who you are. Now take a present hurt that is still percolating and imagine your life ten years hence. Will you most likely be more accepting and forgiving of this hurt? If you can do it then, why not do it now?

LESSON EIGHT: THE POWER OF APOLOGY

Julie Exline found that apology is the single largest predictor of forgiveness. To offer and accept an apology is really one of the most potent and poignant human interactions. More than anything, a sincere apology helps restore a relationship. Apology has the ability to wash away resentment and bitterness. Some researchers feel that the richer an apology is—admitting responsibility for a mistake, expressing remorse, and offering to repair the situation—the more powerful it is. The key to apology, however, is remorse. Remorse truly conveys distress, self-awareness, and regret. It also elicits empathy in the hurt person.

Studies show that someone who imagines an offender offering a strong apology feels more positive and experiences declines in heart rate and other physiological measures of stress. In other words, apology heals the recipient.

And yet, apologies often fail, so we all need to think about giving and receiving apologies effectively. For instance, it does little to repair a relationship if you say, "Okay, if you think I did something wrong, I'm sorry." Nor does it help to give an apology with the expectation that all will be forgiven: "I'm sorry already! I've said I'm sorry! So why don't you let it go?" The goal of an apology is not necessarily reconciliation. It's a gift to another—and to yourself. It needs to be given freely and sincerely.

One reason apologies fail is that the "transgressor" and the "victim" usually see the event differently. Examining personal narratives, researchers have found that those who cause harm tend to minimize the offense—probably to protect themselves from shame and guilt. They often feel that their mistakes or transgressions were mitigated by extenuating circumstances, and they may divide the blame among several people or describe motives that were understandable at the time. They also tend to downplay the consequences of their actions. These tendencies can inflame the anger of the hurt person, who, in contrast, may see an offense as bigger than it really is—simply because when a wound is fresh, it feels that way. Weeks, months, or even years later, we may have a different perspective, but at the time it simply hurts. Those who are hurt tend to see the act as one with severe consequences and as part of an ongoing pattern that is inexcusable, immoral, and gratuitously cruel. Each person has his or her own truth, and there is bias and distortion on both sides. Therefore, to apologize sincerely we must first listen attentively to how the other person really feels about what happened—not simply assert what we think happened.

Researchers have discovered another reason apologies fail: they call it the "magnitude gap." When we've harmed someone, that person loses more than we gain. That means we can never really repay our debt. That is one reason vendettas become permanent over time. After trying to repair the situation, the "transgressor" believes the two sides are now even. But the "victim" may still feel that retaliation is warranted. Forgiveness does not happen all at once. In addition, people sometimes hold a grudge because another person has breached their own standards of justice and moral behavior. Forgiveness depends to some extent on the magnitude of a transgression and its moral burden.

What do we do when we've made a serious mistake and harmed someone? For nearly a decade I chaired the Committee on Students at the Case School of Medicine. I recall several students who almost quit medicine because they'd made a medical mistake with some serious consequences, despite good supervision. Fortunately, they kept on and, in the process, learned a lot about how to tell patients about errors without having patients completely lose confidence in the health care they receive. Medicine is a learning curve. Some years ago, Dr. Aaron Lazare, author of the renowned book On Apology and chancellor and dean as well as professor of psychiatry at the University of Massachusetts Medical School, came to visit our school of medicine and talked to us about apology. The lecture hall was packed, and the next day on grand rounds the hallways were filled with medical students and physicians wanting answers: Should we tell patients when we make mistakes? How do we apologize for these mistakes? How can we say we are sorry without losing our patient's confidence?

Lazare told us that apologies heal because they restore self-respect and dignity for both individuals. Apology assures us that we share the same values, that the error was not purposeful, that we are safe in another's presence, that the one who harmed us is authentically suffering over his mistake, and that we can talk openly about it. What is needed for an apology to be effective is a deeply empathic, heartfelt, hard-won "I am so sorry for what I did."

❧ *Apologize from the heart.* The exercise here is simple: when an apology seems warranted, offer it with sincerity.

A Final Lesson: Become the Good You Wish to Find

Melody LeBaron, now a life coach based in Atlanta, Georgia, was the oldest of seven children in a religious Mormon family. When she left the church and her first husband, her father disowned her. She was devastated, but over time, practicing forgiveness exercises, not only did she and her father reconcile but, he came to her wedding to her current husband, which was held at a Buddhist shrine. LeBaron still marvels at the change she has seen in her father, who delighted in her wedding ceremony even though it was non-Mormon. "Forgiveness," says LeBaron, "is the most freeing act there is." LeBaron practiced a specific forgiveness meditation for an entire year while she and her father were estranged, and they finally reconnected with a loving phone call from LeBaron. She became the loving person she wished her father to be. "These days, when I read a letter from my father, I take in only the love, not the fear and judgment that is still part of his worldview," she explains. "A friend of mine reminded me recently that I used to read his letters to me and cry over the parts that were harsh. Now I just ignore those parts. I have truly forgiven him."

Here is a version of the forgiveness exercise that Melody LeBaron practiced and that she also teaches her clients:

❧ *Sit in a quiet place and relax.* Breathe deeply. Imagine your body filling with light. Now, allow yourself to imagine roots growing out of the base of your spine and the soles of your feet, growing down into Mother Earth, grounding you like a strong tree. And just as trees bring energy or life force up through their roots, imagine that you can feel life force coming up your feet and spine, blessing your body. When you feel safe and strong, visualize the pure soul or essence of the person you wish to forgive. "Soul" does not mean some nonmaterial etheric matter that floats off when we die; you may understand soul as spirit, or you may understand it as that pure essence that shone out of our eyes when we were a newborn, before life and experience altered us. Now, tell that person's soul about your hurt. Tell that soul what you need it to know. Speaking to the soul of the person you have forgiven, set any boundaries you need to set, speak any unspoken truths, give that person permission to show up differently if possible, or wish that person and yourself well.

❧   *Become the love.* Now allow love to fill the space where the darkness had been. Know that you are becoming the good, the love, you wish to see in this other person.

❧   *Offer a gift.* From Shari Delisle comes this simple suggestion: do something small but meaningful to show appreciation for the other person. Do this without expectation of getting something in return. Delisle recalls that one mother, who wasn't speaking with her ex-husband at all, sent him a Father's Day card that said, "Thanx for being such a good dad to our boys." The father reported that after he opened the card, he sat down and wept for half an hour, then phoned her and thanked her for sending it. She was stunned that it was so meaningful to him, and they had a three-hour conversation during which they both agreed to fire their attorneys.

In whatever way you choose, you can turn to the power of forgiveness to set yourself free.

Your Forgiveness Score

It's time to answer the questions on the forgiveness section of your Love and Longevity Scale. We have divided responses into percentiles, or fifths. These are general guidelines; you may score right near the cutoff between percentiles, so please keep this in mind and use the scale as a friendly tool. Remember:

There are two steps to determining your score on a scale. First, determine which items need to be "reverse-scored" (denoted with the ® symbol). For reverse-scored items, see the chart below for how to score.

If you score a . . .	. . . assign yourself a score for that item of:
1	6
2	5
3	4
4	3
5	2
6	1

The second step is to add the scores for individual items *after* the reverse-scored items have been reverse-scored. Take the quiz now, and take it again if you wish after you've finished this book and begun practicing the art of forgiving in your daily life.

Using the scale provided, please circle the one number that best reflects your opinion about whether or not each statement below describes you or experiences that you have had. There are no correct answers, so please respond as honestly as possible to each one.

1. I don't hold grudges when one of my family members does something that hurts me.
    1=strongly disagree   2=disagree   3=slightly disagree   4=slightly agree
    5=agree   6=strongly agree

2. I find it easy to forgive when someone in my family harms me.
    1=strongly disagree   2=disagree   3=slightly disagree   4=slightly agree
    5=agree   6=strongly agree

3. I try to set an example of forgiveness in my family.

   1=strongly disagree   2=disagree   3=slightly disagree   4=slightly agree
   5=agree   6=strongly agree

4. I have grudges against loved ones that I've held on to for months or years.[®]

   1=strongly disagree   2=disagree   3=slightly disagree   4=slightly agree
   5=agree   6=strongly agree

5. It is not very easy to forgive when a family member hurts me.[®]

   1=strongly disagree   2=disagree   3=slightly disagree   4=slightly agree
   5=agree   6=strongly agree

6. I never hang on to grudges when one of my friends does something that hurts me.

   1=strongly disagree   2=disagree   3=slightly disagree   4=slightly agree
   5=agree   6=strongly agree

7. I never let my anger simmer when a friend treats me unfairly.

   1=strongly disagree   2=disagree   3=slightly disagree   4=slightly agree
   5=agree   6=strongly agree

8. My friends would say that I am a forgiving person.

   1=strongly disagree   2=disagree   3=slightly disagree   4=slightly agree
   5=agree   6=strongly agree

9. It is not very easy to forgive when a friend hurts me.[®]

   1=strongly disagree   2=disagree   3=slightly disagree   4=slightly agree
   5=agree   6=strongly agree

10. When a friend hurts my feelings, I act coldly toward him or her for quite a while.[®]

    1=strongly disagree   2=disagree   3=slightly disagree   4=slightly agree
    5=agree   6=strongly agree

11. When a coworker or neighbor does something hurtful, I work hard to forgive.

    1=strongly disagree   2=disagree   3=slightly disagree   4=slightly agree
    5=agree   6=strongly agree

12. I never hold on to a grudge when a neighbor or coworker hurts my feelings.

    1=strongly disagree   2=disagree   3=slightly disagree   4=slightly agree
    5=agree   6=strongly agree

13. I try to set an example of forgiveness in my community and place of work.

    1=strongly disagree   2=disagree   3=slightly disagree   4=slightly agree
    5=agree   6=strongly agree

14. When someone in my community hurts my feelings, sooner or later I will get even.®

    1=strongly disagree   2=disagree   3=slightly disagree   4=slightly agree
    5=agree   6=strongly agree

15. My neighbors and coworkers would probably say that I'm a vindictive person.®

    1=strongly disagree   2=disagree   3=slightly disagree   4=slightly agree
    5=agree   6=strongly agree

16. I encourage people I know to view the conflicts around the world in a more forgiving way.

    1=strongly disagree   2=disagree   3=slightly disagree   4=slightly agree
    5=agree   6=strongly agree

17. Forgiveness should be a much bigger part of foreign relations.

    1=strongly disagree   2=disagree   3=slightly disagree   4=slightly agree
    5=agree   6=strongly agree

18. When our nation is attacked, revenge is the best way to solve the problem.[®]

    1=strongly disagree   2=disagree   3=slightly disagree   4=slightly agree
    5=agree   6=strongly agree

19. We should do more to retaliate when endangered by a foreign foe.[®]

    1=strongly disagree   2=disagree   3=slightly disagree   4=slightly agree
    5=agree   6=strongly agree

20. For the most part, it is impossible for nations to forgive their former enemies.[®]

    1=strongly disagree   2=disagree   3=slightly disagree   4=slightly agree
    5=agree   6=strongly agree

YOUR FORGIVENESS SCORE

High Giver (80th percentile)	93 or above
Giver (60th percentile)	83–92
Moderate Giver (40th percentile)	75–82
Low Giver (20th percentile)	68–74

❧

Six

❧

The Way of Courage:
Speak Up, Speak Out

In 1996, Elissa Montanti visited Bosnia. At the time, she lived in Staten Island and suffered from a debilitating anxiety disorder. "I was shown a letter from a boy who had lost two arms and a leg when a land mine blew up," she recalls. "The letter this boy had written said, 'Somebody help me, please get me new arms and a leg.'" Moved and inspired, Montanti recruited airlines and hospitals and within twenty-four hours had gotten enough aid to bring the boy to New York. "I was single at the time and had two dogs, so he stayed with me for four months, and while I was giving him back his limbs, my anxiety started to disappear. I had been asking God to help me with my anxiety, and little did I know that help would come in the form of a letter from halfway around the world."

Today the nonprofit foundation that Montanti has created, Global Medical Relief Fund, offers medical care and prosthetic limbs to refugee children from war-torn places like Bosnia, El Salvador, Liberia, Niger, Iraq, and Somalia. "The courage of these kids is absolutely amazing," says

Montanti, who seems innocently unaware of her own courage in visiting war-torn places and rescuing these children. "A little boy I just brought here lost his sight *and* arm. I reached out, and twenty different specialists saw him. His sight was too far gone for a cornea transplant, but he got a new arm and when the newspapers asked, 'How do you feel now?' he answered with a big smile on his face, 'Now I can search my way.' This is courage." The first boy she helped, Kenen, now lives with Montanti and her husband and is, she says, "an example for all the children I bring here. They look at him and say, 'If he can do it, I can do it,' because he's a triple amputee." Many of the children return each year as they grow, to have their prosthetic limbs adjusted. "People ask me if anyone can do this. Yes, anyone can do this who has love in his or her heart. That's all it takes."

Courage: Love That Forces Change

Courage is love as action—love on her silver steed, forcing change in the world, rising to challenges, negotiating life with skill, and confronting others with care and wisdom. The qualities that courage draws upon—hardiness and resilience, as well as the ability to bend and alter course when faced with difficulty, to commit oneself to a cause, and to find inner power during times of pain—are *all* associated with mental health. We need a deep, tensile strength to face the tough times in life, to speak out persuasively against injustice, and, above all, to love others wisely and well. To love at all is a risk that requires courage—we risk our safety, letting ourselves be raw and vulnerable; we accept our share of compromise and weather disappointment and despair; and above all, we are willing to confront a loved one even if what we need to say is not easy or kind.

Courage takes many forms. For some, it means changing the world, even risking one's life to do so. For others, it requires standing up for oneself, speaking out in your own relationships about what you need, setting boundaries. For still others, it's the bravery to face each day in spite of difficulties, either psychological, physical, or economic. For all of us, it means developing the resilience and optimism to handle tough circumstances and emerge stronger and wiser. From the landscape of the world to our interior landscape, courage is a necessity—and can be a powerful way of giving, as you'll see.

Courage is the hallmark of every human who has changed the world, from Jesus to Joan of Arc. Real courage is the legendary stuff of history. Martin Luther King Jr., Abraham Lincoln, and Mahatma Gandhi were killed for confronting deep harms embedded in the very structure of society. That they were able to remain free of malice while doing their work is remarkable.

But courage is not just the signature of great historical figures. As Paul Wink—author of one of IRUL's most important studies on giving and health—told me after interviewing nearly 180 individuals late in their lives, "Every life has its moments of quiet heroism. In a sense, we are all heroes. This is what I discovered in interviewing, in depth, so many different folks from so many walks of life."

I like students, and I think of myself as a nurturer, but one time I was forced to confront a student whom we all knew simply did not have the humanity required to be a doctor. He was vividly, palpably racist. His peers were appalled, and his patients terrified. After a series of discussions with this young man, we expelled him. Though we were subsequently flooded with threats from his lawyers, we stayed with our decision. None of us at Case regretted our decision; in fact, his ugly response only confirmed that we'd been correct, even though our decision took a bit of courage.

Courage comes from the Latin for "heart" (*cor*). Courage is also contained in the word *encouragement*—literally, giving heart to another. And so we can look to the roots of language to show us the essence of *courage*.

One of my favorite stories of courage is that of the eighteenth-century Quaker John Woolman, who went to Quaker meetings across all the colonies, witnessing to people, one by one, about the evils of slavery. He visited farm after farm for most of the two decades of his adult life and then traveled to England to continue his work there. Because of his efforts, by 1770, a century before the Civil War, not a single American Quaker owned a slave. Activists like Woolman possess courage in the face of threat, perseverance in the face of indifference, composure in the face of rage, equanimity in the face of hostility, integrity in the face of imprisonment, and, most importantly, love in the face of hate. We in our everyday existence can be inspired to do the same—and our lives will be better for it. For inevitably, when we truly love someone, we are driven at times to confront them.

The very idea of directing an Institute for Research on Unlimited Love is, for me, a way of confronting all those aspects of our society that fail the test of encouraging love. I run up against those who think that, frankly, the whole idea of studying love is insane, partly because they have no confidence that we can be sincerely generous, and partly because they think that real science looks only at human deficits rather than at strengths. I say: love is the only force that makes life worth living. This is my way of confronting the world as we know it with the world as it can become.

"If you want to be courageous, you've got to love. If you want to be powerful, you've got to love," says Otis Moss, the African American pastor at Olivet Institutional Baptist Church in Cleveland, Ohio, and a protégé of the Reverend Martin Luther King Jr. Moss, who is past chairman of the board of trustees of Morehouse College in Atlanta, the nation's only private liberal arts college for African American men, has been active in the civil rights movement for over forty years. "It takes far more strength to reconcile than it does to kill. Out of the context of reconciliation, India gained her independence, South Africa threw off the shackles of apartheid, and Nelson Mandela went from prison to president. So when we look at what bitterness and revenge bring forth and compare that to courage and reconciliation, there really is no comparison at all.

"It was during my college years that the lynching of Emmett Till took place in Mississippi," recalls Pastor Moss, "and Rosa Parks refused to give up her seat on a bus. I became a leader of the sit-in movement in Atlanta and at times risked my life and the lives of those I led. The night before I was to lead a demonstration at the state capitol in Georgia, the mayor of the city and the chief of police appealed to us not to go. I led the demonstration fully aware that we could be seriously injured or killed."

Pastor Moss recalls standing with Dr. Martin Luther King Sr. just after his wife had been murdered. "His wife was shot and killed while she was playing the organ in her church. Here he was, a husband, father, grandfather, a man who had witnessed the assassination of his son years earlier, the untimely death of another son, and now the murder of his wife. And he said, 'I will go on thanking God for what I have left. For the rest of my days

I will not hate. I will not hate. I want to go on record that I will not hate.'
We do not have to surrender to circumstances that would break us. We can
let deep hurts remake us, finding new courage, new strength. There are
people whose faces I look into from Sunday to Sunday who have witnessed
death or gone through triple bypass surgery, and yet they sing 'Hallelujah,'
and they are remarkable witnesses to the power of love. A person in my
hometown once said to me, 'Pastor Moss, I'm living between the "Oh
Lord!" and the "Thank you, Jesus!"' That was her way of saying, 'I live
daily between the forces of hurt and hope, but "thank you" is always the final expression of my life.'"

As Otis Moss so eloquently points out, courage is one of the more challenging ways of love. In this chapter, you'll learn how courage is linked to
traits like resilience and hardiness. You'll learn about tough-and-tender
courage and how to cultivate what are known as "soft skills" to negotiate
conflict. You'll learn about courage as a way of love that can change the
lives of others and fill you with joy even as it demands bravery and risk.
Here are some highlights:

Brave acts are rewarding, according to research on whistle-blowers—those
who speak up against injustice, usually in the workplace. According to a study
in the late 1990s, 90 percent of whistle-blowers said that they would do it *again*
if they had the chance.

People who witness bravery feel inspired to act courageously themselves.

*The willingness and ability to promote justice is linked with the ability to resolve
conflicts.* In one study of two groups who fought in the Korean War, those dec-
orated for bravery also turned out to be socially mature, intelligent, and more
emotionally stable than their peers. In another study of the terminally ill, researchers found that bravery in the face of illness was linked to hope, optimism, and self-confidence.

Hardiness is the core trait of courageous individuals. According to the researcher Salvatore Maddi, founder of the Hardiness Institute at the University
of California at Irvine, hardiness is composed of the three Cs of courage: com-

mitment, control, and challenge. "Hardi-coping," as Maddi calls it, can be taught and protects health and well-being throughout life. One key aspect of hardiness is the ability to view challenges as opportunities to grow.

Courage often requires that people reach a turning point—sometimes a crisis—at which they deconstruct their sense of self and reconstruct it around altered priorities or insights related to the crisis. According to research by the psychologists Richard Tedeschi and Lawrence Calhoun of the University of North Carolina, such change can be fertile ground for growth.

Courage begets joy and connection. Perhaps the finest qualitative, social, and scientific analysis of justice and love is found in the work of Anne Colby and William Damon in *Some Do Care: Contemporary Lives of Moral Commitment.* Colby, a professor of education at Stanford University, and Damon, director of Stanford's Center on Adolescence, studied and interviewed contemporary moral exemplars and activists. The picture of their lives, say Colby and Damon, "is one of striking joy, great certainty, and unremitting faith; one that results in high standards for the self and charity towards others." These individuals, say the authors, inevitably have a support network and exhibit moral courage, faith, and integrity. They share a sustained commitment to their ideals and a willingness to risk self-interest in the pursuit of service and justice. In short, bravery has helped them be successful in their endeavors.

Lessons from the Frontiers of Research

In October 2005, the Institute sponsored a conference called "The Love That Does Justice," which was funded in part by a grant from the Ford Foundation. I facilitated this conference because, as an activist friend of mine once said, "Love is when you pull babies out of the water at the George Washington Bridge in New York City. Justice is when you go north up to the Tappan Zee Bridge to find out who is throwing those babies in the water in the first place." The conference brought together dozens of activists, both young and old, with the abiding theme that a love *not* concerned with justice is simply not adequate.

That conference reaffirmed my intuition that a feeling for justice is linked to courage in what I view as both its core aspects: the willingness to take risks and the ability to heartfully "en-courage" others. Over forty years of research have found that a commitment to justice is linked to a sensitivity to fairness, the ability to imagine oneself in another's shoes, being moved by another's suffering, and feeling morally and psychologically responsive. Here follow insights from research on justice, bravery, hardiness, and transformation—all traits that define courage and allow us to confront harm.

LESSON ONE: COURAGE COMES IN MANY FORMS

The story I am about to tell, of Pastor Carl Wilkens of Milo Adventist Academy in Days Creek, Oregon, is a wonderful example of many kinds of bravery. Says Wilkens: "Real courage comes when you come up against something that far exceeds you. Real courage is about submission and trust. Are we going to rely on something larger than ourselves? We must use the gifts we have been given, but use them in the awareness of a much greater power at work."

Wilkens and his wife had gone to Rwanda as Adventist missionaries in the early 1990s; there they helped to rehabilitate health centers that had been destroyed by the civil war. Wilkens's parents were visiting on the peaceful Easter Sunday the weekend before the infamous mass genocide of 1993 began. The entire family was camped at a lake, "floating in the beautiful sunshine and warm water," remembers Wilkens. "When the genocide hit Rwanda, our whole family could have easily been slaughtered, but when the militia arrived at our gate, our Hutu neighbors spoke up for us to the machete-armed killers. They said, 'When we're sick, they take us to the hospital. Their kids play with our kids.'" Wilkens's neighbors risked their safety to speak up and convince the killers to pass over the home of the missionaries. Because of this, Wilkens decided to stay and help while the rest of his family evacuated with the other Americans. Nevertheless, Wilkens says, "the longer I stayed and the more I saw the scale of this massacre unfolding, the more I wondered if I should stay."

There are different kinds of fear in such a situation, notes Wilkens, and thus different kinds of courage. "There was a physical kind of fear when bullets came into the house, or my car was stopped by killers, or the back window was shot out of my car. But the greater fear is having people's lives in your hands and knowing your decision is going to affect their lives and you don't know whether you are doing the right thing or not. I could have left at any point."

Wilkens also had to summon up courage to face his own hopelessness. "I remember one time I did a word search in my little computer Bible program and put in the word *discouragement*, and this text came up: 'Be strong and courageous. Do not be terrified. Do not be discouraged, for the Lord your God will be with you wherever you go.' " Courage also meant simply continuing to offer daily help and showing that he cared: "The lion's share of my work during the genocide was bringing food, water, and medication to three groups of orphans. I think about what it meant to those people to have someone who actually chose to stay there, even if I was able to do very little for them." This kind of courage required presence above all: "When you talk about love and courage, what was so often underestimated and almost completely missed in the news was the power of presence." Finally, there is the courage required to rebuild after devastation: "The resilience of the people of Rwanda, to be able to pull together the fabric of their society after such a devastating experience and re-create school and government and church and shops and life again, is just phenomenal."

In their book *Character Strengths and Virtues*, the psychologists Martin Seligman and Christopher Peterson note that bravery takes three forms: physical, moral, and psychological. All three forms can be seen in Wilkens's story, and require the ability to act in the face of fear, drawing on ingenuity, mutual aid, social support, and toughness.

Physical bravery in war—like that of Wilkens and his neighbors—has been studied extensively. According to Seligman and Peterson, the most remarkable finding from studies on war and its aftermath is "that people are able to carry on in the face of the extraordinary challenges of life during war."

Bravery also means the ability to take social and economic risks, especially risks guided by conscience. That is *moral bravery*, which requires the willingness to do what one believes is right and just in spite of social or economic consequences—such as losing a job, friends, or status. Again, Wilkens showed great moral bravery in risking his own life. "Telling the truth may set one free," say Seligman and Peterson, "but it does not necessarily make one happy."

Finally, there is *psychological bravery*—the ability to act in spite of the fear of being psychologically destabilized. When Rwandans re-created the daily fabric of their society after the decimation of war, they drew on psychological bravery. Psychological bravery is required for most of us and is often unseen, according to Seligman and Peterson: "Millions of individuals summon psychological bravery every day to face their fears and anxieties," the authors note, "but their courageous behavior can be invisible to others." As Seligman and Peterson point out, psychological courage is required in everything from a physician-patient relationship, where doctor and patient negotiate ill health together, to vulnerability within marriage, since honesty and closeness go "hand in hand with the potential to be hurt and rejected."

Though most of us, thankfully, will never have to live through genocide, we all need to draw on a higher kind of courage at some point, as Carl Wilkens did. To do so, shift your attitude right now and create an inner readiness: be willing to move out of your comfort zone and confront risk. Know that your own trust in yourself to make the right choice is a form of higher courage. Here are some other ways to take action on these ideas.

❧ *Articulate your life purpose.* See yourself as a person on a mission, an individual with a higher purpose. According to the activist Andre Carothers, a great life purpose gives us courage to focus on what counts. A strong sense of purpose is energizing, clarifying, and enriching. Try this exercise: Sit quietly and focus on your breathing. Now imagine that you have just discovered you have one year to live. What will you do with this year? How do you want your friends and family to remember you? What in life are you most proud of, and what would you still like to do in this year? Write your thoughts down and, alone or with a partner, examine your life's purpose and how you would describe it. One person's mission in life might be, "I am here to connect to people through love." Another might be, "My purpose is to protect nature." Yet another might feel, "I was born to be an artist." The point of this exercise is that a life purpose is like a compass's true north: it guides us and gives us courage because it is profound and meaningful.

❧ *Start moving forward.* John Ronstadt, a professor at Babson College, says that in life there is a "corridor principle": those who are willing to take risks—such as individuals who start their own business—move forward as though proceeding down a corridor or hallway, and as they do so doors open to them that they never would have seen had they not been moving forward.

❧ *Take action—again and again.* Psychologists treat phobias through a process called "systematic desensitization." Individuals focus on relaxing while being exposed in a step-by-step fashion to what they fear, beginning with small exposures. Fears lose their power as you confront them. I believe that conquering *any* fear leads to greater confidence. After being widowed, a friend of mine in Manhattan took a sailing course. By the end of the summer, her sense of mastery as a new sailor had given her the feeling that she could rebuild her life as a solo woman. Another friend who considered himself shy volunteered to be a city guide for foreigners one day a month, taking them to see the "real" city that he lived in and loved.

LESSON TWO: LEARN HARDI-COPING

"I've devoted all my effort in my professional life to studying aspects of personality that help people overcome difficulty," says Salvatore Maddi, founder of the Hardiness Institute. Maddi grew up in a gang-ridden neighborhood, the child of Sicilian immigrants. He first discovered the unique protectiveness of hardiness when he and his colleagues began collecting data on workers at Illinois Bell Telephone Company. Six years into the study, in 1981, the company experienced what is still regarded as one of the largest upheavals in corporate history. "They went from twenty-six thousand employees in 1981 to only fourteen thousand in 1982. One manager said that he'd had ten supervisors in twelve months. We continued to collect data for another six years, and we found that although two-thirds of the employees fell apart after the upheaval—suffering heart attacks, strokes, divorces, mental disorders, even suicides—that there was another third who not only survived, they actually thrived."

This group was extremely hardy: they were strong, says Maddi, in the three Cs. "This kind of hardiness is the basis of what we call existential courage. The three Cs are commitment, control, and challenge. If you're strong in *commitment*, when the going gets rough you resolve to stay involved rather than pull away in isolation and alienation. If you're strong in *control*, you keep trying to have an influence on the outcome rather than sink into powerlessness. And if you're strong in *challenge*, you see change and stress as an opportunity to grow and learn, not as a violation of your comfort and security."

Hundreds of studies have been conducted on hardiness. Military personnel on peacekeeping or combat missions are buffered against life-threatening stresses if they score high on hardiness. In one study, Maddi examined hardiness in high school varsity basketball players and found that this trait predicted six out of seven aspects of performance excellence. Hardiness was also the strongest predictor of leadership behavior in West Point Military Academy cadets. In high school graduates about to attend college, hardiness was associated with less alcohol and drug use, according to the students' self-reports.

In one ingenious study of Maddi's, he asked adults to wear pagers; they were paged at random ten times during the day and each time asked to fill out a short questionnaire about the activity they were involved in, with whom, and how they felt about it. Workers who had tested high in hardiness reported that their activities were more enjoyable, interesting, and important, and they felt more support from others than did workers who had tested low in hardiness. Maddi concluded from this and other studies that openness to experience, and even imaginativeness, are associated with hardiness.

Hardy people are very good at what Maddi calls "Hardi-coping." There are, says Maddi, two unhealthy forms of coping. In regressive coping, one denies and avoids stress. The second is catastrophic coping—thinking the worst and striking out at the world. "This is what terrorists do," says Maddi. "But Hardi-coping sees the stressful circumstance accurately, puts it in a broader perspective, understands it's not that terrible after all, and allows you to analyze it deeply to see what you can learn from it. Then you can come up with a plan of action that might be decisive in turning the situation to your advantage."

Not surprisingly, "Hardy people are able to take unilateral action in order to resolve conflicts," says Maddi. "Their social relationships are much better than those of their less hardy peers. They help each other. In fact, hardiness is even related to self-care. We find that the higher you are in the hardy attitudes of courage, the more likely you are to allow yourself relaxation, exercise, and good nutrition."

The good news, says Maddi, is that people can be trained in hardiness. Female swimmers trained in hardiness perform better. Moreover, "we're finding now that when high-risk undergraduates undergo hardiness training, they have higher grade point averages and are more likely to stay in school than similar students who went through more standard approaches like time management and study skills."

Here are some highlights of Hardi-coping that you can integrate into your own life:

❧ *Distinguish between acute and chronic stress.* Acute stress can range from the babysitter's canceling to a change in job responsibilities or an argument with your spouse. Acute stresses may converge and seem overwhelming at times, but you can identify them by the fact that they will end. Chronic stress seems interminable: a relative has a serious, long-term illness; you and your spouse are dealing with infertility; you can't leave a job because it pays the rent. A first step is to separate acute from chronic stress.

❧ *Cultivate "Hardi-attitudes."* Once you have determined what type of stress you are experiencing, start to approach the problem with optimism. For an acute stress, you can expect a relatively quick solution. With chronic stress, you may need to reframe your approach to the problem as you learn to cope with it over time. Know that your life is important enough to engage in fully. Believe that changing your circumstances is a way to deepen meaning in your life. See difficulties as learning opportunities that will expand your talents and capacities. Remind yourself that you can positively influence much of what happens in life. See yourself as capable and as an active participant in your world. Even when a problem has aspects that cannot be changed, trust that if you are resourceful, you will be able to use the situation to learn new ways of responding to it. Welcome change and challenge. Have faith that greater life meaning and satisfaction will emerge from each stressful situation.

✤   *Make sure you have social support.* A social support network buffers you as you meet and overcome challenges in life. Cultivate family, friends, teachers, parents, colleagues, clients, and members of your spiritual community, all of whom you can ask for encouragement and advice, help, mentoring, friendship, and expertise.

✤   *Change difficult relationships.* According to Maddi, many of our relationship challenges can be resolved by *increasing* our commitment to the relationship. Maddi suggests making a list of the significant social relationships in your life. In relationships with significant conflict, determine to resolve the conflicts and replace them with love. Think about the source of the conflict. How much have you contributed, and how much is the other person's responsibility? Listen carefully when the other person expresses anger about an interaction with you. Just how is the person feeling threatened or undermined? Try to assist this person in talking about the problem rather than just expressing your own anger. Think carefully about the feedback you are getting. Make sure to let the person know how much he or she matters to you. Make suggestions about resolving the disagreement that take into account both your needs and those of the other person. Remember that relationships are a two-way street, so it is not likely that you are an innocent victim. Determining who is to blame is less important than improving the relationship. Remember the three Cs of commitment, control, and challenge. Approach this challenge committed to working it out and, believing that you can influence the outcome, and willing to risk your time and effort to do this. As you begin to change your relationships, one by one, you will begin to realize that you can indeed cope with conflict and stress and gain from the effort.

LESSON THREE: "EN-COURAGE" OTHERS

Offering encouragement to others is one way to change the world. Dr. Robert Haynie, an African American and associate dean for student affairs at Case Western School of Medicine, encourages young men who are in a jail diversion program by both confronting and caring about them. Haynie has been volunteering in this program for a decade, after being recruited by a minister named Bishop Prince J. Moultry. The East Cleveland Jail Diversion Program is a substitute for jail time and offers education as well as job training. "I believe we will ultimately be judged by how caringly we deal with three groups of individuals," says Haynie. "Those at the dawn of life, the children; those at the twilight of life, the elderly; and those in the shadows of life, the disadvantaged. The men in this program are in the shadows. At the first meeting I went to," he recalls, "a young man named Duane was ignoring everything I said. I said, 'You don't seem to be interested in what's going on here.' He looked straight at me and said, 'Let me tell you about you. You're a bourgeois nigger from the suburbs coming here to brainwash us.' I said, 'Duane, you look like an intelligent man, so let's analyze every word you just said. Give me the origin and use it in its proper context. So the first thing you said was 'bourgeois.' Tell me, what does that mean? Give me a little history of that word. We're going to examine each word you said in order.' Well, fast-forward six months and Duane graduated from the program. He'd totally changed. I saw him about two years ago, and he said, 'Doc, now I never say something if I don't really know what I mean by it.' "

According to Haynie, whenever he asks a group of young men in the program how many have had a close friend or relative murdered, every single hand goes up. "So I sit there thinking, *Boy, what would happen to me if I was raised in that atmosphere?* I was raised in a complete family unit. I ask these young men, 'What would you do if I gave you a sledgehammer and $5,000 to do the maximum amount of damage you can to tear up this room?' And they usually say, 'Doc, we're on it!' Then I say, 'Okay, tear it up. But what if I give you $500,000 now and a week to repair the room?' They know it's going to be much harder to repair that room than tear it down. I tell them it's easier to build than destroy. The same thing is true with their lives. But the code of the street is 'dis.' If you dis them—disrespect them—it can lead to death. Those two can come together very easily. That's why I've never disrespected any of those men, never raised my voice to them. I understand that under similar circumstances, maybe I could be in their position. East Cleveland has been in a state of physical emergency for eighteen years. One of the guys in my group was murdered eight years ago—just shot dead on Euclid Avenue."

Haynie recalls the time the bishop brought him down to the jail. "It was an absolute dungeon, like the Third World, with only one little light, and it smelled to high heaven. There was one guy who'd been down there for 180 days. I couldn't stay there for 180 seconds! So I wrote a letter to the judge and the mayor and told them this jail was cruel and unusual punishment. These men had not yet been found guilty—they were simply in a holding cell. Well, the city closed the jail and fixed it up."

How can you best encourage others? Here is one way:

❧ *Be willing to confront pain in the world.* Those in Haynie's "troika" of the vulnerable—children, the elderly, and the disadvantaged—need our help, and that requires both en-couragement and courage. We need to be supportive of those who are vulnerable and willing to step up to confront harm. Who in your vicinity can be en-couraged today? What cause can you help, whether with time, a donation, or good ideas?

LESSON FOUR: CONFRONT WITH CARE

Confronting destructive behavior is probably the hardest and most important form of courage. I describe it as "carefrontation," a neologism coined with the help of the Ohio psychologist Jack Marsick, who has carried out remarkable work on skillful reconciliation, including a 110-hour curriculum on leadership for the Ohio School Business Association.

"Carefrontation first creates resonance with the person you're confronting. I use gentle statements. I'm trying to read feelings. I also put my own feelings on the table. 'You know, when I'm near you, I feel anxious, so what do you think is going on here?' Or, 'I feel sad when I come in and your work isn't done, because I know you're really struggling.' In order to change behavior you need to engage people, not attack them."

Carefrontation caringly challenges the destructive tendencies in ourselves, others, and society at large. Sometimes such challenges are almost invisible, and yet they can have a profound impact. Twelve years ago, a forty-year-old woman was admitted to Case Western School of Medicine, and we almost expelled her. She had a gift for taking care of kids, but she was academically unprepared and failed a number of courses early on. Several faculty members and administrators were ready to oust her, so in my capacity as chair of the Committee on Students, I went individually to each person involved in making the decision and quietly advocated for her, encouraging them to look at her a little differently and to give her a second chance. They let her stay on, although she was required to repeat an academic year. Six years later I was having coffee in a local diner and saw this woman with her husband and parents. They came over and thanked me. The former student, now a practicing doctor, told me that her career was flourishing and she was immensely happy.

Carefrontation is a learning process for all of us, and sometimes it requires teamwork. Here's another small, personal story that might resonate with parents. A few years ago, my son and all his friends became addicted to computer games. Even when the sun was shining on a beautiful summer Saturday, he and his best friends would be inside with two game control panels, hardly speaking a word to each other, absorbed in the game for hours at a time. Some of these games concerned me because of their violent content—one, for instance, required dropping bombs on the computer screen. I would try to confront my son caringly and limit his computer time, and in turn he would get upset, even to the point of crying. He reasonably argued that all his friends spent this time on the games, so why should he be singled out? I had no idea how I could change his behavior without ruining our close and special relationship. Then I realized I needed help, so I called the parents of each of my son's friends and suggested a plan for limiting computer time during the week. We all said no to computer games during the week, and miraculously, the intervention worked. No one child felt singled out, and they all happily began to play soccer, practice their musical instruments, shoot hoops, enjoy nature—and still enjoy time on the weekends in front of their computers.

Carefrontation, says Jack Marsick, requires *soft* skills—not the hard skills of competitive prowess and ruthless business acumen. Marsick trained cardiovascular and thoracic surgeons at the Cleveland Clinic to be better leaders and listeners and to handle conflicts well by teaching them the soft skills of empathy and kindness. He was startled to find that each surgeon knew his college class rank and that the climate of the surgical unit encouraged the doctors to compete over the number of surgeries they completed each month. Interpersonal warmth was at a truly low ebb. "One day," Marsick recalls, "the chief of staff came to me and said, 'Jack, what do

I need to do to be a better leader?' and I looked straight at him and said, 'You need to be nice.' That was my way of carefronting him. In that simple statement I was really saying, 'I care enough about you to tell you to stop badgering people. You're such a gifted surgeon. People come to you from all over the world. But you're hard on your colleagues and staff.' " This was a remarkable comment for Marsick to make—and a mark of genuine sincerity on the part of a very thoughtful chief of staff to inquire in the first place.

Carefrontation requires four "soft skills" and four "core concepts," says Marsick:

The Four Soft Skills are:

1. *Learn to listen* and watch for emotional clues as well as content.
2. Show and *cultivate understanding of,* interest in, and sensitivity to another's perspective.
3. *Focus on having a positive impact* on others rather than winning an argument. or fight.
4. *Care as much about others' goals* as you do about your own.

The Four Core Concepts are:

1. *Build trust* by showing nonjudgmental respect for others.
2. *Influence others positively* by being a teacher, coach, counselor, or mentor.
3. *Offer advice* in a caring, inoffensive style.
4. *Offer understanding* of the other person's rationale and feeling without needing to embrace their reasons or diagnosing their problems from your perspective.

How can you carefront others effectively and gently? Here are some ways:

❧ *Explore triggers of fear or pain.* What kinds of interactions are most disruptive to your peace? Do you hate being interrupted while talking? Do the barbs of sarcasm wound deeply? When people ignore you or withdraw from you, do you feel frightened and lonely? Try to visualize a time when one of these triggers caused you discomfort. Share these triggers of vulnerability and pain with a friend or partner. With your new understanding of your-selves and each other, agree to try to avoid that triggering behavior, and if it does occur, discuss it with an open heart. En-courage openness and courage in each other.

❧   *Share what you love and what you don't.* Sit with a colleague, friend, or loved one and tell them (1) what you value in them and your relationship; (2) how it feels to be in their presence and to work, play, or live with them; (3) what you would like to see improved in your relationship; and (4) what you yourself are willing to do to ensure that this improvement happens.

❧   *Let someone know how much they matter before you confront them.* If you begin your confrontation with love and caring, the other person will feel less defensive. Then, as you confront their harmful or destructive behavior, let them know how it makes you feel and ask what they are feeling that might have triggered that behavior. Try to build trust, and offer advice in a caring way. Let them know that if they continue the destructive behavior, you may have to leave until they are willing to change, but that doesn't al-ter your commitment or affection.

LESSON FIVE: TRAUMA CAN
LEAD TO TRANSFORMATION

Forging and fine-tuning courage often occurs when people reach a *turning point*—often a crisis or severely traumatic event—that requires the decon-struction of their sense of self and the rearrangement of their priorities. Richard Tedeschi and Lawrence Calhoun of the University of North Car-olina use the term "post-traumatic growth" to describe positive psychologi-cal change that is forged in the fire of highly challenging life circumstances. They quote Hamilton Jordan's description of battling cancer: "After my first cancer," he writes in *No Such Thing as a Bad Day*, "even the smallest joys in life took on a special meaning—watching a beautiful sunset, a hug from my child." The authors don't bypass the depression, anxiety, and grief associated with trauma. They go on to quote Rabbi Harold Kushner's reflections on the death of his son: "I am a more sensitive person, a more effective pastor, a more sympathetic counselor because of Aaron's life and death than I ever would have been without it. And I would give up all those gains in a second if I could have my son back. If I could choose, I would forgo all of the spiritual growth and depth which has come my way because of our experiences . . . but I cannot choose."

Trauma begins like an earthquake, say Tedeschi and Calhoun. "A psychologically seismic event can severely shake, threaten, or reduce to rubble" the structure of a person's life and his or her sense of meaning. One's safety, identity, and future are threatened. After an earthquake, it requires courage to rebuild. Oddly, say Tedeschi and Calhoun, trauma survivors experience both heightened vulnerability and heightened strength. They have viscerally experienced the fact that bad things can and do happen, and yet they also find that they can survive earth-shattering events. Out of loss comes gain. In the midst of deprivation, one finds gratitude. At a time when one is vulnerable as never before, one finds reserves of strength. And, say Tedeschi and Calhoun, it is by thinking about the event deeply that one slowly processes and reframes it and one's life.

Is this kind of courage linked to health? One study in 1998 found that men with HIV were less likely to have rapid declines in certain immune cells if they processed their situation and reframed it as meaningful. An earlier 1987 study found lower rates of mortality in heart attack victims who derived meaning and life benefits from their illness by reframing it. These are tantalizing hints that the courage required to face and reframe life's greatest challenges may indeed protect health.

Reframing your circumstances is a way of creatively resolving suffering. Kevin Reimer, a professor of psychology at Azusa Pacific University, recalls one teenager from the Pico Union District, a ghetto overflowing with gangs in Los Angeles. "Eliana is fifteen and lives with her mother and brother in a four-hundred-square-foot room," says Reimer. "Almost single-handedly she began a neighborhood program to care for the elderly in a convalescent hospital a few blocks away. Her program involves people in relationships with senior citizens who are ill." Reimer interviewed Eliana in her tiny apartment, where cockroaches scurried across the walls and loud music blasted down the hallway. Eliana told Reimer that she "would like to be a person like my mom. She doesn't judge people by what she sees, but by what they are." She also told him that she'd never known her grandparents, who had been killed in Guatemala, and felt that her outreach to older people helped fill that gap. Kids like Eliana, says Reimer, "understand who they are because they've been forced to go deep and come to terms with their own quirks, strengths, and weaknesses."

If war refugees and ghetto children can find the courage to transform their lives, surely we can learn from their example. "People undergoing traumatic events have a great capacity to help others. Often a trauma survivor can be a great teacher," says Richard Mollica. In Cambodian refugee camps, Mollica visited wooden shacks where "people were overcrowded, had nowhere to go, and were eating the same rice and fish for ten years. They had no temple. Yet they were chanting, praying, and meditating. All over the world people are managing their terrible, extraordinary difficulties with tremendous courage, and the fact is that most people, from the moment of injury, really want to help themselves and others. This is the beauty you find in the experience. I've been humbled as a doctor to see all the work people are doing without help. All over the United States, for instance, there are refugees running community centers for other refugees."

Mirabai Bush, executive director of the Center for Contemplative Mind in Society in Massachusetts, says she first saw true courage when she went to work with Mayan refugee women in Guatemala. "They had lost everything—their husbands, parents, sometimes their children, their homes, and their land. And they were still resilient and finding new ways to grow gardens and still had the capacity for joy and caring for others. At the time, I had gone through a divorce and was upset that I was living in a smaller place, but they taught me some very deep lessons about bravery."

How can you transform your own life in the most difficult times? Betty Rogers, a documentary-maker and activist who has worked to stop sex trafficking, finds that meditation is key. Without a meditation practice, says Rogers, she could not have sustained herself. Traveling in Nepal, Kenya, Zimbabwe, Ethiopia, and other countries, she carried a small Buddhist altar with her and practiced meditation daily. "Anger is not effective if you're going to work in these areas. The stronger my meditation, the wider the space I cultivate every day, like creating a garden. And I carry that space with me so that there's room for love to appear. I remember a little school of young kids in the middle of nowhere on a mountain who had an inspired teacher, and she'd taught them to sing their hearts out, and they were conducting these amazing performances for themselves. I've had moments when I've felt there is a kind of universal force in our makeup, in the fabric of our being, in our very molecules, and that to be open to that is our life's work. There is always grace, there is always love."

❧ *Begin your process of transformation.* Rogers suggests sitting quietly and meditating in whatever way feels comfortable to you. Once you feel that inner quiet, ask yourself:

- What do I see that needs to be changed?
- What needs to be let go?
- Where can I be effective and make these changes?
- How can I find the higher grace in this situation? What might be some ways to redefine this situation, and myself, to find that grace?
- How can others' examples inspire me? How can I sing like the children on the mountaintop—sing my own life—with courage and love?
- Remember that social activism can teach you very profound spiritual truths if you're present and your heart is open.

The arc of courage is a wide one. It can be found in lives of great personal sacrifice, like those of Reverend Martin Luther King Jr., Rosa Parks, Joan of Arc, or Mahatma Gandhi—people who changed history and the world. It can be found in every successful relationship during those times when we confront difficulty with those we love, rise to the challenge, and stay committed. It is there in the smallest, most invisible ways each day— even if it just means the courage to "be" in a world that is often confusing. For all of us, courage requires love, and it allows us to love.

Your Courage Score

It's time to answer the questions on the courage section of your Love and Longevity Scale. We have divided responses into percentiles, or fifths. If you score in the twentieth percentile, that means that 80 percent of people are more courageous than you. Conversely, if you score in the eightieth percentile, that means that you are more courageous than most people. Remember:

There are two steps to determining your score. First, determine which items need to be "reverse-scored" (denoted with the ® symbol). For reverse-scored items, see the chart below for how to score.

If you score a . . .	. . . assign yourself a score for that item of:
1	6
2	5
3	4
4	3
5	2
6	1

The second step is to add the scores for individual items *after* the reverse-scored items have been reverse-scored. Keep your scores for each domain and add them up for a total courage score. Take the quiz now, and take it again if you wish after you've practiced the exercises in courage.

Using the scale provided, please circle the one number that best reflects your opinion about whether or not each statement below describes you or

*experiences that you have had. There are no correct answers, so please
respond as honestly as possible to each one.*

1. When my loved ones are doing something harmful or destructive,
    I encourage them to correct it.
    **1=strongly disagree   2=disagree   3=slightly disagree   4=slightly agree
    5=agree   6=strongly agree**

2. I am willing to confront my family members when they do
    something that is harmful to others.
    **1=strongly disagree   2=disagree   3=slightly disagree   4=slightly agree
    5=agree   6=strongly agree**

3. When you see a family member doing something that's harmful to
    others, it's important to raise the issue.
    **1=strongly disagree   2=disagree   3=slightly disagree   4=slightly agree
    5=agree   6=strongly agree**

4. I'm too timid to confront my loved ones when their behavior is
    hurting themselves or another person.[®]
    **1=strongly disagree   2=disagree   3=slightly disagree   4=slightly agree
    5=agree   6=strongly agree**

5. I have given up trying to make my loved ones treat themselves
    and others with respect.[®]
    **1=strongly disagree   2=disagree   3=slightly disagree   4=slightly agree
    5=agree   6=strongly agree**

6. When my friends are doing something harmful or destructive, I
    encourage them to correct it.
    **1=strongly disagree   2=disagree   3=slightly disagree   4=slightly agree
    5=agree   6=strongly agree**

7. I am willing to confront a friend when I think he or she is
    mistreating others.
    **1=strongly disagree   2=disagree   3=slightly disagree   4=slightly agree
    5=agree   6=strongly agree**

8. It is pointless to confront friends who are doing things that are
    hurtful or destructive.®
    **1=strongly disagree   2=disagree   3=slightly disagree   4=slightly agree
    5=agree   6=strongly agree**

9. I'm too timid to confront my friends when their behavior is
    hurting themselves or another person.®
    **1=strongly disagree   2=disagree   3=slightly disagree   4=slightly agree
    5=agree   6=strongly agree**

10. I may be too accepting when my friends are engaging in
    unacceptable or destructive behavior.®
    **1=strongly disagree   2=disagree   3=slightly disagree   4=slightly agree
    5=agree   6=strongly agree**

11. I have occasionally spoken to a neighbor or coworker when I
    thought he or she was behaving wrongly.
    **1=strongly disagree   2=disagree   3=slightly disagree   4=slightly agree
    5=agree   6=strongly agree**

12. I have attended meetings at my place of work or in my
    community to speak out against unfair policies.
    **1=strongly disagree   2=disagree   3=slightly disagree   4=slightly agree
    5=agree   6=strongly agree**

13. I am willing to take personal risks in my neighborhood or place of
    work to ensure that everyone is treated fairly.
    **1=strongly disagree   2=disagree   3=slightly disagree   4=slightly agree
    5=agree   6=strongly agree**

14. I mind my own business in my neighborhood and community,
    even when someone is behaving badly.®
    **1=strongly disagree   2=disagree   3=slightly disagree   4=slightly agree
    5=agree   6=strongly agree**

15. I'm not the sort of person to attend a meeting to protest an unfair policy.®
    1=strongly disagree   2=disagree   3=slightly disagree   4=slightly agree
    5=agree   6=strongly agree

16. I have supported social organizations that are devoted to correcting injustices in the world.
    1=strongly disagree   2=disagree   3=slightly disagree   4=slightly agree
    5=agree   6=strongly agree

17. I willingly get involved in causes to make the world a better place, even when it involves some risk to me.
    1=strongly disagree   2=disagree   3=slightly disagree   4=slightly agree
    5=agree   6=strongly agree

18. I have spoken out publicly (through protests, petitions, or direct action) against unfair practices in the world.
    1=strongly disagree   2=disagree   3=slightly disagree   4=slightly agree
    5=agree   6=strongly agree

19. The truth is that I'm probably a bit too timid to try to "change the world."®
    1=strongly disagree   2=disagree   3=slightly disagree   4=slightly agree
    5=agree   6=strongly agree

20. I'm too involved in my life to risk making the world a better place.®
    1=strongly disagree   2=disagree   3=slightly disagree   4=slightly agree
    5=agree   6=strongly agree

YOUR COURAGE SCORE

High Giver (80th percentile)	99 or above
Giver (60th percentile)	91–98
Moderate Giver (40th percentile)	84–90
Low Giver (20th percentile)	76–83

Seven

The Way of Humor:
Connect with Joy

Your dad's funeral doesn't seem like the ideal place to play the clown, but for Marie Hanson, a certified "laughter specialist," a funeral was the perfect occasion to bring family and friends together in loving laughter. Hanson, who first put on a clown suit in 1987 and found herself "utterly set free, transformed to be goofy and funny," made a slide show of her father's life for the funeral, where so many relatives and friends had gathered to honor her dad.

"My mission here on earth is to help people lighten up," says Hanson, "because so many of us forget to give ourselves permission to laugh and be silly. My mom liked to make jewelry," she recalls, "and my dad used to love to hunt around for items she could use as a jeweler. The first slide I showed was of my dad at the side of a road, bent over a dead porcupine, extracting quills with a pair of pliers, for Mom to use in her jewelry. That slide got everybody laughing, and we kept laughing with each new slide. After the funeral a woman came up to me and said, 'I want you to do my funeral,' and I said, 'Sure, you want to set up a date now?' which of course elicited more peals of laughter."

Healing through the warm connection of laughter continued later that week. Hanson and her sister drove to the Upper Peninsula of Michigan, where their mother lived, and another sister followed in her own car. "I got stopped for speeding," recalls Hanson, "and my sister began to tell the policeman how my dad had been buried two days ago and my mom had recently had a stroke. The sympathy ploy didn't work, and he gave us a ticket. A few minutes later my other sister got stopped for speeding too, and she plied him with the same story of burying her dad and how her mom had recently had a stroke. Well, this was just too much for the poor officer. He said, 'There is no way I'm going to give two people in the same family a ticket on the same day after all you've been through.' When we got to Mom's house, we called our uncles and cousins and aunts, all the relatives who'd come to the funeral, and told them this story. And it brought us all together with more laughter during our time of loss. That's what we've always done as a family. Laughter helps us get through tough times."

A Remarkable Lightness of Being

Humor is one of my personal favorite ways of love. I really believe in the whimsical heart. I try to take myself a bit lightly, even poke fun at myself. I'm a frequent joker, even if the jokes I tell sometimes elicit sighs of tolerant bemusement from family and friends. My co-author likes to remind me that when she told me one of her nicknames was Jillybean, I immediately regaled her with this joke:

"Do you know what kind of beans never grow in a garden?

"Jellybeans."

Thankfully, she has indulged my humor and even returned with her own; she e-mailed me this little ditty in September 2004:

There once was a fellow named Stephen,
Better known as Stephen the Even.
In matters of love he preached balance,
Though everyone has their own talents.

Henceforth, we were Jillybean and Stephen the Even.

In medieval Europe the virtue most closely associated with love (*caritas*) was hilarity (*hilaritas*). Spiritual traditions like Hinduism and Buddhism worship gods of laughter. If humor is a way of love, laughter is its most buoyant expression. It's a human universal, shared by all humans in all cultures.

Like no other way of love, humor can instantly transform a dark mood. We underestimate the enormous power of humor and the importance of cultivating it as a style. No matter how potent and destructive a negative emotion, it can be melted in a moment by humor. Humor's essence is a spontaneous shift in perception. And its lightness is the secret of its power, because it so deftly sneaks past people's defenses. Humor suddenly frames the world in a new way. Laughter is incompatible with anguish. At the moment you laugh, your burden is lightened, even if just for that moment.

How Humor Heals

Humor is a form of *play*, and as the psychiatrist Kay Redfield Jamison writes in her book *Exuberance*: "Play allows the pleasurable practice of improbable twists and turns in instinctive behaviors . . . it shapes the developing brain in potentially lifesaving ways." Exuberant play nourishes social bonds in animals—and clearly in humans too. "The exuberance of play," she writes, "is a joyous improvisation on the knowledge newly acquired through exploration." In fact, the more playful a child, the more creative he or she tends to be. Research by the Harvard psychologist Jerome Kagan and his colleagues found that certain extroverted children had an ineffable vitality: these children were highly energetic, smiled frequently, and laughed with zeal. Kagan called these children "Ethel Merman types." Similarly, the researcher Nathan Fox of the University of Maryland found that certain infants who smiled, cooed, gurgled, and were eager to explore the world thrived on novelty and social interaction.

Above all, humor requires the ability to be flexible, to frame life anew. As the humor "guru" Swami Beyondananda has said, "Some of us suffer from a debilitating mental disorder called irony deficiency. Seeing a doctor won't help, but seeing a paradox will." Did you smile when you read that? I did. Not only is Swami's wordplay funny, but it is also true.

Humor may be light, but it is also deep. As the comedian Steve Allen once said in an interview in *Laughing Matters* magazine, we are all born with a genetic ceiling and floor, but what we do with our lives determines whether we end up on the ceiling or the floor. When we laugh, we live in the now, delight in being alive, and "let go" of ourselves. Laughter lifts us to the ceiling of our lives.

In this chapter, you'll learn how humor heals. For instance:

One hundred laughs is the aerobic equivalent of ten minutes spent rowing.

Laughter elevates the secretion of our natural mood-enhancing catecholamines and endorphins and decreases levels of the stress hormone cortisol.

One reason laughter is exhilarating may be that it releases the feel-good chemical, dopamine. Researchers used brain imaging to study individuals while they looked at funny cartoons, and they found that a region of the brain with reward centers that involve dopamine was activated. The degree of humor "intensity" was positively linked to bold signal intensity in that area of the brain.

Humor—used in a benign, uplifting way—is linked to better heart health, higher self-esteem, and psychological well-being.

Above all, the power of humor and laughter is spiritual. It powerfully facilitates social bonds.

(S)he Who Laughed First

Though we don't know exactly when in the course of evolution laughter first arose, it is clearly now essential to our being and easily transcends the limits of language. Laughter does seem hardwired to begin young, and it even exists in animals in some form. In a 2005 article in the journal *Science*, Jaak Panksepp, a neuroscientist at Bowling Green State University, reports that when chimpanzees play and chase each other, they pant in a manner that is strikingly similar to human laughter. Even rats seem to chirp while they play. Young children laugh joyously in the midst of rough-and-tumble play, says Panksepp. And little kids laugh when surprised—for instance, at the simple game of peek-a-boo—hinting that the ability to laugh depends on the appreciation of novelty and newness.

If you take a moment and contemplate laughter, you realize how odd the mere physical act is. When psychologist and neurobiologist Robert Provine of the University of Maryland, author of *Laughter: A Scientific Investigation*, brought recordings of human laughter to a laboratory at the National Zoo in Washington that usually analyzes birdsongs or other animal calls, he found that the average laugh consists of short bursts of "ha-ha" or "he-he" lasting about 75 milliseconds and separated by pauses of 210 milliseconds. A typical laugh starts strong, ends soft, and usually occurs as a kind of punctuation to speech, rarely interrupting it.

How does humor—and its most obvious expression, laughter—heal? Think about the times you've just been unable to stop laughing—"I almost died laughing," or, "I laughed until the tears ran down my face." Those fits of laughter are actually good for us. In laughing, the abdominal muscles and diaphragm contract in a respiratory "fit," not unlike sneezing or crying. Your heartbeat accelerates, your blood pressure rises, and your vocal cords may vibrate uncontrollably. It was Dr. William F. Fry, a psychiatrist at the Stanford University School of Medicine, who found that a hundred laughs is the aerobic equivalent of ten minutes of rowing.

After that satisfying belly laugh, muscles loosen up and a delicious, warm relaxation flows through us like honey. Preliminary studies indicate that laughter elevates the secretion of mood-enhancing catecholamines and endorphins and decreases levels of the stress hormone cortisol. Some studies, including one in 1985, have shown that an immunoglobulin in our saliva (S-IgA) is increased when we laugh. And a 1988 study found that those who scored low on a scale measuring humor had the greatest decline in S-IgA during stressful periods. They were more vulnerable to stress, in contrast to high-humor individuals, who showed little change in their S-IgA even when they experienced stress. Another very interesting (if preliminary) 1996 study found that when individuals were asked to create a humorous monologue to accompany a stressful film (of an industrial accident, a film commonly used in lab studies of stress), measures of stress like heart rate and skin conductance stayed lower than when the subjects were asked to create a serious monologue.

Researchers have long speculated that humor activates reward centers in the brain—why else would it be so pleasurable? A 2003 study from Stanford University's Psychiatry Neuroimaging Laboratory confirms this: when researchers used functional MRIs to study individuals looking at funny cartoons, they found that a region of the brain was activated that contains reward centers involving the neurotransmitter dopamine. Dean Mobbs, the lead researcher, writes: "Without humor, life would undeniably be less exhilarating. Indeed, the ability to comprehend and find a joke funny plays a defining role in the human condition, essentially helping us to communicate ideas, attract partners, boost mood, and even cope in times of trauma and stress."

All these results are preliminary but very interesting, and they seem to uncover some of the biomarkers indicating the obvious—that laughter and humor buffer us against stress and provide intrinsic rewards and pleasure. So lighten up. Here are a few insights into how you can do that.

Lessons from the Frontiers of Research

IRUL has not specifically funded studies on humor; however, there is an intriguing and suggestive clinical literature pointing to the benefits of humor and laughter. Here I emphasize comedy and lightness as a way of helping others. If we understand that humor is a very effective way of connecting, of lightening another's life as well as our own, we can have tremendous fun *and* give love.

LESSON ONE: HUMOR HELPS IN HARD TIMES

Death comes to us all. My own dad died in 1996. He was unwavering in his wish to die naturally, at home. A few minutes before he died, my mom said, "Henry, I have to call 911," and he responded with gentle humor, "Marguerite, husbands don't always do what their wives want!" He then passed away. A few days later, after I'd attended Dad's memorial service, a neighbor who knew my penchant for humor approached me, gave his condolences, and added with a wink, "But I must tell you, it's so nice and quiet now. I don't hear your mom's voice echoing all the way down the creek yelling, 'Henry!' " We both had a good laugh.

Peggy Stabholz, a family counselor and a "certified laughter leader," says her love of laughter began with her own father, a Holocaust survivor who "taught my sister and me that laughter was a great way to cope with life. He said one reason he survived the concentration camp was because he was so funny that he kept people's spirits up and they helped in return. He can wiggle his ears, hit his head, make noises, move his mouth in funny ways when he sings. And when I was growing up, he'd often tell funny stories about himself." Stabholz offers laughter training to the young and the elderly. "I find that it makes me feel better. It changes my whole attitude about life. I may wake up in the morning not feeling well, but after a laughter group I feel great. Sharing laughter gives purpose to my life."

In interviews with eighty-four Holocaust survivors conducted by Chaya Ostrower of Tel Aviv University, humor was repeatedly mentioned as a way of surviving trauma. Said one survivor, "Humor was one of the integral ingredients of mental perseverance. This mental perseverance was the condition for a will to live, to put it in a nutshell. This I am telling you as a former prisoner. However little it was, however sporadic, however spontaneous, it was very important. . . . Look, the ghetto showed that people have great vitality—as soon as a moment's time passed separating one trauma from the other, people were already laughing; they maybe even laughed more."

Humor has smoothed the paths of many leaders—and it may be the mark of a great leader. Take Theodore Roosevelt, about whom a *New York Times* reporter wrote: "A hundred times a day the President will laugh, and when he laughs he does it with the same energy with which he talks. It is usually a roar of laughter . . . sometimes he doubles up in paroxysm . . . you shout with laughter with him." And a British diplomat characterized Roosevelt this way: "You must always remember, the President is about six." That effervescence is humor at its most remarkable—and it carried Roosevelt through hard times. Growing up, he suffered from asthma and poor eyesight. In 1884 his first wife died in childbirth and his mother died of typhoid on the same day. Yet he once said, "No man has had a happier life than I."

Ronald Reagan was also adored for his good humor. According to one of his speechwriters, Doug Gamble, Reagan's humor literally "glowed from his very soul. . . . Reagan loved jokes that poked fun at himself. But he also realized that a side benefit of self-deprecating humor, especially as he employed it, is its effectiveness in disarming criticism. When 1984 Democratic presidential nominee Walter Mondale accused Reagan of 'government by amnesia,' the president countered with, 'I thought that remark accusing me of having amnesia was uncalled for. I just wish I could remember who said it.' When it became known that he would occasionally nod off at the White House during the day, he said, 'I've given my aides instructions that if trouble breaks out in any of the world's hot spots, they should wake me up immediately—even if I'm in a cabinet meeting.' " Reagan was equally adept at the quick ad-lib—famously, when he was shot and in danger of dying, rather than worry about himself, he instantly set the emergency room doctors at ease by quipping, "I hope you're all Republicans."

Does laughter actually heal illness? Norman Cousins's influential 1979 book *Anatomy of an Illness* described his daily regimen of laughter—inspired by watching funny movies—and large doses of vitamin C to help him recover from a bout of severe ankylosing spondilitis, a painful rheumatic disease. Cousins found that twenty minutes of hearty laughter gave him two hours of pain-free sleep. The story was inspiring, but a single case history, no matter how unusual, is just that—a single story. Even Cousins himself took care to ask people not to extrapolate too much from his experience.

Robert Provine points out that much of the scientific study of laughter and health "does not involve true controls and solid experimental design. We don't know whether the impact of laughter is simply a distraction effect, and if other distractions, such as jumping up and down, or talking, would work equally well." However, the most promising research in laughter, says Provine, suggests that it *does* reduce stress and physical pain.

Humor seems to help the heart. A 2001 study published in the *International Journal of Cardiology* found that type A personality traits—hostility, aggression, and competitiveness—are linked to coronary heart disease

(CHD) and that the propensity to laugh protects against heart disease in this group. The study of three hundred heart disease patients used questionnaires measuring responsiveness to humor as well as hostility. Heart disease patients tended to be less likely than healthy individuals to laugh in response to life's everyday events. This significant study is simple but elegant.

You can consciously cultivate humor. It's a "fun" kind of discipline and one that can help lighten life. This set of exercises comes from Leslie Gibson, a nurse and the founder of the Morton Plant Mease Comedy Connection service.

❧ *Turn to entertainment.* As obvious as it seems, this really works: watch movies and DVDs that make you and those you care for laugh.

❧ *Reframe your situation and others' situations in a lighter way.* Ask yourself or another you are trying to help, "How would a young child see this situation?" Or ask, "How would your favorite comedian make light of this situation?" Think of a difficult time you went through long ago, a time you are now at peace with and can even joke about, and realize that whatever you or another is going through now might similarly shift and be transformed over time. Reframe any event into a matter that is not so serious and loaded. A childlike and whimsical perspective on life can help keep us young, flexible, and happy.

❧ *Keep a humor notebook.* Whenever you get a chance, write down something that made you laugh. Browse your humor notebook when you're under stress.

❧ *Keep funny truisms around the house.* For instance, "Life is a test. It is only a test. If this were your actual life, you would be given better instructions." Here's another: "Recent research shows that the first five minutes of life are very risky. The last five minutes aren't so hot either." Keep a drawer full of your favorite comics and cartoons and look at them in difficult times.

LESSON TWO: LAUGH TO LIFT, NOT HURT

Humor can elevate or destroy. It turns out, not so surprisingly, that benevolent uses of humor are linked to psychological health and well-being, while detrimental, harmful humor—even if used to enhance the self or relationships—tends to be linked to low self-esteem and poor psychological functioning.

In 2003 the psychologist Rod Martin of the University of Western Ontario in Canada published a framework measuring four functions of humor in everyday life. Do we use humor to enhance the self, and if so, do we use it in a benign or harmful way? Do we use humor to enhance relationships with others, and again, do we use humor this way in a benevolent or harmful way?

"Truly mirthful laughter is a sign of health," says the psychologist Steve Wilson, founder and Cheerman of the Bored, World Laughter Tour. At his first workshop on humor, Wilson said that healthy laughter has four qualities:

1. It sounds warm and inviting, not sneering, jeering, or hollow. It's so inviting that you can't help wanting to join in, even if you don't know what was funny in the first place.
2. There's always a good reason for healthy laughter, even if there is also a quality of "Well, you just had to be there."
3. Healthy laughter is at nobody else's expense and does not embarrass or ridicule.
4. There is a buildup of anticipation and tension before the release of healthy laughter.

"Very early in my discovery of my passion for humor and its healing qualities," recalls Wilson, "I gave a talk at a cancer clinic in Ohio. I brought a box of toys and bubble soap and note cards with jokes. And yet each of the thirty-five people in that room had serious cancer, and I was overcome by the idea that I was in a room filled with people with catastrophic illness, and all I had were toys and jokes. But then one man introduced himself and said, 'My name is Lester, and I'm pissed off! They gave me six months to live, so I gave away my winter coat, and that was over a year ago!' And everybody started to laugh, and I took it as a sign. So I started passing around my toys and telling my jokes and explaining how laughter heals, and pretty soon there was a knock at the door and a woman stuck her head in and said, 'Listen, I'm running a support group next door, and we heard so much laughter from this room that we'd like to come in and join your group.' That was very powerful. That clinched it for me. I knew then that laughter was my mission. Laughter and humor overtook my practice and life. I started telling people, 'Don't postpone joy,' and that got me the nickname of 'joyologist.' "

Quoting two popular clichés, Wilson says, "You'll never die laughing, but you may die of being dead serious." In 1998 he met Dr. Madan Kataria, whose laughter workshops are extraordinarily popular in India. "We were just giddy with each other," recalls Wilson. "We set up a lecture tour, traveled to fourteen cities together, and talked about humor and laughter twenty-four hours a day." Since that time, Wilson has developed a laughter training workshop that is "two days where people learn about the psychology of humor, the physiology of laughter, and how to create laughter." Wilson also created a concept called "Good Hearted Living," which suggests six important steps that lead to healthy laughter: complimenting others, being flexible, maintaining an attitude of gratitude, offering acts of simple kindness, forgiving others, and eating or giving chocolate (and other pleasures). "These simple practices help us be open and joyful, leading the way to laughter," says Wilson.

In his own life, says Wilson, his philosophy has been a great help, especially when his youngest son borrowed his older brother's motorcycle and was thrown through the plate-glass window of a storefront while trying to negotiate a turn. After getting a phone call informing him that his son was in the hospital, Wilson and his wife put together a humor first aid kit. "We took toys, games, a rubber chicken, and clown noses and threw it all in a gym bag on the way to the hospital." Soon their son was giggling and smiling. "Laughing together in a situation like that is about forgiveness and safety," says Wilson. "We both put on clown noses and put the rubber chicken on his IV pole, and as we did laps up and down the hallways, we picked up other patients who wanted to join us. It was a turning point for him, and he recovered very well."

LESSON THREE: BUILD BRIDGES THROUGH JOY

"Humor is the most elemental expression of connection to another person," says Korey Thompson, who is a professional clown in Milwaukee, Wisconsin. Korey has been clowning in hospitals, and for Alzheimer's patients in particular, for over thirty years. "Whenever you are connected to somebody, you inevitably smile, you just can't help it. One time I just held my two hands out to a person with dementia and imagined that in the center of my palms was the softest, most tender love, and she looked up at me and smiled. I think that is the essence of humor. You reach out, the other person reaches out, and you both smile. That's it."

Dressing up in clown clothes is in itself a humorous act, says Thompson. "As a clown, you can experience others in a completely different way. Here you show up dressed like a clown, and that alone is funny."

In fact, according to Robert Provine, one of the most remarkable things about laughter is how common and frequent it is. Provine has found that much of our most ordinary, daily laughter is in response to utterly trivial comments in ordinary social settings, such as, "Got to go now," or, "Hi, how ya doin'?" Provine, who listened in on over twelve hundred "bouts" of laughter in public settings like malls, found that laughter leavens our daily lives so often because we rely on it to help create warm connections with others. In everyday situations, only about 15 percent of laughter follows a joke. People do a lot of giggling and snorting in response to jokes and humor, but they do this as a way of regulating and gauging social bonding. So laughter is really a form of social healing. Laughter and humor enlarge our web of connection and love.

Laughter powerfully facilitates bonding. "I can't tell a joke to save my life," says Sara Laskey, a former clown with Ringling Brothers and Barnum & Bailey Circus who attended medical school at Case Western University. "But when I laugh together with someone, it's really pleasurable, and for that second we're together in the same place at the same time, connected, whether it's at the circus or the dinner table. The feeling of bonding I got in the circus when the audience was laughing is exactly the same as the feeling I get when I bond with a patient in the emergency room." For Laskey, as for the rest of us, laughter is a way of facilitating oneness.

Laughing is an activity shared together, not alone. "I laugh my heart out at a laughter club once a week," says Sebastien Gendry, world operations director of Laughter Yoga International. Gendry, who lives in Altadena, California, believes that laughter helps us "bypass fear, depression, sadness, and anxiety. It puts us in touch with the perfection within, and has given me an easy and powerful outlet for tension and stress. If I've had a hard day and then I go to the laughter club, it completely turns my attitude around. And the bigger the group, the stronger the dynamic. If you have fifteen or twenty people, a few will always be less inhibited and laugh much more easily. And when one person starts laughing, it's like a brushfire—soon the whole group is laughing." Laughter yoga, says Gendry, is not about happiness as an achievement but happiness as a way of living. "You make a commitment to be happy, here and now. You don't need a specific reason to laugh, so you decide to just create joy in your life right now."

Laughter is contagious—another sign that it is in essence a form of group bonding. "We all experience laughing jags and fits when we start laughing and can't stop," says Robert Provine. "And when that happens, we laugh because somebody else is laughing. Like talking, laughter is a way of communicating with other people. It's an important signal you send to someone that says, 'This is play. I'm not going to attack or hurt you.' "

Provine points out that we laugh thirty times more often in social settings than in solitary contexts and that in everyday conversation speakers laugh nearly 50 percent more than listeners. A 2001 study in the *Journal of General Psychology* confirmed findings regarding the social essence of laughter—people watching a funny video laughed more in the presence of others than when they viewed the video alone. We even laugh more when we hear a laugh track on a sitcom.

Provine believes that laughter is a sign of healthy social relationships and that we laugh mostly in the presence of friends and family—and so the health benefits of laughter may actually stem from joyful connection. "It may be that laughter is ultimately a marker for the fact that things are going well in your life," says Provine. Laughter inevitably enhances and maintains positive relationships.

One way to begin connecting to others through humor is to think about your own humor style. According to the nurse Sandra Jones Campbell, we all tend to have one predominant style and do best indulging the style we're comfortable with. Here are some simple questions to help you identify your style:

Are you:

❧ A *spectator?* Do you enjoy watching, observing, or laughing in the crowd or the audience? If so, you may want to connect to others by sharing comedy on the big and small screen or in the theater.

❧ A *visual person?* Do you respond to cartoons, comics, toys, gags, slapstick, clowns, pantomime, funny clothing, funny buttons, and costumes? If so, you may want to volunteer as a clown, send cartoons by e-mail, or buy amusing toys for friends.

❧ A *participant?* Do you want to be in on the action? Do you love to tell funny stories, jokes, and anecdotes? If so, you may connect to others as a raconteur, taking center stage.

Another way to connect is sharing laughter with those you are intimate with. One 2004 study by Carl D. Marci and his colleagues published in the *Journal of Nervous and Mental Disease* found that laughter during psychotherapy sessions was animating and arousing for both patient and therapist and created a shared physiologic response, a kind of sympathetic resonance. This study simultaneously measured skin conductivity in patients and therapists and found that skin conductivity rose sharply when patients and therapists laughed *together.* They concluded that laughter creates a sense of comfort and safety for the patient and enhances rapport.

Finally, sharing laughter and humor turns out to be a key ingredient to a successful, long-term marriage, according to The University of Washington psychologist John Gottman, author of *The Mathematics of Marriage.* Gottman is famous for videotaping couples and analyzing the videotapes in depth, arriving at parameters that allowed him and his colleagues to predict, with great accuracy, which couples would still be together three years hence. Apparent conflict or lack of conflict was not the important the health of a marriage; it was whether the couple coped with their issues through dialogue, laughter, and affection. According to Gottman, the conflicts and differences at the beginning of a marriage will often last through the whole marriage—but it is not the differing viewpoints that matter so much as learning the skills of using positive emotions like humor and gentle teasing to deescalate conflict and keep marital magic intact.

Here are some ways you can share humor with those you love:

❧   *Start a humor history.* With friends, family, or other significant individuals in your life, talk about and write down the funniest events that occurred on vacations, at special gatherings, or just on ordinary days.

❧   *Tickle gently.* Use what Robert Provine calls the most "potent, ancient, and controversial laugh-stimulus." That is, the tickle. "The tickle is a part of physical play that is most appropriate for children, close family, friends, and lovers," says Provine, "and never strangers." Of course, make sure that the tickling is gentle and that the recipient is willing and even eager. Let yourself be tickled in turn.

LESSON FOUR: APPRECIATE ABSURDITY

One of the world's greatest humorists was the physicist Richard Feynman. His deep appreciation for the universe was woven through with a humorous sense of the absurd and the miraculous. His humor led to enormous creativity: Feynman's thesis adviser wrote, "Discussions turned into laughter, laughter into jokes, and jokes into . . . ideas." And that humor was part of a larger joyfulness and appreciation. Feynman linked laughter and the beauty of the cosmos this way: "It is a great adventure to contemplate the universe . . . To view life as part of this universal mystery of greatest depth, is to sense an experience which is very rare, and very exciting. It usually ends in laughter and a delight in the futility of trying to understand what this thing . . . [is] . . . that looks at itself and wonders why it wonders . . . where did the stuff of life and of the earth come from . . . what a wonderful world!"

We can feel Feynman's palpable delight in the universe and even our seemingly absurd place in it. Here are a few ways to cultivate the absurd:

❧   *Surround yourself with visual humor.* Buy books of cartoons, keep funny photos handy, and save amusing captions on your computer desktop as a background or screensaver.

❧ *Go back to childhood knickknacks*. Keep your favorite childhood toys on your desk—the kind that make you laugh, like trolls or gnomes. Or buy new toys that make you smile. Wear something silly, like rabbit ears, and enjoy the laughter of others.

LESSON FIVE: FIND HOPE IN A HIGHER GROUND

Hope has been defined as the passion for the possible, and humor is a delightful way of offering hope to others. According to research by Samuel Oliner of Humboldt University, whose work on Holocaust rescuers we highlighted in our chapter on courage, humor is part of an "approach" coping style. Those who are skilled at using humor as a coping mechanism are able to focus on problems without becoming overly emotional, and they also report less stress. Indeed, humor seems to be essential to human thriving, whether the hoped-for outcome is trivial or cosmic. Humor brings us to the higher ground where hope lives.

Dr. David H. Rosen is a professor of psychology, humanities in medicine, and psychiatry at Texas A&M University. He views humor as a way to help us move toward hope, no matter our circumstances. In a 2003 study published in the *International Journal of Humor Research*, Rosen reported on the ability of a movie comedy to increase hope. One hundred and eighty folks, aged eighteen to forty-two, watched a fifteen-minute comedy. Before and after, they took the Snyder Hope Scale, as well a scale measuring humor and one measuring stress. Those who watched the comedy felt significantly more hope than those who didn't, and that feeling of hope reduced the perceived intensity of recent stress.

In a 1993 study by the researcher Kay Hearth, 94 percent of "high-hope" individuals indicated that lightheartedness is a necessary component of dealing with difficult life events. And in a more recent classic study of twenty-three exceptionally altruistic individuals conducted by Anne Colby and William Damon of Stanford University, in-depth interviews found that a lively sense of humor was key to these altruists' ability to work successfully with others. As Damon and Colby discovered, successful altruists have a sense of humor that "helps them bounce back from disappointments, discouragement, and setbacks." For all their seriousness of purpose, these altruists share a whimsy that fosters hope even when they are taking enormous risks and facing danger.

Have you ever seen somebody check his watch while laughing uproariously? It's simply impossible. Humor releases us from time, and a moment of laughter is a hint of eternity. In the Buddhist tradition, the first experience of enlightenment is often associated with an outburst of laughter. The Buddha himself is often portrayed as laughing. In Judaism the very word *Isaac* means "laugh." Why? Because Sarah, the elderly wife of Abraham, laughed when three angels appeared and predicted that she would have a son. Or as Harry Emerson Fosdick, the great Protestant preacher at Riverside Church, once wrote of Jesus in *The Manhood of the Master*, "He never jests as Socrates does, but He often lets the ripple of a happy breeze play over the surface of His mighty deep."

Cultivate humor as a higher path—a cosmic contentment that is truly lighthearted and full of joy. You will lighten the lives of others simply by the radiance of your good humor. Even the briefest laugh reminds us that we have available a kind of spiritual gold anytime, anywhere.

❧ *Keep a joy jar at home.* Fill it with positive "laffirmations"—a term borrowed from Joel Goodman, author of a book by that name—that have a certain humorous sparkle. Share laffirmations like these with others when they need a lift:

- THINGS TO DO TODAY: 1. Inhale. 2. Exhale. 3. Inhale. 4. Exhale. 5. Inhale. 6. Exhale. 7. Inhale.
- "Sir, what is the secret of your success?" "Two words." "What are they?" "Right decisions." "And how do you make right decisions?" "One word." "What is that?" "Experience." "And how do you get experience?" "Two words." "And what are they?" "Wrong decisions."
- Out of my mind, back in five minutes.
- Give me ambiguity or give me something else.

❧ *Look to the larger picture.* Frame your life not as a tragic drama but as a romantic comedy. Search for the inherent humor in situations, from relationships to careers. If you or someone you love is anxious or worried, exaggerate the worst outcome in a funny way. Exaggeration is a key element of humor, and it helps us all realize that whatever is happening right now is probably not so bad and could even be seen as a little bit amusing.

❧ *Laugh at life, but not at yourself or others.* Humor uplifts while reminding us that we, and life, are really okay.

Your Humor Score

It's time to answer the questions on the humor section of your Love and Longevity Scale. We have divided responses into percentiles, or fifths. These are general guidelines; you may score right near the cutoff between percentiles, so please keep this in mind and use the scale as a friendly tool. Remember:

There are two steps to determining your score. First, determine which items need to be "reverse-scored" (denoted with the ® symbol). For reverse-scored items, see the chart below for how to score.

If you score a . . .	. . . assign yourself a score for that item of:
1	6
2	5
3	4
4	3
5	2
6	1

The second step is to add the scores for individual items *after* the reverse-scored items have been reverse-scored. Take the quiz now, and take it again if you wish after you've finished this book and adopted a light-hearted lifestyle.

Using the scale provided, please circle the one number that best reflects your opinion about whether or not each statement below describes you or experiences that you have had. There are no correct answers, so please respond as honestly as possible to each one.

1.   I'm good at making members of my family laugh when they need to relax.
     1=strongly disagree   2=disagree   3=slightly disagree   4=slightly agree 5=agree   6=strongly agree

2.   I use humor to try to give my family a fresh perspective and hope.
     1=strongly disagree   2=disagree   3=slightly disagree   4=slightly agree 5=agree   6=strongly agree

3.   I try to use humor to help my family cope with problems in life.
     1=strongly disagree   2=disagree   3=slightly disagree   4=slightly agree 5=agree   6=strongly agree

4.   I do not use humor to help my family be more optimistic.[R]
     1=strongly disagree   2=disagree   3=slightly disagree   4=slightly agree 5=agree   6=strongly agree

5.   I don't find much to laugh about when spending time around family.[R]
     1=strongly disagree   2=disagree   3=slightly disagree   4=slightly agree 5=agree   6=strongly agree

6.   I use humor to try to bring a fresh perspective and hope to friends of mine.
     1=strongly disagree   2=disagree   3=slightly disagree   4=slightly agree 5=agree   6=strongly agree

7. I think it's healthy to find things to laugh over when spending
    time around friends.
    **1=strongly disagree   2=disagree   3=slightly disagree   4=slightly agree
    5=agree   6=strongly agree**

8. Sharing funny experiences with friends is uplifting.
    **1=strongly disagree   2=disagree   3=slightly disagree   4=slightly agree
    5=agree   6=strongly agree**

9. I don't try to make friends laugh when they are stressed out.[R]
    **1=strongly disagree   2=disagree   3=slightly disagree   4=slightly agree
    5=agree   6=strongly agree**

10. Telling friends entertaining stories is not something I'm good at or
    interested in doing.[R]
    **1=strongly disagree   2=disagree   3=slightly disagree   4=slightly agree
    5=agree   6=strongly agree**

11. I'm good at making neighbors or coworkers laugh when they need
    to relax.
    **1=strongly disagree   2=disagree   3=slightly disagree   4=slightly agree
    5=agree   6=strongly agree**

12. I try to use humor to help coworkers or neighbors cope with
    problems in life.
    **1=strongly disagree   2=disagree   3=slightly disagree   4=slightly agree
    5=agree   6=strongly agree**

13. Sharing amusing experiences with people at work or in my
    community is uplifting.
    **1=strongly disagree   2=disagree   3=slightly disagree   4=slightly agree
    5=agree   6=strongly agree**

14. I don't try to make neighbors or coworkers laugh when they are
    stressed out.[R]
    **1=strongly disagree   2=disagree   3=slightly disagree   4=slightly agree
    5=agree   6=strongly agree**

15. I do not use humor as a way to help make people at work or in my neighborhood feel optimistic.[®]
    1=strongly disagree 2=disagree 3=slightly disagree 4=slightly agree 5=agree 6=strongly agree

16. I use humor to try to give people a fresh perspective and hope.
    1=strongly disagree 2=disagree 3=slightly disagree 4=slightly agree 5=agree 6=strongly agree

17. I usually try to break the ice or improve the atmosphere with humor or comical stories.
    1=strongly disagree 2=disagree 3=slightly disagree 4=slightly agree 5=agree 6=strongly agree

18. I always approach new people with a smile.
    1=strongly disagree 2=disagree 3=slightly disagree 4=slightly agree 5=agree 6=strongly agree

19. I do not like to use humor when trying to make a point or motivate people.[®]
    1=strongly disagree 2=disagree 3=slightly disagree 4=slightly agree 5=agree 6=strongly agree

20. I don't tend to find much to laugh about around strangers.[®]
    1=strongly disagree 2=disagree 3=slightly disagree 4=slightly agree 5=agree 6=strongly agree

YOUR HUMOR SCORE

High Giver (80th percentile)	107 or higher
Giver (60th percentile)	100–106
Moderate Giver (40th percentile)	95–99
Low Giver (20th percentile)	84–94

Eight

The Way of Respect:
Look Deeper and Find Value

We had only our bare hands and backpacks when we went in against enemy fire," recalls ninety-year-old Cleveland neurologist Joe Foley of the invasion of Normandy, where at age twenty-eight he served as head doctor in the beach battalion. It was June 6 and 6:40 A.M. when he got off a small boat in three feet of water while machine guns exploded around him. Within minutes Joe and his eight men had set up an aid station and a flag, and within an hour "we were taking casualties." Foley found a bulldozer and dug a massive hole under the seawall, which became their permanent aid station for the next month. "I made it through in great part because of loyalty to the doctors I was with," he recalls. "Your buddies are the ones whose respect you cherish. I had to have whatever it took to give confidence to the men working with me. On a beachhead like that, you have God's own number of physical and mental casualties. But I felt that each one of those people was very important. I had affection for every single person with whom I dealt." Some of the American soldiers showed unthinkable courage and good humor, even to the very end. Joe recalls an infantry captain with whom he'd trained and whom he'd often kidded. "I'd assure him that the infantry was composed of a group of mental defectives, and he'd assure me that the navy was utterly incapable of working onshore. We shared a lot of good-humored banter. In my third hour on the beach, he came to my aid station with a great gash in his carotid artery and a huge hole in his liver. He said, 'Am I going to make it?' I said, 'I wish I could say you are, but you're not.' He grinned at me and said, 'Isn't it just my luck when I need a real doctor to have a quack like you around.' He died with that grin on his face."

Joe was born to poor Irish immigrants in Boston and eventually ended up at Harvard, then at Case Western Reserve University as head of neurology. One of his protégés, James Corbett, is now chairman of the Neurology Department at the University of Mississippi in Jackson. "I remember when a woman came into the emergency room with severe headaches and no obvious neurologic signs of a disorder," says Corbett. "The staff assumed she was crazy and decided to transfer her to a psychiatric ward. While she was waiting to be transferred, she died. She had a brain tumor that swelled up and herniated. Not long after, we all gathered in the small auditorium where we had grand rounds, and all of us, internists, psychologists, and neurologists, were beating our breasts and wringing our hands and saying, 'Mea culpa, mea culpa, we missed this brain tumor,' and Joe stood up and said, 'What is wrong about what happened to this woman is not that she had a brain tumor that would have killed her anyway. It was that she was treated as if she were crazy. She died without anybody consoling her or showing her true concern or respect. That's what we need to learn from this.' I never forgot that. I just love the man, and I try to emulate him. I have an open door because he always had an open door."

I owe my life at Case Western to Joe. He was a member of the search committee that interviewed me for my job there, and I still recall how we sat down on a soft, cracked red leather bench in the lobby of Hanna Pavilion, the psychiatric unit of University Hospitals, and talked of everything from euthanasia and neurological illnesses such as Alzheimer's to the Nazi doctors of the Holocaust. After meeting Joe, I knew I would take the job if it were offered, and when I moved to Cleveland in June 1988, Joe took me under his wing and introduced me to everyone in town who knew anything about older folks with dementia. One morning in the clinic Joe said to me, "You know, you have to call them by name and expect a response! It may not come, but expect it, because sometimes it will, and they deserve to have names and be called by those names, however demented they are. And speak directly to them, and above all, bend down and make eye contact. There is more there than you might think sometimes." Joe's moral sense of inclusion was a marvelous model for me.

Another morning, in August 1996, we drove together to Mount Vernon, Ohio, where the state has a large institution for people with the most severe forms of retardation. Inside we were surrounded by patients who were incontinent, incapable of speech, malformed of limb, or in various other ways difficult to behold. It was pure mayhem. And suddenly a disheveled man in his forties stood up and said, "Hello, Doctor Foley!" And of a group of about twenty patients in the room, nearly half chimed in with big smiles, in unison, "Doctor Foley, Doctor Foley." Joe took their hands, each one of them, and spoke slowly and lovingly to each one, and at the end of our stay the mayhem had literally turned to peace.

From Joe Foley I learned many things, but the most lasting lesson was that the foundation of all love is respect.

The Basic Insight: Rank Counts

Respect is love's careful guardian. Its essence is acceptance—to hold another as "irreducibly valuable," as the Christian philosopher Gene Outka puts it. The Latin root of "respect"—*respectare*—means "to look again." That's a lovely image that reveals the essence of respect. It requires us to look again, past first impressions and unconscious biases, to gaze deeply in order to understand another person's history, struggles, life journey, and perspectives. Without respect, even the most sincere love can become coercive, driven to absorb the beloved into oneself or to reshape him or her. And so, its way is freedom, for self and other. (I will pause for a caveat here that should be taken for granted throughout this chapter: respect never means accepting beliefs or actions of others that are genuinely harmful or evil.)

From macaques to managers, birds to baboons, toddlers to teachers, respect—in the form of rank—is important for health. Status matters. It determines not only how people regard themselves but how others treat them. Rank is directly related to stress hormones and illness. The money you make, the years you've spent in school, and your standing in comparison to others in your career and community—all these matter.

Your risk for everything from cardiovascular disease to diabetes, infections, and even cancer varies with your social rank—and this is not simply a matter of being rich or poor or having access to the best health care. This is about status and thus about respect—your rank influences your health even at the upper reaches of society, where everybody already has money and power. A middle manager with a nice house in a nice suburb is statistically more vulnerable to illness than his or her boss. According to the Swiss economist Ernst Fehr, an expert on altruism at the University of Zurich, this is called "relative rank." The British economist Andrew Oswald of Warwick University agrees: "We're very driven by a concern about rank," says Oswald, "and there is only so much rank to go around in any society. Wages, for instance, are relative. In my own life, on a university faculty, I find that my colleagues are incredibly interested in what others are earning. Status comes from where you are on the ladder."

The groundwork for this remarkable insight was laid in the late 1960s with a famous study of men in the British civil service that is still widely discussed and applied. Called the Whitehall Study, it was directed by Dr. Michael Marmot, director of the International Center for Health and Society at University College in London. Marmot has since become justifiably famous for this work, which tracked mortality rates over a decade for over seventeen thousand men in the British civil service.

Marmot and his colleagues were astonished when they analyzed the data, because they showed that rates of mortality—from all causes, and separate from other risk factors such as smoking or drinking—consistently and steadily decreased as men's civil service grade increased. Every single man had equal access to health care, but men on the lowest rung of the ladder had three times the mortality rate as those who had the highest positions. A twenty-five-year follow-up of these men published in 1996 found that this connection persisted even after retirement and even among men who were in their late eighties.

Marmot concluded that stress—which affects our hormones, immune system, and vulnerability to disease—might be the hidden factor. The lower your social status, the more stressed you feel: you're treated with less respect, and you have less control over your life. In 1985 Marmot and his colleagues launched another large study, which is called Whitehall II and includes both men and women. Questions were added to illuminate how employees felt about control at their jobs. The researchers found that a lack of a sense of control accounted for at least half of the increasing mortality rates. And a 2004 study that appeared in the *New England Journal of Medicine* was simply, bluntly titled: "Class—The Ignored Determinant of the Nation's Health." Even when unhealthy lifestyles and diet are factored out, the poor are more likely to die prematurely. In another intriguing, if short-term, study at Carnegie Mellon University in Pittsburgh, the psychologist Sheldon Cohen asked individuals to rate their relative standing in their community and then were exposed to a respiratory virus. Those who had ranked themselves low were more likely to get a cold.

Social exclusion—whether because of race or status—has a strong, negative effect on health. Social trust, which is predicated on respect, improves health. Dr. Ichiro Kawachi, director of the Harvard Center for Society and Health, has correlated mortality rates with the percentage of individuals who agree with the statement "Most people would try to take advantage of you if they got the chance." In contrast, an individual with high "social trust" may be more connected to others and likelier to give and receive help and to feel less stress. Says Kawachi, "In political science and sociology there is a notion of social capital, which refers to resources to which people have access. Social capital helps people find jobs and handle personal emergencies, and it turns out it helps their health."

Social status is complex and multidimensional. It can include gender, ethnicity, age, income, education, and occupational status—as well as less measurable qualities such as social network, cultural orientation, and strength of community. It even includes one's childhood, because our childhoods influence the ways in which we interpret life events. Early abuse, neglect, or stress can alter the way the brain and body respond to stress, creating bigger spikes in hormones like cortisol in response to obstacles and challenges. The Harvard physiologist Erik Louks, who studies the biological pathways by which social circumstances influence health, says there is strong evidence that low socioeconomic status is linked with depression and that depression itself is a risk for disease. Looking at cholesterol, blood pressure, body mass, and inflammatory markers in their blood, Louks and his team have followed hundreds of thousands of people over time, asking them about everything from their education to their parents' education to their social relationships.

If we look to animals, we can actually find out *how* stress and rank affect hormones. Profound hormonal changes result in animals when they are stressed by subordination. One great pioneer in this arena is Bruce McEwen of Rockefeller University in New York, whose research into stress and status stands out in the field. McEwen coined the concept of "allostatic load" to measure stress. Allostasis refers to the ability to maintain stability through change. When we measure stress hormones, we can tell how much "load" an individual is enduring. "Social support and cooperation may decrease allostatic load," says McEwen, "while social conflict and competition for resources may dramatically increase it."

With this novel concept in mind, McEwen and his colleagues studied male and female rats housed together for two weeks. Inevitably, a hierarchy of dominance formed. Dominant rats stayed at their original body weight, while control animals housed in male-female pairs actually gained weight. But subordinate rats showed a rapid, prolonged weight loss. Their insulin and blood glucose levels plummeted. Testosterone levels also decreased in the subordinate males, suggesting that, overall, being subordinate is a severe stress. And yet, interestingly, in the same study, dominant rats were slightly more stressed than their happily mated controls. Maintaining dominance is not always stress-free. Other research has shown that, in animals at least, low rank is most stressful when food is scarce and therefore competition is high. When an abundance of food is available, there is less stress for all the animals. Similarly, the biologist Robert Sapolsky studied male baboons in the savanna. Dominant males had lower stress hormones (and allostatic load) than subordinates—because, say the researchers, they were rarely challenged by the subordinates.

What is the final take-home message of this research? There's still a lot to be learned, but what I believe is that:

Hierarchies are inevitable in the insect, animal, and human world. Hierarchies are, in part, the natural outcome of evolution: we all specialize in certain tasks, from the bee that disseminates pollen to the cardiothoracic surgeon who dissects aortas.

Rank is significant. The profound link between social status and health shows us that our rank among our peers—and thus, in part, the respect they accord us—is very important.

Respect is more important in tough times. McEwen says that the stress of being subordinate "may depend mainly on how much a subordinate individual suffers from physical or psychological threats from dominant individuals." Even being dominant can be stressful when dominance requires struggle or conflict in order to maintain that status.

Offer respect routinely: it reduces stress. Offering respect to others and respecting ourselves can reduce the overall load of stress on us all. We can't eliminate hierarchies from human life. Neither can we eliminate our craving for rank. And tough times come to us all. So what is the answer? Let's try to unhinge our respect for ourselves and others from all these inevitable factors. One of the most healing acts of life is to value and respect yourself and others. Begin with respect, rather than ending with it.

Lessons from the Frontiers of Research

In this chapter, we look at respect on an ascending curve that has four elements:

Tolerance. Tolerance is respect in its essential and universal form. It can come naturally or be a conscious, rational choice, depending on our disposition and circumstances. Its foundation is humility, because we begin the subtle shift to intolerance when we assume that our own perspective and experience define the norm or even the ideal. And the hard fact is that we inevitably *do* favor our own experience and preferences—often without noticing. So tolerance is often a necessary, conscious, and rational choice. In October 2004, IRUL convened a conference on justice and tolerance at which the psychologist Adam Seligman of Boston University presented two decades of research. In 1998 Seligman established the Toleration Project (in part with a generous grant from the Pew Charitable Trusts) to explore religious resources for tolerance and pluralism. He discovered what people actually do and believe to arrive at tolerance, whether they wear Stars of David or Buddhist bracelets, or whether they carry rosaries and crosses or Muslim prayer books. What he learned can be applied universally, and I discuss it later in this chapter.

Civility. Doing small things with great kindness: that is the essence of civility. We seem to have lost our commitment to civility in public life, from politics to entertainment. Paparazzi deploy long-range camera lenses like sniper's guns to snap celebrities naked in their own homes, politicians drag their opponents through the political and personal mud, children taunt each other in schoolyards, and strangers shove each other out of the way to push ahead in line or let a door slam in the next person's face instead of holding it open. Since even a moment of rudeness contains contempt, lack of civility frays our lives. Civility is a form of love, and one we can cultivate.

Acceptance. Here we begin to move into emotion and a more profound experience of respect. Tolerance and civility are rational choices, but acceptance is a deeper embrace of another human being, and it requires intimacy and attentive listening (in itself a way of love). When we accept, we affirm the preferences and experiences of the other as meaningful, and if we can, we bend in order to let ourselves be guided by that person's values and desires. A great, if difficult, metaphor for this is informed consent for patients, an issue that, as a bioethicist at a medical university, I have seen up close. Patients want and deserve to be listened to, and to have a choice in the medical decisions that guide how they live and die. I explore the science and reality of this issue later in this chapter.

Reverence. Reverence is the most evolved manifestation of respect: it's a state of awe or amazement over the existence of another. I don't mean reverence as worship, but a deeply egalitarian honoring of the uniqueness of the other—an honoring that is instinctive and natural. Sometimes we may look at someone we cherish and feel a kind of holy wonder over their being and life. The naturalist E. O. Wilson captures reverence in his line: "The flower in the crannied wall—it *is* a miracle." The Jewish mystic Martin Buber expressed it beautifully when he coined the phrase "I-thou" to express true relationship. Reverence stands before the mystery of another and silently bows its head in appreciation. The state of reverence has not been researched much, perhaps because it is ineffable, but there are a few very interesting studies I discuss later.

LESSON ONE: TOLERANCE—CELEBRATE YOUR DIFFERENCES, CELEBRATE EACH OTHER

Yes, we live in hierarchies, embedded within further hierarchies. And I hesitate a little here to even say that, because I well understand that many people in the world, and a large segment of our own population, receive too little respect because of the relatively low rung they occupy on the ladder of power. That's why the expression "dis" arose on the street in the early 1990s among inner-city youth. For a class that had already suffered searing disrespect in every aspect of their lives, "Don't dis me, man," was a demand for respect. Don't "get in my face" either. (Incidentally, both "dis" and "in your face" made the latest edition of *Merriam-Webster's Collegiate Dictionary*.)

I remember my own starting experience of the power of "dis." My daughter Emma had invited me to a "values clarification" skit based on the story of Hansel and Gretel, performed by her third-grade class. After the skit was over, the teacher asked the class, "Was the witch right to try to cook and eat Hansel and Gretel?" I smiled, profoundly amused by the question, but an African American boy was frantically waving his hand in the back of the class, and he simply blurted out, "Yeah! They dissed her by eatin' on her house!"

As Emma and I walked home, I thought about this child, who lived in a tough inner-city neighborhood of Cleveland and was bussed into Emma's Shaker Heights school as part of a special program intended to foster educational equality. I realized that, for this child, whose parents never seemed to show up at school family nights and whose clothes were frayed and worn, "Don't dis me" was a cry for respect—and more than anything, this boy craved the respect of others.

According to the Yale psychologist Jonathan Bargh, author of *The New Unconsciousness*, emotions tinge perceptions and "there's nothing that's neutral. We have yet to find something the mind regards with complete impartiality, without at least a mild judgment of liking or disliking." Even when Bargh tested preferences for nonsense words, he found that "juval-umu" was pleasing to English speakers, "bargulum" was moderately so, and "chakaka" was considered unpleasant. We may instantaneously, without even understanding why, react to people with pleasure or displeasure, with an inexplicable passion in either direction. So what do we do after acknowledging that there is no individual—let alone any nonsense word—we are ever going to be neutral about?

This is where I return to the concept of *tolerance*—and one of the most inspiring individuals I know in fostering tolerance—Adam Seligman, who created the Tolerance Project. Seligman has undertaken remarkable work in war-torn areas of the world. At first, he and his colleagues worked in both Israel and Bosnia to teach tolerance to students in religious schools. Seligman feels that religious traditions have been hijacked by ethnic and nationalist ideologies and that those who go back to the ancient texts will not only learn more about their own traditions but understand that pluralism and tolerance are very possible. Since so-called religious intolerance has led to genocides, it's a good model with which to begin. "We're not making any claims about what's right, what's true, we're just saying, look at your own religious traditions and their concepts of tolerance," says Seligman. From Orthodox rabbis to Franciscan priors in monasteries, the Tolerance Project is having a profound impact, and Seligman's unique approach is working. "In certain programs," he says, "we join rabbinicial students and those in Islamic seminaries and have them study together once a month. It's a simple but brilliant idea if you realize that these students are living only eighty miles from one another and are virtually at war. So have them study together! The handbook we developed for Bosnia has now been translated into Bulgarian, Albanian, and French." Students in Israel study parts of the Torah and the Koran together in order to better understand each other. "[Their] curriculum was developed by Muslims, Jews, and Christians, and they were working during the most difficult of circumstances, the *intifada*."

"Let's say, in the Jewish case," says Seligman, "there was a text that said a non-Jew is less than human. And they were challenged, 'Okay, how will you present this text to your Palestinian colleagues in half an hour? This is not just an abstract discussion. You are going to have to present this text to a Palestinian when it says that non-Jews are not human beings. And this is somebody you just ate lunch with.' The teachers inevitably wrestled with these passages, and many ended up saying, 'Even if it is the word of God, I cannot agree with it.' Then the facilitator brought in other texts that showed how the religious tradition itself had dealt with this difficulty. That allowed these people to find a place within their own tradition that was tolerant, and yet to reject a particular passage that fostered intolerance."

One recent summer, says Seligman, Jews, Muslims, and Christians met together inside the Dome of the Rock in Israel. Individuals prayed alongside each other in their own traditions and in their own languages. "Many of us were crying. Being able to hear the others in the background was extremely moving. We're not trying to erase boundaries. We're not trying to say everyone is the same. We're saying that even with our differences—and these differences may go all the way down to our core—we can live together."

The Tolerance Project has produced unexpected and amazing results. "Albanians opened a library three years ago for religious dialogues," says Seligman. "Bosnians who participated in Jerusalem opened a similar center in Sarajevo. People go back to their home countries with new tools to address intolerance." In another remarkable project, Seligman and his colleagues are bringing together Israelis, Turks, French, and Americans to rebuild both a Russian Orthodox church and a mosque that were destroyed in the wars in Bosnia. "They will see that, even if they disagree about absolutely everything from democracy to women, they still can work together to rebuild a thing of physical beauty."

Celebrate your differences—and you can still celebrate each other. You can honor yourself and your own values and tradition and still honor another human being. "We've confused respect and boundaries in a horrific way," says Seligman. "It is not that our only two choices are to dissolve all boundaries or to erase all respect. Modern, secular culture tends to want to erase all boundaries and say we're all the same. But the fact is that boundaries constitute societies and communities, and we just have to recognize that." Religion, says Seligman, is membership in a sacred tradition, a response to the mystery and challenge of life and being. Religion is part of our identity, but it is not our whole identity.

A spiritual catalog of the family of humanity includes everyone from Jews, Muslims, Christians, and Buddhists to atheists and all other perspectives. The Tolerance Project teaches us a truth we can bring home to our own lives: that you and I can be different, even radically different, and yet still respect each other. So the next time you find yourself "dissing" someone, even in your own mind, pause. Think of Muslims, Jews, and Christians praying together, in their own languages and traditions—and some of them crying to realize, for the first time, that this is possible. Think of them rebuilding mosques and churches together. Start to rebuild the bridges in your life from the first rung of respect: tolerance.

❧ *Cultivate tolerance by traveling.* Travel to other countries, to other parts of your city, or to other cultures in your own environs. When you travel to foreign countries, immerse yourself in the ways of that culture, from cuisine to fashion to politics. Take an afternoon with friends or family and travel to another part of your city with the intention of discovering something about another culture. For instance, eat dim sum with the Chinese for breakfast on Sunday morning, or stop in a Spanish bodega to ask about the spells that different potions cast.

❧ *Increase tolerance by seeking out difference.* Find friends of different nationalities and share each others' different worlds.

❧ *Practice tolerance by learning about other cultures.* Watch foreign movies and documentaries about other places and cultures. Learn a new language. Attend a religious or cultural ceremony that is new to you. Allow yourself to be fascinated by other approaches to life.

❧ *Join in a project with others.* Try adapting Adam Seligman's innovative exercises from the Toleration Project. Create a community project to build or repair something with those of a religion, culture, or style vastly different from your own.

❖ *Help those from other walks of life.* Take a few hours a month to volunteer to help those who are handicapped or impaired, mentally or physically. As you help them, try to open your heart to their humanity, not their disability. As you do that and feel that, shine that same tolerance on yourself.

CONSIDER BEING CONSIDERATE

Kathleen DeLoach was five years old when her younger brother Daniel was born and they brought her to the hospital to see him naked on the table. "He was born fourteen pounds, but he was only a seven-pound baby," she remembers. "The other half was all tumor. He had mangiomas, webbed feet, all sorts of deformities." Daniel had been born with Proteus syndrome, an extremely rare disease that is best known by the story of "the Elephant Man." "I looked at him and turned to my parents and said, 'Oh! He is so cute.' I didn't see one difference at all, and I wasn't a shy child. I just looked past all the tumors, and that in a nutshell sums up my reaction to him my whole life. He's always been my cute little baby."

Now eighteen, Daniel has had ninety surgeries at the time of this writing. But perhaps the hardest thing Daniel has endured is lack of civility and kindness from others. "Daniel is Mr. Social," says DeLoach, "so when people get to know him, it doesn't take them long to get past differences. But every time we go on a vacation, it's so hard. People stare, they ridicule. They tap each other and whisper and say, 'How ugly.' The other day a guy in his twenties said, 'Did you see that ugly kid?' and his girlfriend laughed and said, 'You're so bad!' My mother used to say, 'Tell them you're fine, that's how God made you.' Sometimes he shouts out, 'Take a picture!' And it literally breaks my heart."

Kathleen DeLoach's experience with her brother has shaped her life and her ideas about consideration for others. Because of Daniel, she got a master's degree in bioethics and wrote and self-published a book about him. She and her mother also raise funds for a foundation for Proteus syndrome. And not surprisingly, she joined an organization called Operation Respect. "They developed a project called 'Don't Laugh at Me,' which uses songs to lessen bullying in schools. My respect for others comes from loving my brother and seeing his challenges. His experience made me realize that everyone has chaos and hurt and that alone is why they deserve respect. The other day I saw a woman crying in a coffee shop and hyperventilating, and every single person was walking by her, just walking by her. And you know, lack of consideration can be shown through mere silence. Being ignored can hurt more than words. I walked up to her and said, 'I don't know what happened, but whatever it is, I'm sure it will get better.' And she told me everything about her ex-husband, her therapist, her kids. Love and respect for each other, shown in the simplest ways, mean everything in life."

Daniel himself is an inspiration to his family. "This may sound farfetched," he says, "but this disease actually forced me to have a good outlook on life. Sometimes I wonder if God gave me this disease so other people with little illnesses or small surgeries can think of me and draw courage. I've learned a really deep lesson from this disease: it's not the way people look, but the way they act toward others that counts. I remember when my family and I went to Lourdes on a pilgrimage when I was twelve, and I saw people a lot worse off than me. And I'm not a hippie type, but I have to tell you, it was very spiritual. We went up the hill at night, and there were five thousand people with candles, all praying for themselves or the ones they loved. Each candle was for a person."

LESSON TWO: CIVILITY—PRACTICE THREE WAYS

Civility begins with language, a unique invention of humans (although recent research on dolphins suggests that they may identify themselves with their own specialized, sonic songs). It then moves into actions—for which we have a code we call etiquette, or manners. At the level of society at large, civility is enshrined in documents like our Constitution, which guarantees the equal rights of all human beings.

Kind words smooth our way. "Words are magic," says Yale law professor Stephen Carter, author of the best-selling book *Civility: Manners, Morals, and the Etiquette of Democracy.* "We conjure with them . . . with words we report the news, profess undying love, and preserve our religious traditions. Words at their best are the tools of morality, of progress, of hope. But words at their worst can wound . . . the way we use words matters. This explains why many traditional rules of etiquette . . . were designed to govern how words—those marvelous, dangerous words—should be used."

We all know the art of verbal kindness: saying "please," "thank you, " "excuse me," with a warm smile and respectful body posture; letting others finish their sentences without interruption; refusing to taunt others. Too often our words are hasty and discourteous—in all the obvious ways.

Etiquette uplifts, and true etiquette is a form of ethics. My grandfather's first wife was Emily Post, the author of the definitive book of manners, *Etiquette in Society, in Business, in Politics, and at Home.* My grandfather, Edwin Main Post, had been a wealthy stockbroker who lost all his money; shortly afterward, his first marriage, to Emily, fell apart (rumor has it that he left her for a chorus girl), and he later married the woman who became my grandmother. It wasn't until after her divorce from my grandfather in 1906 that Emily turned to writing. The story goes that when her editor suggested she write on etiquette, she said, "But it will be a small book. The whole subject can be reduced to a few simple rules." The final product was more than six hundred pages long. The book has been updated by her great-granddaughter by marriage, Peggy Post, whose nearly nine-hundred-page seventeenth edition was published in 2004.

My grandfather died in a boating accident at sea when my dad was just eleven years old, so I didn't get a chance to sit at Granddad's knee and hear stories about Emily, and I don't know that branch of the family well at all. But I do have the 1945 edition of *Etiquette* at home, and it's a favorite.

It's almost a shock to browse through Emily's *Etiquette*—and to reimagine a world where custom dictated the nature of an invitation, the seating of a gentleman of "first rank" at a table, the necessity of a bedroom sofa, or the way to eat fruit. (Plums and bananas were eaten in "fingers"; apples were "quartered with a knife"; peaches were held "with a fork"; and the blade of a fruit knife had to be "silver or gold plated with a sharp point for removing seeds.") Reading *Etiquette*, I find that the world of Fred Astaire and Ginger Rogers, for all its excess, beckons with the glow of a long-lost utopia.

Delicious and antiquated details aside, what is striking about Emily Post is that she understood something much deeper about etiquette: it's actually a branch of ethics. "Charm cannot exist without good manners," she writes, "not so much manners that precisely follow particular rules, as manners that have been made smooth and polished by the continuous practice of kind impulses." Etiquette is the art of considering the rights and feelings of others—a "code of instinctive decency, ethical integrity, self-respect and loyalty . . . not only to friend, but to principles." Emily Post's dictum was: "Courteous people enrich their own spirits by making other people feel good." Or as Jonathan Swift wrote, "Good manners is the art of making people comfortable in our presence." I find it interesting that one of the most renowned philosophers of our time, the Talmudic scholar Emmanuel Levinas, defines ethics as "opening the door for others." Thus, common courtesy can also be seen as a powerful metaphor for letting others into our own hearts.

Civility means social conscience. Stephan Carter calls civility "the sacrifices that we make for the sake of living together, for the sake of our common journey with others, and out of love and respect for the very idea that there *are* others." Civility goes deeper than manners; as Emily Post understood, it's a kind of moral code. In its broader social context, civility was the undergirding of the civil rights movement. Carter recalls when his family moved into an all-white neighborhood. He was twelve, and on moving day he and his siblings sat on the front step of their new house. "Our new white neighbors passed by on the street, some driving, some walking, looking at us, some of them stopping and staring for a while, and walking on, not saying hello, not greeting us," Carter told David Gergen, editor-at-large of *U.S. News & World Report*, in a 1998 interview. Then, recalls Carter, "from across the street came this booming voice of welcome." It was a Jewish woman, who soon brought the children a tray of cream cheese and jelly sandwiches. "I would say those are the finest sandwiches I ever tasted in my life," says Carter, who notes that those sandwiches introduced him powerfully to the notion of civility.

❦ *For a single day, decide to be courteous, even openly and buoyantly so, to everyone in your daily life*—neighbor, doorman, mailman, the stranger at the street corner or in the coffee shop, the cashier, your colleagues. Consciously greet people, ask how they are, hold a door, give a smile and a compliment. At the end of the day, sit down and examine how you feel. If you feel more buoyant, connected, and happy, choose to hold a "civility day" at least once every few weeks.

❧   *Just for fun, hold a formal family dinner.* Dress up as if for a party, lay out the fine china, and have a meal that the author of *Etiquette* would approve of. Play at the old ways of civility, and enjoy the experience with a dose of levity.

❧   *Meditate on civility in the deepest sense.* Read about the lives of Rosa Parks, the Reverend Martin Luther King Jr., the Dalai Lama, Mahatma Gandhi. Consider how you can reach out and include others in a deeper civility in which social rank does not count. Treat each person you encounter, from a taxi driver to the cable repairman, as someone with a meaningful history, as an individual you can learn from.

LESSON THREE: ACCEPT ANOTHER— LET IT BE, LET IT GO

In the name of love, we impose our own desires on another. To take an example from an area I know well as a bioethicist, there can often be a rift between what a family member wants and a dying person's own wishes. I've seen very loving parents who, even when their child has undergone several rounds of chemotherapy with no lasting success, want to do everything possible to keep the child alive. And sometimes that child, wise beyond his or her years by virtue of painful experience, wants to let go. In the last decade our courts have increasingly recognized the rights of teenagers in this arena. Many pediatric institutions now mandate that children over seven years be involved in discussions of whether they will participate in a clinical trial with an experimental drug. Even so, the law still states that parents and a physician have a right to override a child's wishes. Here, when parents heed a child's wishes, they are not admitting defeat but instead offering deep acceptance.

Jamie Talan, a writer for *Newsday* in New York, tells the story of her stepfather Jimmy's death. "At 70, he was handsome, ageless . . . his skin was smooth, with no evidence of a smoking history. But colds took something out of him. And one particular virus choked his pipes and pushed him to the ground in fear of dying." At the hospital he was placed on a respirator. "I would place a pen between my dad's fingers and touch the point of it to paper and hope he would write something that made sense. 'I want to die,' he scribbled. 'Please.' The next day his young doctor said that his lungs were so damaged that his only hope was to replace the respirator with a tracheotomy tube. He would then have six months of rehabilitation and go home to ward off the next cold. 'My dad wants to die,' I said. The doctor said that was depression speaking. I said, 'He is in the final stages of chronic pulmonary disease. He is on a ventilator and odds are he will have to live on machines for the remainder of his life. He's said no. What part of that don't you understand?' " The doctor said Jamie's father would have to talk to a psychiatrist, and when the psychiatrist agreed that Jimmy was not depressed, the pulmonologist allowed them to sign papers that read: "Do Not Resuscitate." "He actually seemed angry," recalls Talan. "Soon, the respirator was removed, and my dad made his only request. Orange juice. He let out an enormous sigh of pleasure. More, more, he demanded . . . nurses began a morphine drip, and he and I held hands as I watched him close his eyes . . . my dad passed peacefully—and on his own terms."

Acceptance is the foundation of informed consent—and what happens in a hospital can teach us how to have dialogues with others anywhere. The latest research shows that, across all ethnic and racial groups, the level of patient satisfaction is tied to whether the patient feels that he or she was treated with dignity and involved in decision-making. In fact, in one fascinating study of 7,730 patients published in the *Annals of Internal Medicine*, physicians who were rated in the lowest 25 percent in terms of involving patients in treatment decisions had lost one-third of their patients to other doctors in the following year. In contrast, the doctors who most involved their patients in decision-making retained 85 percent of their patients.

The bioethicist Christian Simon of Case Western Reserve University has been studying the informed-consent process through an IRUL-funded project that looks specifically at the decisions made by children and their parents to participate in new cancer research following a diagnosis of childhood cancer. Simon and others in the field have pointed out that sometimes doctors are coercive with patients and suggest to them that their participation in a clinical trial will help others in the future. A doctor might say to a parent, "This will be your child's contribution to science," or, "We will learn something from this study and be able to help others in the years to come." However, whether or not doctors are subtly coercive in this way, the study showed that parents' decisions to enroll their children in clinical trials were not affected at all. This finding, to me anyway, is a relief, and it suggests that parents care above all for the welfare of their child. And yet, amazingly, as Simon says, "Over eighty percent of kids diagnosed with leukemia in this country end up in clinical trials. Clinical trials aren't even alternative treatment anymore—they are the standard of care. And we've found that when children get to participate in discussions of their treatment, the dynamics change. Sometimes they ask very simple, important questions like, 'What will happen to my hair? Will I be able to be on the volleyball team?' "

How does informed consent apply to all of us, since we will all be patients at one time or another? Says Simon: "We're people first, with fears, concerns, and hopes that can be diminished in a clinical setting where there is too little time and where there is the enormous tendency of biomedicine to reduce people to illnesses. The body has a complexity that is amazing, that we can glory in, but we shouldn't elevate it beyond this much more ethereal thing, which is the person."

We need to grab on to and resurrect the humanity of the interaction between a patient and a clinician—just as we need to do with each other in every setting in life. Just asking a few simple questions like, "Where did you go to school?" or "How do you feel about this?" or "Why are you making this medical choice?" can profoundly change the patient-doctor interaction. I remember an elderly lady who had refused cataract surgery. Her doctor asked for her consent, she said no, and that was the end of the story, until a more responsible doctor said to her, "This simple surgery will restore your vision. Why don't you want it?" She responded, "Because I've seen *Star Wars*, and laser beams scare the hell out of me!" The doctor laughed and told her she had no need to worry about *Star Wars*. "These are tiny beams of light that aren't going to hurt you, and you will be able to see much better." The woman opted for the sight-restoring surgery.

Acceptance requires authentic conversation, and we engage others by first asking why they are making certain choices. We conscientiously raise penetrating questions for someone we love, offer our own perspective, and then accept their final choice. As this kind of caring conversation unfolds, we are accepting the other as just that—other, unique and different. Besides, how are we to know the final outcome of someone's decision? As the science-fiction writer Mary Doria Russell once said in an interview, "What seems like bad luck at one point in our lives can turn out to be the best thing that ever happened to us. And what seems like a wonderful thing can turn into a nightmare. My belief is, the story isn't over until it's over. Often events and decisions echo for centuries, and even millennia; they have unimagined consequences that can show up long after everyone has forgotten about them. Whether an event is ultimately a good or bad thing depends on when you decide the story has ended. To use a Christian example, the crucifixion of Jesus was bad news on Friday, but by Sunday, it became good news." As Russell notes, we mostly live in that metaphorical Saturday in between—when we're not sure about the right step on the road to a happy ending, and when we know that Sunday may bring a whole new interpretation. Acceptance, of ourselves and others, is therefore crucial.

In this way, acceptance is more joyful than tolerance. When I tolerate another, I carry a certain burden of rational choice; when I accept another, I feel celebration and trust.

❧ *Start a respectful dialogue with another person.* Ask how they feel or why they are making a decision. Remember that, as Mary Doria Russell put it, "whether an event is ultimately a good or bad thing depends on when you decide the story has ended." Since we are not omniscient, we cannot know how someone else's story will unfold, and it's wise to err on the side of acceptance.

❧ *"Seek to understand, not to be understood."* Respect requires understanding another person's story. Make discovery the goal of your relationship with another, rather than being right or wrong. When you're seeking to understand, you only want to be sure you know what someone's belief is, so there is no need to argue or engage in conflict.

❧ *Acceptance of ourselves helps us accept others.* It's easiest to offer respect to others when we feel good about ourselves. The clinical psychologist and meditation instructor Tara Brach offers this guidance for what she calls radical acceptance: "Our fear is great, but greater yet is the truth of our connectedness." According to Brach, we spend too much time at war with our-selves and others, judging and blaming; if we meditate on self-acceptance, we will naturally begin to include others in a sense of peace and caring. She says, "The biggest fear we have is that somewhere we are failing or are going to fail." Then, she says, we fear we will be rejected. To foster accept-ance, the two most important questions you can ask yourself daily are: "What is happening inside me right now?" and "Can I meet this with kind-ness?" Keep pausing to ask yourself those questions and extend yourself kindness, says Brach, and eventually you will begin to accept yourself and others more easily.

LESSON FOUR: REVERE LIFE

Reverence is respect's final flowering. It's a peak experience with a sense of the miraculous at its core, the place where we marvel at the mystery, beauty, complexity, and simple existence of life. Although we have virtually no sci-entific studies of reverence, Jonathan Haidt and his colleague Dacher Kelt-ner, whose work I discuss in the next chapter on compassion, have written about awe. In a 2003 essay published in *Cognition and Emotion*, they suggest that the two core features of awe are vastness and accommodation. Vastness is a reference to anything we experience as far larger than ourselves and our ordinary frame of reference. We can feel awe about anything from Niagara Falls to childbirth to a tsunami. We can feel absorbed into this vastness. At the same time, we need to shift so that we can accommodate this vastness. Awe is a challenge to settled assumptions, and it even has a touch of terror to it. As the poet Rainer Maria Rilke wrote, "For beauty is nothing but the beginning of terror, which we are still just able to endure."

Haidt, whose work in the field of positive psychology is truly pioneer-ing, also touches on reverence in another article from the year 2000. Haidt found that when we see people helping others in a very generous way, we often feel surprised and emotionally moved. That inspires us to then help others ourselves. One woman in Haidt's study recalled how a man from her church jumped out of his car to stop and shovel snow from an elderly lady's driveway. "I felt like singing and running, or skipping and laughing," the woman recalled. Just watching another person be generous gives us that elated sense of the miraculous in human nature. In another study, Haidt showed a group of participants a film about Mother Teresa's life, a comedy, or a simple documentary. Those who watched the film about Mother Teresa reported feeling loving and inspired, and they were more likely to volunteer afterwards in charitable activities.

I'd like to think that, since we've all had the experience of being swept away by reverence—whether seeing the Grand Canyon, falling in love, or witnessing the birth of our child—we can try to apply this transported, transforming state to those whose lives may seem in tatters. Reverence motivated Gandhi, Mother Teresa, and Martin Luther King Jr., and it shapes the lives of the Dalai Lama and Jean Vanier. I'm always amazed and comforted when I see the Dalai Lama's absolutely buoyant mirth. Rather than complain about being a leader in exile who was taken from his parents when he was little more than a toddler, he encounters others with joy. Years ago the late John F. Kennedy Jr. interviewed the Dalai Lama for his magazine, *George*. On seeing Kennedy's bandaged hand, the Dalai Lama held it in both of his own, rubbing and patting it. After the Dalai Lama and his entourage had left, Kennedy described watching them until they were out of sight down the hill and feeling "content but oddly deflated. It was as if we were all in a dark room and the fellow with the lantern had just left." The Dalai Lama's reverence for all life had inspired everybody in the room. Moral "saints" like the Dalai Lama are immensely important to the fabric of civilization. The thought of Mother Teresa bathing a leper, of Martin Luther King Jr. risking his life for his people, of the Dalai Lama rubbing JFK Jr.'s injured hand, inspires a kind of awe.

Dr. Esther Sternberg, director of the Integrative Neural Immune Program and chief of the Section on Neuroendocrine Immunology and Behavior at the National Institute of Mental Health, speaks of reverence for life's preciousness and fragility, that sense of awe and terror, in recounting an incident that shattered her when she was a young resident in Montreal. "A woman came in with an uncomplicated bladder infection, and instead of sending her home with a prescription, for some reason I decided to admit her and watch her overnight. And right before my eyes she went into septic shock and cardiac arrest and we had to resuscitate her. She was probably around thirty years old, not much older than me, and she'd seemed perfectly fine, and then her life was suddenly almost snuffed out, and then just as suddenly we brought her back to life. And that is the most spiritual experience anybody can ever have, and what it made me realize was the incredibly fragile thread by which we all hang. We need to remember to hear the background music of what makes us live, what makes us be, because life itself is incredibly precious and can be lost in the blink of an eye." Later, when Sternberg began to work in biology, "I was thrilled by macrophages under a microscope," she says. "I'd see them as living beings and come into the lab on the weekends with my daughter to 'feed' them, as if they were pets. At the same time, I'd look up at the stars and feel the immensity of the universe. I remember how my father used to sit with me on the terrace in summer and look up from his book and say, 'Listen to the sounds of peace,' which were the tennis ball bouncing in the court across the street, the dog barking, the birds chirping. Both he and my mother would do that. She used to say, 'Look at this sunset as if it were your last.'" From immune cells under the microscope to a young woman's life to the overwhelming beauty of nature in a backyard or a night sky, Sternberg's evocation of reverence says more than I ever could.

🌿 *Spend time in beautiful surroundings and let yourself be transported.* (Yup, I've said this before!) Take time, if you can, to travel to natural wonders, from the Grand Canyon to Niagara Falls to coral reefs, and keep a few videos or DVDs around the house that depict these natural wonders to refresh yourself when you can.

🌿 *Listen to transcendent music.* Handel's "Messiah," Beethoven's "Ode to Joy," and other such music can literally send chills of ecstasy up your spine. Watch the famous opening sequence to A *Sound of Music.* Music is one of the quickest ways to shift into a state of reverence and joy.

🌿 *Meditate on or write a description of a time when you were moved to awe, even to tears of appreciation.* Was it the birth of your child? A moment of marvelous physical intimacy with your spouse or significant other? The experience of visiting a cathedral like Chartres or viewing the Sistine Chapel?

🌿 *Seek out the quality of the miraculous.* Some of us see the miraculous in the sinuous movement of cells under a microscope; others find it in a toddler's pride and excitement as he first learns to walk, in a baby's birth (including kittens, puppies, even guppies), in seeds sprouting in a flowerpot, in the crystalline teardrops flowing from branches after a winter ice storm, in the pellucid dewdrops on a blade of grass in the morning.

❧ *Let reverence reverberate.* In all these instances, once you are in a state of reverence, try to extend that feeling to those you love, realizing that they too are remarkable, unique, and even transcendent at times.

Your Respect Score

It's time to answer the questions on the respect section of your Love and Longevity Scale. We have divided responses into percentiles, or fifths. These are general guidelines; you may score right near the cutoff between percentiles, so please keep this in mind and use the scale as a friendly tool. Remember:

There are two steps to determining your score. First, determine which items need to be "reverse-scored" (denoted with the ® symbol). For reverse-scored items, see the chart below for how to score.

If you score a . . .	. . . assign yourself a score for that item of:
1	6
2	5
3	4
4	3
5	2
6	1

The second step is to add the scores for individual items *after* the reverse-scored items have been reverse-scored. Take the quiz now, and take it again if you wish after you've finished this book and begun practicing the art of respect in your daily life.

Using the scale provided, please circle the one number that best reflects your opinion about whether or not each statement below describes you or experiences that you have had. There are no correct answers, so please respond as honestly as possible to each one.

1. In discussions I make it a point to really listen to my family members' opinions.
    **1=strongly disagree   2=disagree   3=slightly disagree   4=slightly agree
    5=agree   6=strongly agree**

2. I believe that I always can gain something from considering the perspectives of my family members.
    **1=strongly disagree   2=disagree   3=slightly disagree   4=slightly agree
    5=agree   6=strongly agree**

3. I make it a point to acknowledge the efforts and aspirations of people in my family.
    **1=strongly disagree   2=disagree   3=slightly disagree   4=slightly agree
    5=agree   6=strongly agree**

4. Even when I don't get my way in family decisions, I let my family members know that I respect their right to their own opinions.[®]
    **1=strongly disagree   2=disagree   3=slightly disagree   4=slightly agree
    5=agree   6=strongly agree**

5. I don't think it's that important to let my family members know that I respect them.[®]
    **1=strongly disagree   2=disagree   3=slightly disagree   4=slightly agree
    5=agree   6=strongly agree**

6. I believe that I always can gain something from hearing a friend's perspective.

    1=strongly disagree   2=disagree   3=slightly disagree   4=slightly agree
    5=agree   6=strongly agree

7. I try to make my friends feel important.

    1=strongly disagree   2=disagree   3=slightly disagree   4=slightly agree
    5=agree   6=strongly agree

8. Regardless of a friend's origins, upbringing, or background, I try to communicate my respect for them.

    1=strongly disagree   2=disagree   3=slightly disagree   4=slightly agree
    5=agree   6=strongly agree

9. I have trouble seeing the value in a friend's opinion when it is very different from my own.®

    1=strongly disagree   2=disagree   3=slightly disagree   4=slightly agree
    5=agree   6=strongly agree

10. I can get disrespectful when it comes to talking to friends about issues we disagree on.®

    1=strongly disagree   2=disagree   3=slightly disagree   4=slightly agree
    5=agree   6=strongly agree

11. In discussions I make it a point to really listen to the opinions of my neighbors or coworkers.

    1=strongly disagree   2=disagree   3=slightly disagree   4=slightly agree
    5=agree   6=strongly agree

12. I believe that I always can gain something from hearing the perspective of my coworkers or neighbors.

    1=strongly disagree   2=disagree   3=slightly disagree   4=slightly agree
    5=agree   6=strongly agree

13. I try to communicate my respect for people at work or in my community, regardless of their origin, upbringing, or background.
    1=strongly disagree   2=disagree   3=slightly disagree   4=slightly agree
    5=agree   6=strongly agree

14. I don't see the value in the perspective of a neighbor or coworker when it is so far from my own.®
    1=strongly disagree   2=disagree   3=slightly disagree   4=slightly agree
    5=agree   6=strongly agree

15. It's not that important to treat people at work or in my community respectfully when we admittedly disagree on things.®
    1=strongly disagree   2=disagree   3=slightly disagree   4=slightly agree
    5=agree   6=strongly agree

16. The world would be a better place if everyone tried to understand the point of view of other people.
    1=strongly disagree   2=disagree   3=slightly disagree   4=slightly agree
    5=agree   6=strongly agree

17. Every person has unique value.
    1=strongly disagree   2=disagree   3=slightly disagree   4=slightly agree
    5=agree   6=strongly agree

18. People should make it a point to acknowledge the efforts and aspirations of others around them.
    1=strongly disagree   2=disagree   3=slightly disagree   4=slightly agree
    5=agree   6=strongly agree

19. I don't see the value in other people's perspectives when they are far from my own.®
    1=strongly disagree   2=disagree   3=slightly disagree   4=slightly agree
    5=agree   6=strongly agree

20. I can become somewhat disrespectful when talking with someone with whom I disagree.®

    1=strongly disagree   2=disagree   3=slightly disagree   4=slightly agree
    5=agree   6=strongly agree

YOUR RESPECT SCORE

High Giver (80th percentile)	106 or higher
Giver (60th percentile)	99–105
Moderate Giver (40th percentile)	93–98
Low Giver (20th percentile)	83–92

Nine

The Way of Compassion: Feel for Others

Susan Scott Krabacher is founder of the Mercy and Sharing Foundation, headquartered in Aspen, Colorado, and Port-au-Prince, Haiti.
Krabacher, a former Playboy model, started the foundation with
$12,000, and now, along with her lawyer-husband, she runs three orphan-
ages in Haiti that house and feed 2,300 children. Together, they raise
money for monthly purchases of 6,000 diapers, 14,000 pounds of rice,
7,000 pounds of bean, and 250 pounds of toothpaste, just to name a few
items.

"One of my orphanages is for children awaiting adoption, and another
is for babies whose mothers died in childbirth or abandoned them. A third
is for handicapped and terminally ill children. That's really where my heart
loves to be," says Krabacher. "I love those kids so much, and I don't always
know if I'm going to get to see them again. Almost always when I go there,
there's an empty bed, and I know that means somebody had to buy a small

casket. There's an incredible poem that is my motto, and it goes like this: 'God, let me be aware, stab my soul fiercely with another's pain. . . . Give me the heart that divines and understands. . . . Flood me with knowledge and drench me with light.' "

Krabacher's compassion was born in part from her own suffering. "I had a horrific childhood," she admits. Sexually abused by her grandfather, she was put in foster care when her mother had a psychiatric breakdown. Her third foster family was abusive, so she went back home. "When I was sixteen, I quit school, got a job, and had my little brother move in with me, but later he killed himself. Then, at seventeen, I was given the opportunity to do a centerfold for *Playboy* for $15,000, and it was more money than I had ever dreamed of in my life. I moved into the Playboy mansion, and for the next ten years I did nothing but play very hard. And yet I was going through such depression. I married a guy who turned out to be one of America's most wanted men, and now he's in prison. I remember when they picked him up in a roadblock just outside of Aspen, and I walked on into Aspen and started knocking on people's doors telling them I could cook, clean, babysit, and just needed a place to sleep. Nobody would take me in, so that night I slept in a barn. The next day I knocked on more people's doors, and I found a paraplegic lady in a wheelchair. I lived with her for a year. I decided to find a lawyer to help me divorce from my husband, and I ended up at the office of the man who is my husband now. And this is going to sound a little corny, but my husband is the wind beneath my wings. He's nearly seven feet tall, he's absolutely gorgeous, and he could have a wife staying home wearing Fendi purses and spike heels and raising 2.2 children here in Aspen, but he's never complained, not once, about my mission. When one of the children in my orphanages dies, he cries with me."

Today Krabacher's foundation employs 150 Haitians and raises half a million dollars a year. Krabacher puts it this way: "I work long hours, put up with unbelievable sacrifice, bury too many children, and get no compensation but love, which is the greatest freedom you can know and the most important thing in the world."

Pati Cum: Offer Empathy to Another

Pati. Cum. These two Latin words blend together to form the root of "*compassion*," and they literally mean "to suffer with." While we can empathize with a whole rainbow of emotions in others, compassion requires the capacity to tenderly feel another's pain.

When I think of compassion, the figure who inevitably comes to mind is Abraham Lincoln. There is a story about a town drunk who was sleeping on the road in his own vomit one winter night when Lincoln and his friends walked by. Lincoln took the man home. And in his second inaugural speech, he made this remarkable and unforgettable statements "With malice toward none, with charity for all, with firmness in the right as God gives us to see the right, let us strive on to finish the work we are in, to bind up the nation's wounds." It is in binding up another's wounds that we offer true compassion.

Compassionate acts are innumerable: a hug to a friend, a donation to victims of a disaster, volunteer work, thoughtful advice, or in a rare case like that of a Mother Teresa, an entire life spent tending others in pain. Compassion is a way of living that you can cultivate, and it will soften and brighten your world.

Everyone from the Dalai Lama to the towering thinker Adam Smith has pointed to compassion as the most human, and humane, quality. David Hume, possibly the greatest of all Enlightenment philosophers, stated that though reason guides ideas, math, logic, and fact, it cannot move us to act. Only emotions stir us in that way. The German philosopher Arnold Schopenhauer stated it bluntly: "Compassion is the basis of morality."

Compassion is immediate. We are moved by suffering that is right before us, and we're less likely to be stirred by pain halfway across the world. In that case, we might need to make a little extra effort to "feel" our way into lives that are unconnected to us.

Of all the research on compassion, I find new brain imaging studies most fascinating. These studies allow us to see the act of compassion lighting up certain areas of the brain. There is a neurocircuitry that seems necessary for compassion. In this chapter, you'll learn that we're hardwired to open our hearts and to care—and in fact, compassion is important for the survival of the species, especially newborns and young children.

Compassion begins at birth. Compassion is the hallmark of perhaps the most important kind of love in our species: that of mother for child. The brains of moms show a distinct and powerful response to their baby's distress—certain parts of their brains light up in response to a just-born infant, and different parts of the brain light up months later as the relationship evolves.

Compassion calms and connects up. The wellspring of compassion may be in the hormone oxytocin—a neuropeptide produced in a part of the brain called the hypothalamus, which penetrates the whole nervous system and has become famous for its link to pair-bonding, devotion, and nurturing attachment. Some researchers now feel that oxytocin represents a unique axis of the nervous system that they call "calm and connection"—the exact opposite of the well-known fight-or-flight hormones.

Compassion allows us to mirror others' feelings. New research at Princeton is beginning to show that a brain area called the insula, located within the cerebral cortex, is associated with empathy and compassion. It's a hot topic in neuroscience right now, because it is the place where mirror neurons—neurons that "mirror" an experience another person is having, almost as if we're having it ourselves at the same time—seem to be located.

Compassion increases positive emotions. We may be able to cultivate compassion through regular meditation and visualization and permanently shift our brain patterns. Pilot studies with Buddhist monks show that regular compassionate meditation may permanently change brain patterns, leading to greater happiness. Compassionate feelings and actions, even when they involve the ability to sense and empathize with another's pain, help trigger positive emotions.

Compassion is linked to spirituality. One researcher's new findings suggest that compassion and spirituality are hardwired and linked. He has measured the "attachment" hormone, oxytocin, and the activity of the vagus nerve, a major nerve extending from our heart area to our brain, and found that both correlate with high compassion and intense spiritual experiences. Though these findings are preliminary, they hint that compassion is linked with other powerful, feel-good experiences like connectedness and spirituality.

Lessons from the Frontiers of Research

Compassion is emotionally powerful and engrossing. And as a research topic, compassion is unique among all the ways of giving in that we have begun to use sophisticated imaging techniques to watch the brains of moms, dads, monks, and others during states of empathy and caring. Compassion is so much more than a buzzword that has inspired best-sellers and Buddhists. It actually stops us from imposing suffering, and in that sense it is our moral compass. If you are a person who naturally reacts to the pain of others with empathy and care, the idea of willfully causing suffering is unthinkable.

LESSON ONE: COMPASSION BEGINS AT BIRTH

If there is one image that is archetypal across all cultures, it's that of a mother holding her newborn. Most mothers report an overwhelming feeling of devotion and tenderness when caring for their babies; the sound of a baby's cry triggers an immediate response from the mother. For fathers too, a new baby sparks a time of being deeply engrossed. According to Dr. James Swain of Yale University, two weeks after childbirth mothers report spending nearly fourteen hours a day exclusively focused on their baby, while fathers spend about half that time. During this period of falling in love for both parents, the new child is idealized: 73 percent of mothers and 66 percent of fathers report having the thought that their baby is "perfect." At the same time, couples report anxiety over the safety of their newborns and work hard to create a safe, clean, secure environment.

I asked Swain and his Yale colleague Dr. James Leckman to study the neurobiology of parental love for IRUL. Swain says, "I wanted to use neuroimaging to find out how brain activity reflects the huge emotional changes people go through when they become parents and include a whole new person in their lives who is utterly dependent on them. We've been studying breast-feeding moms, stay-at-home dads, and now moms who are using formula. Our initial data show that stay-at-home dads' brains function more like moms' brains." Swain and Leckman asked parents to listen to the cries of their own child, another child, and various "control" sounds and to view infant pictures of their own baby, another baby, and "control" photos—while their brains were being monitored. "We actually used the cries of stranger babies that were in the same range of spectral frequency pattern and volume as the parents' own babies," Swain notes. He himself was surprised at the obvious difference in brain-wave response: "I'm not yet a parent. It's an experience I'm really looking forward to, but I have to confess I didn't believe a parent would be able to distinguish between the recorded cry of their own baby and that of a strange baby. To me they all sound the same. I was wrong. There was such a profound difference in the brain's response.

"Every day in my work I am reminded of the enormous compassion that is such a huge part of becoming a parent," says Swain. "We're just beginning to understand the brain circuitry, but the research certainly supports the idea that love and compassion are necessary for the survival of our species. We hope to expand our research to find out how love and compassion change us in positive ways. I look forward to finding out more about how positive emotional attachment can transform us."

Brain-imaging studies show that when a breast-feeding mother listens to a baby's cry, all the brain areas known to be responsible for maternal behavior in animals light up. In the first month after childbirth, primitive areas of a mother's brain that govern emotion light up when her baby cries. Even seeing photographs of her own baby or unfamiliar babies can stimulate this brain circuitry. The power of this response is ancient and enormous.

Compassionate care turns out to be crucial for the baby too. Nurturing and care spurs the development of healthy nervous and immune systems. Pups that are licked and groomed frequently have reduced stress hormones and "startle" responses, and their ability to learn and remember is enhanced.

Even later in life, these differences in stress responses are evident—showing that tender care in infancy shapes lifelong resilience. A 2005 study by the psychologist Seth Pollak and his colleagues at the University of Wisconsin at Madison found that severe neglect and isolation change the levels of two hormones associated with attachment and nurturing. The scientists worked with eighteen four-year-olds from Romanian and Russian orphanages who had been adopted into Wisconsin homes. They found that the kids had markedly lower levels of these hormones than normal. Normal kids who were tickled and held had a spike in the attachment hormones, while children from the orphanage did not. Personally, I believe that repair of the nervous system is possible in these children—it just takes some time and care.

❧ *Spend time with babies and young children.* Knowing that new moms and dads are in a state of blissful love, consider spending time volunteering to assist with newborns or young children—whether babysitting for a neighbor's baby, volunteering on a maternity ward, or giving time in an orphanage or children's hospital. We've all seen a baby's smile bring out a kind of tenderness and happiness in strangers. We are clearly hardwired to care for the innocent and helpless, and spending time caring for babies can only spark our own compassionate brain.

LESSON TWO: LET COMPASSION CALM AND CONNECT YOU

Let's look at the biology of a new mother a little more closely. The wellspring of compassion in a new mom begins with the hormone oxytocin, often called the attachment hormone because of its role in pair bonding and nurturing. After the tumultuous experience of childbirth, women are often flooded with a new calm that is actually the result of an increase in oxytocin. Oxytocin rises during breast-feeding and massage. Animals injected with the hormone will immediately calm down, and mother rats injected with oxytocin will start licking and protecting nearby pups. In fact, oxytocin will stimulate full maternal behavior in virgin female rats—within just a few minutes of injection.

According to the Swedish endocrinologist Kerstin Uvnas-Moberg, mothers with higher levels of oxytocin are calmer and more sociable. Uvnas-Moberg and other scientists suggest that oxytocin represents an entirely unique axis of the nervous system, what they call "calm and connection." It is, they suggest, the opposite of our fight-or-flight hormones and may be just as important in helping us survive and flourish. I think of this as a compassion axis.

Sue Carter of the University of California at Irvine is famous as the doyenne of research on this potent hormone of attachment, which she has studied extensively in the prairie vole. Carter began studying the prairie vole—which lives in monogamous pairs for life—back in the 1970s. She discovered that oxytocin has a particularly powerful effect on the vole's brain after stress. Carter has also found that injections of oxytocin in male prairie voles stimulates nurturing behavior. IRUL funded Carter to examine the role of oxytocin in positive social interactions. She found that in male prairie voles oxytocin is necessary for nurturing behavior. So both male and female votes have a hormonal system that fosters compassionate caring behavior. When this "calm and connection" system is operating, there is reduced stress.

The "calm and connect" axis is good for our health. New research shows that compassion may be a key to religion's health benefits. In a 2005 study, the psychologist Patrick Steffen looked at 441 very religious individuals and found that compassion significantly reduced depression and stress. Even after factoring out religion, the link between compassion and mental health remained strong. In contrast, when Steffen eliminated compassion from the analysis, the link between religion and health fell apart. "Just going to church on Sunday, or synagogue on Saturday, isn't sufficient for good health," Steffen says. He believes that it's incorporating compassionate action into your life that counts—and will protect your health even if you are not religious. Again, this is a preliminary study and will need to be followed up by others.

Mothering doesn't simply occur at childbirth—we can mother people our whole life long. Amy Ai is an affiliated researcher at the University of Michigan's Integrative Medicine Program and an associate professor at Washington University in St. Louis. "Back in the winter of 1990," she recalls, "I had just been accepted to the University of Michigan, and that summer I met Mary, the wife of a professor and a mother of three adult children." At the end of the summer, having worked too hard and eaten poorly, Ai fainted and was taken to the emergency room, where she was diagnosed with dehydration. "When Mary learned about my illness, she took me to her country home. I could barely walk and immediately fell into sleep on her couch. When I opened my eyes, her mother, a white-haired granny, held a bowl of chicken soup next to me. 'Honey, you must take care of yourself. If you do not, nobody can do it for you,' she told me. I felt the deep love from her that I had felt from my own granny. That week Mary's family took care of me as their own child, and I recovered very quickly. And that Christmas Mary took me to their home again to spend the holiday together. While exchanging our presents, Mary told me: 'We help you not for rewards but for you to pass this love and help to others.' Today Mary's mom has passed away, but her compassion stays with me always."

Another wonderful story of "mothering" care comes from Kit Sawyer, a Cleveland massage therapist and healer deeply moved by the events of September 11, 2001. For nine months she visited New York monthly and—along with one thousand other massage therapists—offered massages to rescue workers at St. Paul's Chapel downtown. "I worked on National Guardsmen, highway patrol men, marines, construction workers, policemen, firemen, guys down in the pit. It was such a privilege to be there for all these workers thrown into this unimaginable horror. There was so much that went unsaid. People serving food would say, 'Do you want pancakes or eggs this morning?' and the worker might answer, 'Hey, pancakes sound great,' and you know what's unsaid is, 'You have no idea what I saw this morning.' I could feel these unsaid words in their bodies as I massaged them. Then when I'd go back home to Cleveland, I'd meet with a group of women friends who are healers, and they would work on me. They'd take care of me, and I could go back again renewed the next month." This was compassionate care in every direction.

Here are some ways to calm and connect in your own life:

✧ *Visualize your day anew.* At night before sleep, think back about your interactions during the day. You'll probably think of a few moments when you spoke or acted hastily, perhaps rudely, without genuine compassion. Replay that moment and visualize your response differently, as one that is deeply heartfelt and caring. Let peace fill you.

✤   *Turn to compassion to calm and connect you and another.* Exchange massages, a long, tender bear-hug, or spontaneous presents with a spouse or friend.

LESSON THREE: LIGHT UP YOUR BRAIN

Buddhism sets compassion at the center of the universe. Edie Irwin knows that from a remarkable encounter she had as a college junior in 1967, when she spent the year as a volunteer teacher of Tibetan refugees in Darjeeling, India. "Many of the children were ill with tuberculosis," she recalls. "The school was understaffed, and I became tired and jaded by the constant poverty, illness, heat, monsoon rains, leeches, and demands of beggars. One day a friend and I were walking on a cloud-wrapped, winding mountain path, deeply absorbed in conversation, when we heard a voice behind us, calling insistently. I did not really want to turn around. I felt intensely irritated. But then I saw a Tibetan monk with a two-year-old child in his arms, and blood flowing down the child's face. The monk could not speak English, had no money, but wanted to help the child. My friend and I took them to the hospital, paid to stitch up the child's head, and were awed by how much happier we felt, having helped where help was needed. Now, nearly forty years later, I look back on decades of involvement with Tibetan Buddhism and its ideals of universal compassion, with joy and peace."

Dacher Keltner, director of the Berkeley Center for the Development of Peace and Well-being at the University of California, is studying Buddhist monks because they spend hours a day meditating and cultivating empathy for all living beings. The remarkable findings about the brains of Buddhist monks—and what sets them apart—have been widely discussed in the last few years.

"I remember a long Buddhist meditation exercise I took part in at a summer institute," recalls Keltner. "For once in my life, I felt like my mind was still. And the words I felt were, 'I love people. I love human beings.' At the core of me was this tremendous feeling of care for others. And when I feel that, I feel my whole life is better. I'm glad we've begun to study compassion, because there is stunning potential in this line of research."

In 1992 monks living and meditating on the slopes of the Himalayas agreed to allow scientists to study them. The Mind and Life Institute and the John Fetzer Institute supported this research, which has been led by Alan Wallace, a leading Buddhist scholar, and the psychologist Richard Davidson of the University of Wisconsin. Using positron-emission tomography (PET scans) and functional magnetic resonance imaging (fMRI), Davidson has found that Buddhist monks have a remarkable and unique brain-wave signature.

In a 2005 study Davidson compared eight Buddhist monks and ten college students and found that the parts of monks' brains that lit up on imaging were ones known to be associated with positive emotions. The monks had practiced meditation for between fifteen and forty years. The students were given a mere week of meditation training, for an hour a day, in which they focused on love and compassion. Then, on a full-day retreat, all eighteen individuals meditated, focusing in particular on a state of unconditional loving-kindness and compassion. When Davidson used fMRI to study the monks, he found that, compared to the less experienced meditators, monks showed heightened activity in the left prefrontal cortex, the seat of positive emotions. He also found lowered activity in the right prefrontal cortex, which is often linked to anxiety and negative emotions.

This small and fascinating study seems to suggest that years of daily meditation create permanent shifts in the brains—in other words, that, as Buddhism has always promised us, we can cultivate loving-kindness and well-being through meditation. Perhaps the brain can change in response to practicing compassion in the same way that it changes when a pianist plays arpeggios or a guitarist plays tremolos—brain imaging shows a merging of the neurons that control the index and middle fingers. Of course, right now researchers are cautious. But they're hoping that cultivating compassion can actually change our neurocircuitry—permanently.

Of course, monks don't simply meditate on loving-kindness—they offer their lives in service to others in many ways. Many healing techniques and chants originated with Tibetan monks, and they are often willingly present to help people as they die. After September 11, a group of Tibetan monks visited New York and Washington and created beautiful "sand mandalas" as a gesture of compassion and caring. These mandalas are intricate paintings made with colored marble powders. The monks ceremonially create and then destroy them to remind us of the beauty and impermanence of life. Buddhist wisdom might be summed up in this statement of the Dalai Lama's to T. George Harris in the magazine *Spirituality and Health*: "If you engage in some service to others, give at least a short moment of happiness to others, including animals . . . then you get deep satisfaction. You get fulfillment of your existence."

Another study of meditation's power to increase compassion comes from the psychologist Jeanne Tsai of Stanford University. Tsai and her graduate student Jocelyn Sze studied how people would respond to a letter from a prisoner serving a life sentence for murder. Using excerpts from real-life letters, they designed a letter that explained why the prisoner was in jail and how he felt about his crime. "It's a very emotionally mixed letter," says Tsai, "designed to create distress for participants after they read it." Would these readers feel compassion? Would they write the prisoner a letter themselves? The study found that college students who meditated were more likely to write the prisoner—and that regular Buddhist meditators wrote even longer letters. IRUL then funded an expanded version of that study to look at individuals between twenty-five and sixty years old who had meditated for a minimum of three years—and whose overall average was eight years. Once again, mediators were more likely to write the prisoner and to write longer, more compassionate letters. As Tsai says, "This is not a definitive study about the effects of meditation, but it powerfully suggests that Buddhist meditators are more compassionate. Now, were these people already compassionate, and therefore drawn to meditation? We don't know, so we're collecting data right now to see if there are any differences in how much these two groups of folks feel empathy in general."

Speaking of letters from prison, as head of an institute, I sometimes receive letters from strangers. Here is one I received the other day that shows how compassionate care can melt even a hardened prisoner: "I was in jail, and two women approached me, said 'Merry Christmas' in broken English, and handed me a little bag. Inside was a brown teddy bear. I was overwhelmed with joy, and didn't feel I deserved this kindness, for I had been sentenced to five years for hurting someone. Why were these strangers caring about someone like me? I knew I couldn't keep the gift because even holding it would land me a trip to higher security . . . on the way back to prison from the factory I passed a house with a small child and mother, kissed the teddy bear, and left it in front of the door. My spirit leapt with a feeling of joy. Even if I only had that teddy bear for an hour, that act of kindness by two strangers showed me that love is not love until you give it away."

Here is a Buddhist meditation, centered on compassion, that you can try:

1. *Begin with yourself.* Sit in a comfortable relaxed position. Let yourself totally relax, and as you breathe in and out, imagine a wave of relaxation and peace washing over your body. Turn your awareness toward your heart; whatever emotions you find there, regard them as your starting place, without any judgment. Now, wish yourself well. Wish yourself happiness and freedom from suffering. Let yourself feel love for yourself.

2. *Merge with others like yourself.* Begin by thinking of a source of suffering in your own life and imagining others suffering from the same illness or problem. Many of them are suffering more than you. Just like you, these people want to be free of their suffering. Feel yourself connected to all those like yourself until a warm feeling of compassion arises in your heart. Now, imagine this: you can take on the suffering of all these people and free them of their pain instantly. Imagine yourself having that tremendous kind of courage. Imagine their suffering dissolving and melting away. Imagine the extraordinary happiness of all these people who no longer suffer, and let their happiness fill your whole being.

3. *Let compassion ripple outward.* Feel warmth and love in your heart, think of all your friends, and feel yourself embracing them with your love and wishing them well. Then extend your love and warmth to people who protect you who don't even know you—soldiers, volunteers, firefighters, police officers. Extend your love to all of them. Then imagine people you haven't met who have been hurt, who are suffering, and try to broaden your love to all these unknown people.

4. *Offer love to all creation.* With that feeling of love for yourself, your friends, the strangers who protect us all every day, and the people you don't know who are suffering, extend your love to what the Buddhists call all sentient beings. Here are some phrases that may

help, or invent your own: *May you be happy. May you love and be loved. May you find whatever healing you are seeking. May you find peace and joy. May all beings everywhere find perfect peace.* Then come back to your awareness of yourself, sitting in your room, and feel the change that has taken place in your heart during this compassion meditation.

Lesson Four: Look Right in Front of You

Is compassion the basis of human morality? Remarkable work by the scientists Joshua Greene and Jonathan Cohen of Princeton University has found that when people contemplate harm done to others—in this case, victims of violence—the same networks light up in their brains as in mothers responding to suffering in their own children.

In one experiment, individuals were asked what they'd do if, while driving their car, they came upon a seriously injured man who needed to be taken to the hospital but who would bleed all over the upholstery of their car and ruin it. Most of us would take the man to the hospital and ruin our upholstery. At the same time, people may know that their money might save lives halfway across the world, but those lives are so abstract that they don't engage us with the same urgency and immediacy. "If we think about this in terms of evolution," says Greene, "it makes sense. I don't think we'll ever respond to the concept of someone starving in Africa the way we respond to someone bleeding to death right in front of us."

Margarethe Laurenzi of Mountain Lakes, New Jersey, is the current president of the Medical Needs Foundation. Mountain Lakes is a small community of 1,500 families, and eight years ago a mother there was stricken with a serious form of Lyme disease. "She had three small children," recalls Laurenzi, "and her medical coverage would not allow her to have certain kinds of treatments, and she was so sick she was actually dying. So her friends and neighbors banded together to take care of the children and help pay for her treatments. They ran a race to raise funds. In fact, there was such an outpouring in the community that they raised far over $100,000 in that first race alone. And there has been a race every year since, and they disperse those funds through a nonprofit foundation they founded. A woman named Judy Halter was the first president. We're a very bare-bones organization that gives away over 90 percent of our funds to individuals with catastrophic or chronic medical conditions. You know, there are so many people in need all around us, and we don't have to go to Sri Lanka to find them. They are right next door to us. And people get into circumstances beyond their control, they get tough breaks, and it's so wonderful that we can help a few families this way. I am very inspired by those who are active in community life and in giving."

So what happens when someone in need is not right next door, or when a situation is woven with complexities? Joshua Greene's work points to a higher-order kind of compassion that can help broaden our care in such cases. "In one of our experiments," he explains, "we ask people what they would do if a bunch of folks are hiding in a basement during a war, and there are enemy soldiers outside, and a baby starts to cry. You know if the soldiers hear that baby cry, they'll find you and kill you all. The only way to prevent this is to smother the baby to death. And the awful question is, is this okay to do, ethically speaking?"

Brain imaging shows that it takes folks a long time to come up with an answer. A part of the brain called the anterior cingulate cortex lights up. "One thing we know about this area of the brain is that it lights up when you feel conflicted about your response," says Greene. "And we also see a part of the prefrontal cortex light up—a part that is responsible for cognitive control."

With two parts of the brain lighting up together, Greene notes, it's as if people's first response is pure compassion for the baby. At the same time, they can reason out that one death is better than many. "Their brain is spending time choosing the less automatic response," says Greene. And those people who finally agree that one death, even an innocent baby's death, is better than a whole group dying have higher activity in the cortex, the executive control area, than the folks who just finally say, "No, don't smother the baby, no matter what."

Greene is quick to add that these scenarios are not the kind we normally encounter, but they help us understand the way our brains are built and structured, so that we can gain insight into how we actually live. When those nearby suffer, we are stirred to help by a kind of visceral response. But in more complex situations, we reason out a higher-order compassion that benefits those who are far away or is geared toward the greater good.

- *Look next door.* Where do you see suffering up close? What small gesture of care can you offer to someone going through a difficult time, whether a family member, friend, colleague, or neighbor?

- *Look far afield.* How can you contribute to the greater good of the country and the world? Can you volunteer for a suicide hotline, join a group that offers outreach into the larger community, or, if inspired, volunteer for Red Cross training to partake in disaster relief?

- *Read or recite this Navaho Indian prayer:*

In beauty may I walk . . .
In beauty may I walk.
All day long may I walk.
Through the returning seasons may I walk.
On the trail marked with pollen may I walk.
With grasshoppers about my feet may I walk.
With dew about my feet may I walk.
With beauty may I walk.
With beauty before me, may I walk.
With beauty behind me, may I walk.
With beauty above me, may I walk.
With beauty below me, may I walk.
With beauty all around me, may I walk.
In old age wandering on a trail of beauty, lively, may I walk.
In old age wandering on a trail of beauty, living again, may I walk.
It is finished in beauty.
It is finished in beauty.

Pause after reciting this prayer, and imagine wrapping yourself and those you love in that same feeling.

Your Compassion Score

It's time to answer the questions on the compassion section of your Love and Longevity Scale. We have divided responses into percentiles, or fifths. These are general guidelines; you may score right near the cutoff between percentiles, so please keep this in mind and use the scale as a friendly tool. Remember:

There are two steps to determining your score. First, determine which items need to be "reverse-scored" (denoted with the ® symbol). For reverse-scored items, see the chart below for how to score.

If you score a . . .	. . . assign yourself a score for that item of:
1	6
2	5
3	4
4	3
5	2
6	1

The second step is to add the scores for individual items *After* the reverse-scored items have been reverse-scored. Take the quiz now, and take it again if you wish after you've finished this book and begun practicing the art of compassion in your daily life.

Using the scale provided, please circle the one number that best reflects your opinion about whether or not each statement below describes you or experiences that you have had. There are no correct answers, so please respond as honestly as possible to each one.

1. When someone in my family experiences something upsetting or discouraging, I make a special point of being kind.
   1=strongly disagree   2=disagree   3=slightly disagree   4=slightly agree
   5=agree   6=strongly agree

2. I can't resist reaching out to help when one of my family members seems to be hurting or suffering.
   1=strongly disagree   2=disagree   3=slightly disagree   4=slightly agree
   5=agree   6=strongly agree

3. When my loved ones are having problems, I do all I can to help them.
   1=strongly disagree   2=disagree   3=slightly disagree   4=slightly agree
   5=agree   6=strongly agree

4. I'm probably a bit too preoccupied to be as compassionate as I could be with my family members.[®]
   1=strongly disagree   2=disagree   3=slightly disagree   4=slightly agree
   5=agree   6=strongly agree

5. I don't give my family members the kind or quality of attention they need when they are feeling sad, lonely, or frustrated.[®]
   1=strongly disagree   2=disagree   3=slightly disagree   4=slightly agree
   5=agree   6=strongly agree

6. When friends are sick, I make of point of paying them a visit.
   1=strongly disagree   2=disagree   3=slightly disagree   4=slightly agree
   5=agree   6=strongly agree

7. I drop everything to care for my friends when they are feeling sad, in pain, or lonely.
   1=strongly disagree   2=disagree   3=slightly disagree   4=slightly agree
   5=agree   6=strongly agree

8. When friends of mine are experiencing problems, I do everything
    I can to help them.

    1=strongly disagree 2=disagree   3=slightly disagree 4=slightly agree
    5=agree 6=strongly agree

9. I may be too busy with my own concerns to be as compassionate
    as I could be with my friends.®

    1=strongly disagree 2=disagree   3=slightly disagree 4=slightly agree
    5=agree 6=strongly agree

10. I don't give my friends the amount of attention they need when
    they are feeling sad, lonely, or frustrated.®

    1=strongly disagree 2=disagree   3=slightly disagree 4=slightly agree
    5=agree 6=strongly agree

11. When neighbors and friends are ill, I make a point of paying them
    a visit.

    1=strongly disagree 2=disagree   3=slightly disagree 4=slightly agree
    5=agree 6=strongly agree

12. I drop everything to help my neighbors and coworkers when they
    are having problems.

    1=strongly disagree 2=disagree   3=slightly disagree 4=slightly agree
    5=agree 6=strongly agree

13. When people in my neighborhood or place of work are having
    problems, I do all I can to help them.

    1=strongly disagree 2=disagree   3=slightly disagree 4=slightly agree
    5=agree 6=strongly agree

14. Sometimes I notice myself being unsympathetic when coworkers
    or neighbors seem to be having problems.®

    1=strongly disagree 2=disagree   3=slightly disagree 4=slightly agree
    5=agree 6=strongly agree

15. It's hard for me to feel sorry for people in my community or place of work who are struggling in life.®
    1=strongly disagree   2=disagree   3=slightly disagree   4=slightly agree 5=agree   6=strongly agree

16. I frequently donate to charities that are working to ease the plight of the unfortunate around the world.
    1=strongly disagree   2=disagree   3=slightly disagree   4=slightly agree 5=agree   6=strongly agree

17. I have often come to the aid of a stranger who seemed to be having difficulty.
    1=strongly disagree   2=disagree   3=slightly disagree   4=slightly agree 5=agree   6=strongly agree

18. I do not hesitate to lend my support to causes around the world that seek to help people who are unfortunate.
    1=strongly disagree   2=disagree   3=slightly disagree   4=slightly agree 5=agree   6=strongly agree

19. It's hard for me to feel compassion for complete strangers, even if they seem to be having problems.®
    1=strongly disagree   2=disagree   3=slightly disagree   4=slightly agree 5=agree   6=strongly agree

20. When I hear about people who are suffering in other parts of the world, my typical response is to ignore it.®
    1=strongly disagree   2=disagree   3=slightly disagree   4=slightly agree 5=agree   6=strongly agree

YOUR COMPASSION SCORE

High Giver (80th percentile)	99 or above
Giver (60th percentile)	91–98
Moderate Giver (40th percentile)	84–90
Low Giver (20th percentile)	73–83

Ten

The Way of Loyalty:
Love Across Time

Once upon a time there was a boy named Chester who lived on a rice farm in Arkansas, not far from a country church. One day Chester was sitting with his brother outside church when he saw a girl pass by with a group of visitors and said to his brother, "I'll have a date with her someday." Two years later Chester's family moved across the road from a cotton farm owned by that girl's family. He told her that he'd seen her two years before, when she was fourteen, that she had worn a white dress with green polka dots, and that he had never forgotten her.

"I like to tell people I chased her until I got her right where she wanted me," says Chester Dilday today, after more than seventy years of marriage. Or as his wife Mildred puts it, "We just loved each other from the time we met."

Chester and Mildred have been happily married for seven decades. Never once, by their own admission, have they argued, gone to sleep mad, or entertained the idea of divorce—not when they were separated for years at a time, not when he was in and out of the hospital, not even when their child died.

They first got engaged in the early 1930s, the nadir of the Great Depression. Chester's family moved frequently, renting different rice farms, and soon after he got to know Millie he had to move again. For a year, Chester walked fifty-six miles round-trip to see Millie on the weekends. "I would leave on Saturday as early as I could," he recalls. "You couldn't see anything but prairie, rice fields, and once in a while a home or some trees around a pond." A year later his family moved yet again, but now he was a hundred miles from Millie's home—too far to walk.

"We didn't have telephones then," recalls Chester. "So we wrote letters. And I bought a house and built some furniture for us." They married on August 26, 1935, and that first year he worked for a dollar a day, clearing forest. "I had five dollars in my pocket, and I spent $4.98 at Sears and Roebuck for a wedding ring." Millie still wears the ring: a white gold band engraved with flowers, and has informed her family that, "when I am laid to rest, this ring is to be left on my finger." She also has a stick of Doublemint gum that he brought her on one of his fifty-six-mile-walk visits, and she keeps it in a cedar chest that was his first Christmas present to her. She has a six-inch wooden guitar that he whittled, with strings that are actual string, and a sculpture he carved after the birth of their two girls but during a time—1944 to 1946—when he was away in the marines. "I was caught in the hold of a ship in a storm for over nine hours, and they didn't know I was down there," says Chester. "So I took a knife and cut a piece of wood off the ammunition box and carved two links that represent she and I."

Of Chester's time away in the marines, Millie says, "it was terrible, it was a long two years, but I felt all the time he would return to me, and he did." He was injured during the war and spent the next four years in and out of the hospital. "I had to have an operation on my back," he recalls, "so I sold my farm to pay for it. I was going to do everything I could to keep going. Millie was at home working on a sewing machine to earn money, and I was laying in a body cast. I could only use my arms from the elbows down, but I managed to make leather goods and sell purses, billfolds, and key cases. We never drew a dime of unemployment. We never asked for help. Then I sold my home and business to enter college, and Millie worked for

Oberman Manufacturing Company making clothes, and I worked at two jobs while going to college. That college degree changed my life. I was able to get a good job as a design engineer."

The most difficult moment of their life came when they lost their first-born daughter, Patricia, at age eleven. A stranger ran over her with a bicycle, severely damaging her lungs, and she died three years later. Chester recalls Millie crocheting some items for her daughter before they brought her to the hospital for the final time, and their daughter saying, "Mom, I won't need those. But don't cry." "She didn't cry," says Chester. "She waited until after our daughter died, and then she fell apart."

Today the couple have apartments in both their son's and their daughter's houses. "We spend about half the time in one place and half the time in the other," says Chester. Of their long marriage, says the couple, "one of our philosophies has been, don't let the sun go down on your anger. Realize deep down in your heart your love for one another, and that will give you the willingness to overlook inconsistencies and flaws."

Loyalty Is Love Across Time

I learned the loveliness of loyalty from my dad. I regard him as one of the most loyal men on earth. He was eleven when his dad, Edwin Main Post, died in a boating accident on Fire Island. For the rest of his life my father continued living on Long Island's Great South Bay, and every time there was a big storm or gale wind he'd take our schooner, the *Golden Eagle*, up and down the bay looking for sailors in trouble. My dad was a glass designer, and he was once offered a position as executive vice president of design at Corning, but he refused to move. I asked him why, and he said quietly, "My father died in a storm here." He remained forever and exquisitely loyal to the place where his dad had passed away. So for me, if there is a visual image of loyalty, it's Dad on his boat, year in, year out, doing his best to prevent other fathers from dying in boating accidents—after all, they might have an eleven-year-old boy at home like he had been.

Loyalty is love that lasts—and that's what we all want. The commitment inherent in loyalty defuses our deepest existential anxiety. Broken covenants are hard to restore and never quite attain their state of original trust. It's not easy to find loyalty in our society. Back in the 1960s, sociologists defined the typical American as "protean"—after the Greek god who constantly changed his identity. As the Columbia law professor George Fletcher writes: "Shifting loyalties is an increasingly common way of coping with a weak friendship, a shaky marriage, a religious community that takes the wrong stand on an important issue, or a nation that has come into the hands of the wrong political party."

Loyalty lives on a continuum: it begins, to coin Fletcher's ingenious phrase, with "minimal loyalty: thou shalt not betray me," and at its most profound it blossoms into "maximal loyalty: thou shalt be one with me." We all order our loyalties in descending importance—family, friends, community, and the world. This is known in Latin as *ordo caritatis* (the order of love). Usually we learn loyal love in the crucible of family, where we must stay committed to people long enough to discover their inevitable human imperfections—and then continue loving them anyway. This steadfast love is a challenge; as Zosima in Dostoevsky's *The Brothers Karamazov* puts it: "A true act of love, unlike imaginary love, is hard and forbidding."

Loyalty demands a huge amount of us—especially at times when our emotions and inclinations run in another direction and love becomes a subdued form of duty: flat, empty, even onerous. We anguish over how to keep love's commitments alive and authentic during such times; we try to find a commitment that, in the words of the theologian and ethicist Margaret Farley of Yale University, "binds our sense of freedom without destroying it." But all love is tested this way, and if we stay constant, we build a beauty into love that can only be created with the passage of time. As the poet Robert Frost put it: "But I have promises to keep,/And miles to go before I sleep,/And miles to go before I sleep."

In Judaism, loyalty is called *chesed*—which is translated as "steadfast love." The great philosopher of love Pitirim Sorokin said that "duration" is one of the five most important dimensions of love. Though a soldier may save a comrade in a moment of self-sacrificing heroism, a loyal parent may care for a sick child for decades. And of course, loyalty to a mission is necessary if we're really going to create great change. As Thomas Edison said, "Genius is one percent inspiration and ninety-nine percent perspiration." When a friend consoled him because of his repeated failures, Edison responded, "I have not failed, I've just found ten thousand ways that don't work." So in part the genius of creativity is a kind of loyalty—to never give up. "Never despair," counseled Edmund Burke, "but if you do, work on in despair."

That does not mean, of course, that loyalty is blind to error or wrongdoing. Sometimes protest is the highest form of loyalty. As Mark Twain put it: "Loyalty to petrified opinion never broke a chain or freed a soul." And of course, loyalty needs to be guided by reflection and wisdom. Keeping our commitments and vows is hugely important in loving and being loved, but at times the ethic of "first do no harm" requires moving on from a commitment or seeing it in the embrace of a larger loyalty.

Research shows that loyalty is good for us, as couples, parents, children, and friends. Here are some of the most powerful loyalty-research highlights:

- A survey by the National Opinion Research Center (NORC) at the University of Chicago, published in early 2006 and funded in part by IRUL, found that those in healthy, happy, long-term marriages were highly giving and felt strong love toward others in general.
- Both married men and women are less likely to die than their single counterparts—and this is especially striking in the case of men.
- In "low-conflict" marriages (which, it turns out, the majority of marriages are), children are happier and more resilient if their parents stay together.
- When individuals who were unhappy in their marriages but stayed in them were surveyed five years later, 80 percent were now happy, indicating that if we stick out tough times in a marriage, it's often to our benefit—though not always, of course.
- Friendship can be beneficial to health, protecting against depression and boosting self-esteem. In a ten-year study of people age seventy and older, a network of good friends was found to be more likely than close family relationships to increase longevity in older folks— by an impressive 22 percent.
- Women in particular are good at connection and loyal relationships. In fact, new research shows that women respond to stress with an outpouring of brain chemicals that include not only the typical fight-or-flight hormones but also oxytocin, the attachment hor-

mone. Thus, women may be hardwired to respond to hard times by tending their children and bonding with others.

Lessons from the Frontiers of Research

Loyalty is not a widely studied trait, unlike forgiveness, gratitude, and generativity. Since loyalty is love that shows itself over time, we'd need the gold standard of research—longitudinal studies that look at folks over many decades—to really understand the profound impact of loyalty on health and well-being. There *is* one area of research that stands out, however, and that is the impact of loyalty on marriage and family. Otherwise, I draw on philosophy and experience to offer insights about loyal love that can change your life.

LESSON ONE: A LOYAL MARRIAGE LIFTS YOUR LIFE

What is the source of our good fortune? In many cases, it may be a loving marriage. When the eminent psychiatrist George Vaillant followed 456 inner-city men whose lives had begun in extreme difficulty, he found that by their middle fifties the nine men leading the happiest, most generative lives reported that the single greatest factor in their good fortune was a loving marriage. The science supporting the health benefits of a long-term marriage is compelling. It seems that marriage is one of the most supremely balancing and healthful commitments we can make in life.

Good marriages contribute to the well-being of both men and women, in part because a slow alchemy occurs during marriage that transforms the initial passion into deep, trusting love. To adapt the wonderful insights of Pitirim Sorokin again, I would say that the best marriages embody Sorokin's three levels of love: *eros, philia* (friendship that blends self-interest and benevolence), and the deeply loyal, unselfish *agape* love, sometimes translated as "charity." We may fall in love, but we rise into *agape*. Marriage begins in an enthusiastic burst of commitment, but it lasts through times that are sad, difficult, arid, and conflicted. The vow "for richer and for poorer, in sickness and in health," is actually quite blunt and honest.

Marriage can flourish only if we are giving. In fascinating new research published in 2006 and sponsored by IRUL, the National Opinion Research Center found that those in healthy, happy, long-term marriages tend to be givers and to express a strong love for others in general. Tom Smith, director of the General Social Survey at NORC, notes that it is our country's most comprehensive nationwide scientific survey on empathy and giving. Smith found that individuals who score high on questions asking them about whether they love and care for others ("I'd rather suffer myself than let one I love suffer," or, "I'm willing to sacrifice my own wishes to let the one I love achieve his or hers") were more likely to describe their lives and marriages as "very happy." In fact, 57 percent of those who scored high reported they were in very happy marriages.

Emotional engagement and commitment in marriage are both keys to wives' happiness, according to a study of five thousand couples by sociologists at the University of Virginia. "Wives care about how much quality time they spend with their husbands," note the authors of the study, W. Bradford Wilcox and Steven Nock. They also report that the happiest wives are those who believe that marriage "is a lifetime relationship and should never be ended except under extreme circumstances."

Linda Waite of the University of Chicago is one of the country's most distinguished demographers, or population researchers. She is the co-author of *The Case for Marriage: Why Married People Are Happier, Healthier, and Better Off Financially*. I had a chance to talk with her a few years ago at a small research meeting in Chicago, where a group of scholars had gathered to discuss Waite's remarkable findings on marriage, health, and longevity. Most notably, she had determined that *both married men and women—but especially men—are less likely to die than their single counterparts*.

Waite and her colleague Lee Lillard drew on data from more than six thousand families that had been studied since 1968. They followed the changes in the lives of couples as they married, separated, divorced, remarried, or lost a spouse. She found that, in particular for the men in the study, avoiding wedlock was risky. "Almost nine out of ten married men alive at forty-eight would still be alive at age sixty-five, but only six out of every ten never-married men alive at forty-eight would make it to retirement age," notes Waite. "Divorced and widowed men were almost as likely as confirmed bachelors to die before age sixty-five." For women, the results were not quite as strong: "Nine out of ten married women alive at age forty-eight reached age sixty-five, compared to eight of ten never-married and divorced women." So for women, an extra 10 percent will die early if unmarried, while for men, the marital "premium" is simply huge. This huge "marital advantage" is what propelled Linda Waite into this field in the first place. She had been asked in the early 1990s to analyze a large database of deaths— nearly fifty thousand individuals—and had found that marriage has a profound impact on well-being.

Waite's co-author on *The Case for Marriage*, Maggie Gallagher, is an affiliate scholar at the Institute for American Values. When I interviewed Gallagher, she told me their research showed that married people "are physically healthier, live longer, earn more money, and build more assets than similar singles. They experience less anxiety, depression, hostility, and loneliness, and are more likely to tell you that they're happy with life in general. They have more sex than single people of the same age." Gallagher says one reason long-term marriage benefits us is that contracts in general are good for us: "If you are married and committed to a long-term time horizon, you can do what economists call specialization and exchange. Each of you gets really good at some part of the whole business of life together. And marriage makes you really, really important in someone else's life, so you are not as likely to do something dumb or risky. Even though we live in a culture which celebrates autonomy, independence, and freedom as a pathway to happiness, this research on marriage shows that for most of us it's much more important to be someone who really matters to other human beings. And once you are someone who really matters, you have to be reliable and dependable. That ends up being good for others and for you." Gallagher also notes that for men the real commitment to a woman comes with engagement or marriage, not cohabitation. "When men agree to marry, they commit to the idea that they and their wives are a team, together."

"Commitment to the relationship is a very powerful force," says the sociologist Vincent Jeffries of California State University in Northridge, whose work IRUL has supported. Jeffries studied over fifty couples who had been married for over twenty-five years and for as long as fifty-nine years. He found that "these couples were happier and more in love after many years than when they married, and that the love was deeper and more solid. They'd come to feel that their marriage itself was a good thing that needed to be preserved and protected."

In a 2005 study of 147 couples who had been together over twenty years, the psychologist David Fenell of the University of Colorado found that lifetime commitment was the most important quality of a happy marriage. "If a couple is committed to their marriage," says Fenell, "they can weather the storms that inevitably occur."

And yet, of course, we must make the inevitable caveat: not all marriages lead to health benefits. High-conflict marriages, in which couples openly fight in the presence of children, have been shown to lower immune function dramatically, according to a 2005 study that capped three decades of research at the Ohio State University's Institute for Behavioral Medicine Research.

Sometimes it is not possible to stay married and the conflict is so intense that the entire family is better off if the parents separate. Even then, when a relationship is damaged beyond repair, in leaving it we can make a point of remembering the better times—to forgiving each other and ourselves in the sense of letting go and moving on without letting bitterness eat away at us for years.

I've been married for twenty-four-years. Here are a few insights I pass along that have helped me through the hard times in my own marriage:

❧ *Fill in the gaps.* No human being can resonate to every facet of our being. In fact, complementary differences and abilities are part of what makes a marriage work. But if parts of you feel "silent" in the marriage, cultivate friendships with those who have qualities or interests that your spouse does not. Be grateful to these friends for refreshing you and strengthening your marriage.

❧ *Expect surprises.* Years into a marriage, one partner may divulge a "secret" from the past—perhaps a tough illness, an illegitimate child, or a previous love affair. And over time we each change in ways that may completely surprise us. Try to commit to personal growth for both of you, whether in new fields of work or study or in physical, emotional, and intellectual transformations. You don't have to leave a relationship in order to explore new aspects of life. So, to quote an old cliché, expect the unexpected and go with the flow.

❧   *Spend time together* now. When a spouse actually walks out the door, it's the final step in a dance of departure that has been in full swing for a long time. So cultivate loyalty by spending time together in the present, taking time for what the Yale psychologist Robert Sternberg has called the triangle necessary for good romantic relationships: passion, emotional intimacy, and commitment.

❧   *Give without expectation.* Giving should not come with a price tag.

❧   *Take time to play.* Stay whimsical. There's no need to be a complete fool, and there are times when you need to stand up for yourself, but in general, offer the good joke, the warm smile, and the playful comment.

❧   *Keep the vow.* You vowed "for better or for worse," not "maybe for better or for worse." Marriage encompasses times of consummate, soaring love, quiet cordiality, mere tolerance, and intense hostility. The lows can be a real test, and both partners may be unsure about who is to blame. But if both are committed to the idea of a lasting marriage, it's quite possible you'll get through the darkness and reemerge closer and happier.

LESSON TWO: MARRIAGE MAKES A CHILD'S WORLD WHOLE

"Marriage makes one world for a child. Divorce makes two," says Elizabeth Marquardt, affiliate scholar at the Institute for American Values. "Nobody quite understands the job the child has to do. Even in a best-case scenario, when divorced parents don't fight and both stay involved in the child's life, conflict gets transferred to the inner life of the child." Marquardt, who conducted a national survey of 1,500 young adults between the ages of eighteen and thirty-five, found that children in "low-conflict" marriages did better if their parents made the effort to stay together rather than divorce—even if those marriages were not extremely close or happy. And according to Marquardt, two-thirds of divorces end low-conflict marriages, while only one-third end high-conflict marriages. In those low-conflict marriages, divorce catches children by surprise.

"We know from research that if you adopt permissive attitudes toward divorce, your marriage gets unhappier," says Maggie Gallagher. "The analogy I would make is to parenthood. I don't know what it would be like to be a mother if I had in the back of my mind that I could become a not-mother if motherhood wasn't making me happy. It's difficult for you to get what you seek in marriage with that frame of mind."

Men in particular see marriage and children as a package deal, says Gallagher, and many who hold their marriages together during difficult times say they "stuck it out because they didn't want some other man living with their children. They turn their marriages around for the sake of the kids. Fatherhood is more unstable, culturally, than motherhood."

Gallagher's interest in loyalty and marriage grew out of her own personal experience. "I had a baby right out of college. The father decided he couldn't deal with the situation when my son was three, and I haven't heard from him since 1985. I'm one of four children, and my dad was a magnificent family man. And I learned from my experience as a single mother that, even with all his advantages, my son has had a certain set of struggles that I never had. The fact is that if your mother and father announce that they're no longer part of the same family and you now have two households, it's difficult. It has become more and more vivid to me that the thing we call fatherhood is very much related to lasting love between men and women in the ordinary, reliable context of marriage."

In most marriages good times follow bad. Marquardt notes that even when one spouse says he or she is unhappy at a given point in time, in interviews five years later with those who stay married, 80 percent of the formerly unhappy spouses report being happy. "We have this idea in our culture," says Marquardt, "that if a marriage is unhappy, it's going downhill fast and there's no hope left. But the majority of marriages go in cycles, like life does." In many cases, people can outlast their problems—and loyalty can help see them through. The bottom line for kids is this: four loyal hands are better than two.

✻   *Turn to other couples*. If your marriage is in a tough spot, consider seeking out couples who have saved their marriages. They may have been through wrenching upheavals—adultery, the death of a child, job loss, periods of escalating misunderstandings—and repaired their trust and closeness. Their stories can serve as inspiration, and they may have suggestions to offer.

✻   *As parents, spend regular time together with your children*. Create family wholeness through activities and shared time, a wholeness that can support the marriage.

✻   *Fix problems before they become overwhelming*. Many times marriages go through a dry spell—couples may be absorbed in responsibilities for children and career and feel they have become more like roommates than romantic partners. These are times when marriages are vulnerable to love affairs or increasing emotional distance. If this starts to happen, address it before a serious rift occurs.

LESSON THREE: LOYALTY CAN SAVE ANOTHER'S LIFE

July 25, 1995, was a day like any other for George Bennett, who ran a petroleum equipment business in the town of Slinger, Wisconsin, that he'd bought in 1978. George was inside a petroleum tank applying a special coating to its interior, and it looked like the day was going to be short and easy when he heard a popping noise and saw a sheet of flames racing across the top of the tank toward him. The paint started to ignite, and before he knew it he was fully engulfed in flames. "I thought of my children, my fiancée Vivian, and I knew that I was going to be found dead at the bottom of this tank. So I sat down to wait, and I don't want to say I was serene, but somehow I couldn't feel the pain. And though I was not extremely religious, I heard a voice, and I knew it was God, and it simply said, 'Stand up, George.' I knew when I heard that voice I was going to get out of that tank. People will say to me, 'George, you must have just imagined that was God's voice.' And I tell them, 'I had a whole lot of things on my mind, and I certainly didn't think I was going to hear a crystal-clear voice in my ears.' I must have passed out then. The guys apparently blew fire extinguishers in the tank, and the next thing I knew it was October 3.

"Before the accident, Vivian and I were planning our wedding for October 14. I had been in a coma all those months. I spent six months in the burn unit. I got pneumonia, and then a kidney infection. I was burned over nearly 70 percent of my body. I was on morphine and versed and floating in and out of dreams and consciousness. But when I got more stable and they began grafting skin, then I realized how bad things were. The first time I tried to stand—I couldn't bend my joints at all, my skin was full of scars and adhesions, and I was terribly weak. I stood for seventeen seconds, with my nurses supporting me. I slept the rest of the day. But they wouldn't quit, doggone 'em. Every day I had to stand. It hurt so badly I threw the nurses out of the room one day. I said, 'You're not touching me, I'm just not doing it.' And then my pastor came by, and I said, 'It hurts too much, I can't do it.' And he said, 'You have to, to get back to your family and your life.' So then I just made the commitment. I said to the nurses, 'I'm in your hands.' I knew I was going to live, so it was up to me to make the best of it. And I had so much support. My kids, Vivian, my brothers and sister. My daughter came to visit every day. If you're hurt physically or down and out and flat busted and not a nickel to your name, it doesn't matter. What matters is you have to ask for help and know how to appreciate it. You have to know how to say thank you. You have to commit to someone and something. The first time I walked between parallel bars, all the nurses clapped for me, and I said, 'Okay, if you're going to work that hard for me, I'll work that hard for you.' Sure, I cried a lot of times. But they became my friends, and they're still some of my best friends. You know, when you get burned, the injuries are everlasting."

There was a time, says George, when he wanted Vivian to leave him. "She's a beautiful lady. I didn't want her to waste herself on me. I didn't deserve her any longer because I was so screwed up. I hated myself. We went to my cabin one time, and I couldn't even tie my own shoe, and I was in a lot of pain, and I wanted to quit. I told her, 'I hate myself, I want you to go on with your life.' She didn't say much as I ranted, raved, swore, cursed, and cried. She just stayed there with me. Eventually I got tired and went to bed, and there she was, still with me. And I said to myself, 'I am damn fortunate.' Because of her loyalty, I began to realize I was going to make it, whatever it took, more operations, more struggling, Velcro shoes, splints to bend my hands, pressure garments. She went through it all with me. She'd cut my food for me until I could finally feed myself. My relationship with her keeps improving. It's just better and better. I am such a lucky guy, and I want to give her so much."

Vivian, in turn, never once considered leaving George. "I fell in love with him because of his sense of humor, his big blue eyes. He was very handsome and smart. We were living together by the time of his accident. I remember walking with great fear and trepidation toward his room. His head was the size of a beach ball. His whole body was swollen, and there were tubes of all kinds coming out of him. His nose was burned away, he didn't have nostrils, he just had two black holes. And I lost it, my knees buckled, and I kind of fell into a chair. And I lay down in an empty room next to his, and I just could not reconcile it. It didn't look like him. And during the whole period he was in a coma I was very lonely. I was working morning, noon, and night at my own job and then helping with George's business."

During that time, because he had so little skin to keep his body warm, George was given fifteen thousand calories a day through an IV line. "When he came out of the coma, he called me. It was 5:30 A.M., and he sounded like a little old lady because he had a tracheotomy, a little valve in his trachea to help him talk, but he said, 'Hey, darlin', when you come, can you bring my huntin' socks and my glasses.' And when I walked into his room, he was sitting up. It wasn't him. But it was him."

People sometimes asked Vivian if she wanted to leave George. "That shocked and angered me. I can't imagine what I would do without him. Even driving to the hospital, I'd think, 'Who could I ever be with? He's the one. He's it. He's my one and only.' Even up at the cabin in the middle of the woods, when he couldn't get his own shoe back on, when he told me to get the hell out, I knew he had to vent and he'd calm down. Finally he got quiet and I cooked dinner, and it was kind of like a dinner with a pouty child. And then we got into bed and that was that. There were hundreds of incidents like that. Sometimes I went into a kind of mother mode, trying to shield him. I didn't want him to feel hurt or ashamed. When we finally went back to church, people would stare and my heart would just break." Though he has scars all over, says Vivian, "I've gotten so used to it, it's as if he's always been this way. Now he just looks to me like the man I fell in love with, that's all I can say."

George's occupational therapist, Eileen Riordan, recalls the first time George was well enough to go home. It was Thanksgiving. "Viv came and got him, and they gave each other a hug, and that was a really wonderful moment. You could tell they were crazy about each other. And his daughter used to come and read aloud to him when he was unconscious. She'd go and visit every day and read out of a book. I have to say that faith, family, love, and the drive to live are all huge."

George says the most important lesson he's learned is how fortunate he is. "I appreciate life a lot more. I look forward to tomorrow. It sounds so trite, but I smell the roses. And I try to give in any way I can. I go talk to burn victims. I never charge anything, it's just all I can do to share my perspective with them. I almost don't think of the old George anymore. I look at a picture of myself before I was hurt, and I say, 'Yup, I used to look like that.' And I let it go."

Vivian and George's story sends chills up my spine, but their experience is backed up by research funded by IRUL at the University of California at San Francisco. The psychiatrist Robert Hierholzer, the psychologist Bita Ghafoori, and their colleagues found that veterans of war experienced significantly less post-traumatic stress disorder if they had a secure, loving relationship in their life—particularly with a spouse. The two-year study looked at 110 veterans with PTSD and found that feeling attached to others and loved had a significant impact in reducing PTSD. "To a certain extent," says Hierholzer, "this seems so obvious. But I think the research is exceedingly important, because for many veterans the war is not over when they come home, and this opens up new pathways of exploration for treating trauma."

What are the lessons you can take from the research on loyalty and trauma? Here are three:

❧ *Love heals over time.* Know that even in the worst circumstances your continuing love for a family member or friend may help convince them to fight for their life.

❧ *Loyalty is a buffer against stress.* For yourself and those you love, the security of steadfast caring is one of the great buffers against stress.

❧ *You can offer loyal love with confidence*. Over time love can and *will* dissolve the hardness of difficulty and despair—like a stream that carves away indomitable rock.

LESSON FOUR: LOYALTY IS NOT PERFECT

Ours is a mobile, ever-changing, and rapidly aging society: we live on average into our late seventies, and many of us move several times in our lives. Having this remarkable extension of life, along with families that may be scattered around the country and the world, brings difficult decisions.

Loyal love gets tough, for instance, when a spouse or aging parent becomes ill. What happens to the health benefits of marriage when a spouse becomes clinically depressed and stops working, bathing, or helping with the children? What happens when serious illness strikes a partner? "Take a man who loses his job," says Maggie Gallagher. "He's middle-aged, he's got children, he's depressed about it all. His wife is very sympathetic, and then after a time she begins to get upset. And the husband helps less around the house. There is research showing that unemployed husbands do less housework than full-time executives, and we think this is because they're not feeling manly, and so they don't want to do what they consider woman's work. A wife will only put up with this for a while. There is a significant amount of divorce triggered by male unemployment." The same can be true if debilitating illness strikes a spouse: "If you signed up for marriage hoping it would make you happy, taking care of a disabled spouse can seem profoundly unattractive," Gallagher points out. "There are people who bail. And the people who stay do not necessarily find it an uplifting experience. It's quite difficult. Usually people hunker down and do what they believe is the right thing, but I don't know of any research showing that their marriages become happier as a result."

One of the most loyal and inspiring men I know, retired Cleveland neurologist Joseph Foley, who is now ninety-three, suffered through the disability of two of his five children: "At the age of nine," says Joe, "my son, Joseph Michael Foley, was riding a bicycle at the wrong time, into the path of an oncoming car. He got his head caught under the wheels of an automobile and became mentally retarded, crippled, and epileptic for the rest of his life." His son's intractable seizures required institutional care. I met Joe

Junior once. He was in a wheelchair, and his expression was strained and agitated. His dad was able to take his hand and settle him down with a gentle tone of voice and smile. I remember Joe kneeling down as he spoke tenderly with his adult son, knowing that Joe Junior might not understand every word he was saying, but that his love would be understood. "My second child," says Joe, "was born with severe scoliosis and needed multiple surgeries. She's now sixty, a professor in Texas, and on oxygen all the time. But she is cheerful as can be about life. I can tell you, it's a helluva moment when your child turns sixty. It gives a man pause. I called her on her birthday, and I got her cell phone, so I crooned into it, 'You're sugar, you're spice, you're everything nice, and you're daddy's little girl. You really are.' " Joe Foley doesn't walk on water—no human does—but he has become gentler because of his suffering. He made house calls to people with dementia for instance, long after house calls were out of vogue.

Loyalty is often a delicate balancing act that evokes a whole range of emotions, from joy to despair. One particularly complex compromise involves our aging parents. Although many times we care for our parents out of pure love, sometimes it is loyalty alone that nudges us, and we may sometimes wonder why we are trying so hard to help and if there will be even a penny left of an inheritance after nursing home bills are paid. Are we really supposed to be our parents' keeper?

I've seen this difficult situation many times in my intensive work with Alzheimer's associations around the country. Reports from the National Alliance for Caregiving and the American Association of Retired Persons show that 70 percent of all in-home care for the aging is provided by adult children or spouses. Adult children tend to step in when a spouse cannot meet the challenge. Daughters are more likely than sons to provide this kind of primary care. Even daughters-in-law are more likely than sons to help. Sons tend to handle financial affairs, logistics, and bills. This means that caretaking roles are still hugely influenced by gender. Interestingly, race and culture matter too. African American and Asian American families view care for frail parents as important and often keep that care within the family.

Those who meet the challenges of loyal love when family members become ill and disabled are the unsung heroes of everyday life. Consider these thoughts from a Chinese American friend of mine who willingly cares for his aging parents—who are not yet disabled—and wonders if his own children will do the same for him someday: "The quiet sounds of running water and conversation drift in from the kitchen, punctuated by the occasional clacking of dinner plates. I cannot make out the words, but no doubt my mom is holding forth on the difficulty of life while my wife nods and listens. My children and father are elsewhere in this house, this house that my parents bought just months ago. For years we had asked them to move closer to us—so that we would not have to give up our careers and sever the children from their schools and friends. But my parents had lived in the same area for the entirety of their life together. Their roots went deep. There is no easy calculus for such sacrifice. But they bought a house only a few miles away, and now, with teenagers at home and aging parents nearby, we have entered what some call the 'sandwich' generation. I feel out of sync. I had not expected the years to slip away like this. When did my parents become old? When did I stop being young? Just as we did when I was young, we sit once a week, three generations around a table, playing mah-jongg, a game that seems as ancient as the Chinese culture itself. I sit across from my father, who is now well into his eighties, as animated and happy as I ever see him. Dad loves this game. But he almost died a few years back, when his heart raced out of control and he collapsed in a bowling alley. A few short decades from now, what will happen to me, and how will I respond? I realize that in some way, as I perform the role of the dutiful son, I perform it for my own children: see, kids, this is what is right, this is how to act when your parents get old. But I don't want my children to act out of compulsion. I want them to visit me, care for me, and talk to me because they want to. I love my parents. I do not think of them as a burden. But my affections are not unalloyed. Loyalty to my parents wrestles with loyalty to myself. As a family, I know we have not yet faced our deepest challenges. As I lie awake in bed at night pondering, while my wife sleeps beside me, I think to myself, 'Take good care of that mah-jongg table, just in case.' "

Orien Reid, who was chair of the Alzheimer's Association national board when we first became friends, lost her mother to Alzheimer's disease. She beautifully expresses the bond of loyalty when it shines as love: "Some call it a living funeral—a stunning irrevocable event—when the person you love," she says, "the keeper of your childhood stories, of precious memories that were only shared between the two of you, whether husband and wife, brother and sister, aunt and uncle, or parent and child, are lost in the tangles of Alzheimer's disease." Four of Reid's family members have been struck by Alzheimer's: her grandmother, mother, an uncle, and an aunt. "The one quality that resonates through each of us who are caregivers," she says, "is a strong sense of commitment. The physical and emotional cost of the earnest, unconditional love that caregivers offer, day after day, can't be measured in dollars. Listen to these words," says Reid, "that one caregiver, Lani Kaaihue, wrote for her dying husband:

> "He laughs and I feel joy.
>   He speaks and the sound of his voice
>   Frees something inside me
>   That soars up to the heavens
>   Proclaiming a bond
>   That can never be broken."

We all live our lives as best we can. We need to strike a balance of loyalties that is right for each of us.

❧ *Find compromises that benefit everybody.* When one family member is failing, for whatever reason, compromises must be openly and thoughtfully discussed among all family members. In the case of aging parents, for instance, they may move closer to one of their children. I know of one man who, wealthier than either of his two siblings, built a house for his mother on his property, while she took up babysitting duties for his newborn. Chester and Millie Dilday's children built apartments for their parents so that the couple could live part-time with each of their children's families.

❧ *Understand that loyalty has limits.* If a child or parent is completely unable to care for themselves, it is not disloyal to put them into institutional care. This decision may actually protect their well-being and lengthen their lives.

❧ *Stay involved.* Even when a parent is in a long-term care facility, family caregivers can be deeply involved in their parent's life and in collaborating with health care professionals throughout the final years.

It is important for the aging not to simply become the passive recipients of others' care. I encourage even impaired older folks to try to give to others and to volunteer—for as research mentioned elsewhere in this book shows, volunteering can improve their well-being and state of mind.

LESSON FIVE: FIND A FRIEND, BE A FRIEND

Another kind of loyalty is that of long-term friendship, which turns out to be beneficial to health, protecting against depression and boosting self-esteem. In a ten-year study of people age seventy and older, researchers at the Centre for Aging Studies at Flinders University in Adelaide, Australia, found that a network of good friends is more likely than close family relationships to increase longevity in older folks—by an astounding 22 percent. The study looked at nearly 1,500 older individuals and followed them from 1992 to 2002, assessing their contact with children, relatives, friends, and other confidantes. Researchers found that the positive impact of friendship on lifespan continued even for individuals who experienced profound losses like the death of a spouse or other close family members. "The central message," said one of the researchers, Lynn Giles, "is that maintaining a sense of social embeddedness through friends and family appears important, and it seems that nonkin relationships are particularly important."

One of the most respected researchers on friendship and health is the sociologist Rebecca Adams of the University of North Carolina. Editor of the journal *Personal Relationships*, the official journal of the International Association for Relationship Research, Adams became interested in studying friendship in part because she moved a lot as a child. "By the time I got to college," she says, "I'd been to thirteen different schools, and my hunch was that I'd learned to be gregarious and good at making new friends, but perhaps not as good at maintaining them. I was also interested in the topic because I'd noticed that my grandparents were living far apart from the rest of the family, but doing quite well with the support of their friends. It made me realize how important friends could be to older adults."

Adams and her colleagues found a strong link between friendship and psychological well-being in seventy men and women between the ages of fifty-five and eighty-four in North Carolina. "The study asked in great detail about friendship dyads and networks, and we were particularly interested in what people feel, think, and do in their relationships, as well as whether there are power and status discrepancies between friends and how close they feel. I think of it as a small but deep study. We were able to paint a rich notion of friendship. One counterintuitive thing we found is that people perceived only two-thirds of their relationships as egalitarian in terms of decisionmaking or status. That was surprising, as we tend to think of friendship as egalitarian— it's almost the assumed definition. Even so, we found that the invisible hand of society does guide us to choose people who are similar in terms of characteristics and values. That's a very robust finding. Every study on friendship has found that. Although it's possible the Internet could break down those barriers, and there hasn't yet been enough research on that."

Like other researchers, Adams found that there is a strong relationship between the quality of friendships and one's mental well-being. "In fact," says Adams, "it's been shown over and over again that friendship is more important to psychological well-being than family relations are. We all think our older relatives are just waiting for us to show up and visit them. I'm sure they enjoy our visits, but their relationships with their friends are more important." Why is this? "Friendships are voluntary. So we'll choose friendships that support our psychological well-being. Although our families are important, and we're more likely to get help from our relatives during a chronic illness, our friends are more likely to be important for our psychological well-being." If we're going through a divorce or the death of a spouse, friends can help us. We're likely to choose those who have had similar experiences. In one of Adams's studies on Chicago women over time, she found that these women often went through a change when their husbands passed away or they themselves stopped working. "A change in status in later life sometimes liberates people to reshape their friendship networks," says Adams.

Are friendships more important to people now than they used to be? "We don't really know," says Adams, "because we haven't studied it, but the likelihood is that the more things change, the more they stay the same." One study of neighborhoods in Indiana found that back in the 1930s neighborhood networks were much the same as they are today. "It's good that friendship is finally getting attention by scholarly researchers," says Adams. "Friendships turn out to be a lot more important than we thought."

"Friendship," writes National Book Award nominee Beth Kephart in her book *Into the Tangle of Friendship*, "isn't all big gestures, ecstatic moments. It is also the littlest things, the humanity that happens between people when you find yourself way out of context and someone reaches out and pulls you in. . . . I am who I am because my friendships keep on growing. . . . Because all friendships are finally mirrors. One thing I think it is really important for us to realize, especially as we reach middle age, is that as you get older, you cannot make old friends. You carry them with you. And it's your friends and family who've known you over time, who know you best. So over time, even if someone's qualities begin to grate on you, if you have that long history, you're not going to give up easily. The thing that breaks a friendship is betrayal. And the thing that saves a friendship is forgiveness. And the fact is, if you commit to being a friend, you have to find the resources and time to be there for them. You can't apportion your care. Therefore, you can't have three thousand friends. You can't swim in a sea of acquaintances if you're serious about being there for people. All the philosophers who write about friendship talk about loyalty—and it's hard, to be 100 percent loyal."

Friendship is a domain where we exercise an extraordinary amount of choice, and as Kephart says, loyalty is what distinguishes casual friendships from deep ones. Casual friendships, like those with neighbors or colleagues at work, are the lubrication of everyday life, but they last only as long as the demands made on them. Deep friendship is woven of entirely different cloth. "Friendship," says Kephart, "is a benefaction and a weight. It's an instruction and a tool, a risk, a therapeutic, a happenstance, a philosophy. In our friends we see the best and the worst of ourselves. We refine our character, where we'll go and won't go, through conversation with people we trust. It's a great blessing and a great burden."

Here are some insights on friendship drawn from the research:

Friendship keeps us whole over time. Cultivate friendships that last over time; they will sustain you through tough circumstances and even protect your well-being if you lose a family member.

Friends feel joy. A good friend wants the best for you. He or she feels genuine joy when something great happens in your life, and you feel the same reciprocal joy for them.

Repair friendships when possible. Not all friendships can or should last forever, but recognize the value of true friendship, and try to repair rifts, even if it requires some time.

Rekindle old friendships. We may lose track of friends over time, especially if they move away, and then reconnect later in life. With the connections provided by the Internet, it is easier to track down lost friendships.

Reshape your friendship networks. If your circumstances, status, or values in life change, reach out and find new friends. Friends provide a supportive mirror for our values and paths in life.

Human history has been shaped and changed by remarkable friendships—from the explorers Lewis and Clark to the conqueror Alexander the Great and his lifelong friend Hephaestion. (It's said that Alexander literally dipped into insanity when his friend died.) Without Lincoln, there was no Grant, and without Roosevelt no Churchill. Synergy between friends is transformative.

A wonderful description of a life-altering friendship comes from the psychologist Daniel Kahneman, who shared a Nobel Prize with his colleague Amos Tversky for changing the way that psychologists and economists around the world view human decisionmaking. Kahneman was born in Tel Aviv in 1934, and he met Tversky while teaching a graduate seminar in 1968. As Kahneman writes, "Amos was often described by people who knew him as the smartest person they knew. He was also very funny, with an endless supply of jokes appropriate to every nuance of a situation. In his presence, I became funny as well, and the result was that we could spend hours of solid work in continuous mirth. . . . I have probably shared more than half of the laughs of my life with Amos. . . . At the beginning of our collaboration, we quickly established a rhythm that we maintained during all our years together. Amos was a night person, and I was a morning person. This made it natural for us to meet for lunch and a long afternoon together, and still have time to do our separate things. We spent hours each day just talking. When Amos's first son, Oren, then fifteen months old, was told that his father was at work, he volunteered the comment, 'Aba talk Danny.' We were not only working, of course—we talked of everything under the sun and got to know each other's mind almost as well as our own. We could (and often did) finish each other's sentences and complete the joke that the other had wanted to tell, but somehow we also kept surprising each other. . . . Amos and I shared the wonder of together owning a goose that could lay golden eggs—a joint mind that was better than our separate minds."

This kind of friendship is on a higher plane, one that the Greeks called *philia—friendship love*. Aristotle devoted two of the ten books of his *Nicomachean Ethics* to friendship: he and the Greeks in general elevated the dyad of friendship to the pinnacle of moral life.

We're lucky to have a few such friends in a lifetime—they are, in a sense, "loveships," because they are so deep. Their cornerstones are benevolence, shared interests, and loyalty. At the same time, such a friend can offer loyal dissent when necessary, sometimes telling us tough truths when we might be headed in the wrong direction. As Ralph Waldo Emerson wrote, "Better be a nettle in the side of your friend, than his echo." And so:

❧ *Cherish your "loveships."* These friendships are rare and precious; they sustain themselves because of deeply shared values and interests. They may become lifetime partnerships. If you have such a friendship, treat it with care, and nourish it often.

❧ *Be willing to disagree on occasion.* Friendship does not preclude dissent. Sometimes the kindest friend is one who offers a viewpoint that may be surprising or even seem a bit contrary.

LESSON SIX: LEARN FROM WOMEN

Women have a talent for making friends—for doing what the psychologist Laura Cousino Klein, now at Pennsylvania State University, calls "tend and befriend." A study that Klein co-authored found that women respond to stress with an outpouring of brain chemicals that include not only the fight-or-flight hormones but also oxytocin, the attachment hormone. As suggested earlier, women may be hardwired to respond to hard times by tending their children and bonding with other women. This response is calming in women, says Klein, who notes that "there was this joke that when women who worked in the lab were stressed, they came in, cleaned the lab, had coffee, and bonded, while men holed up somewhere on their own."

Pregnant women who bring a friend to the delivery room have fewer complications and an easier delivery, according to a 1980 study in the *New England Journal of Medicine* carried out by a senior colleague of mine at Case Western Reserve University, the pediatrician John Kennell. And the famed Nurses' Health Study from Harvard Medical School, has shown that the more friends a woman has, the less likely she is to develop physical impairments as she ages. In fact, when the researchers in this study looked at women's functioning after the death of their spouse, they found that those who had even one close friend and confidante were less likely to suffer any new physical impairment or ongoing loss of vitality.

Rebecca Adams has also found a gender divide in friendship styles. "Men define their friendships in terms of shared activities, and women define them in terms of conversation. For men, a friend is their fishing, golfing, or bowling buddy. For women, a friend is someone they can confide in." But it is the intimacy, the "tending" care, that is most nourishing in a friendship.

❧ *Soothe stress by tending to a friend.* Especially if you're a woman, tending to others will calm you and help you feel connected to the world.

❧ *Cultivate a confidante.* Find at least one friend you can be truly open with, sharing your difficulties. For men, this can be difficult. Sometimes men's support groups can help them open up and share.

LESSON SEVEN: SIBLINGS AND PETS ARE FRIENDS

Loyal love among siblings is an intriguing topic. Sibling relationships are a complex weaving of the bond of family with that of friendship. Once we grow up, and especially if we move away for college and career, our siblings become friends of a deeper order—*if we are lucky*. At other times sibling relationships are rent by rivalries and resentments forged in the kiln of family. It's interesting to speculate about whether the idea of "kin altruism" stretches to our siblings—for even though they share our genes, there are as many brothers and sisters who don't get along as there are those who do. Blood loyalty seems to be a choice. So in the end, I look at the sibling relationship as more elective than not—as a kind of friendship that, when it succeeds, is especially powerful because it is bound by such a long common history.

And before we leave this section, let's not forget that animals can provide extraordinary friendship. It's an old and powerful cliché that dogs are immensely loyal, perhaps because they are descended from wolves, which are pack animals. There's a famous Japanese story of a dog, Chuken "Loyal" Hachiko, a white Akita who met his master at a train station outside Tokyo every evening. In 1925 Hachiko's owner died of a heart attack, but Hachiko went to the train station every evening for the next nine years, and himself died there. By then, he was the most renowned dog in Japan, and a statue was made of him; it was melted down during World War II when metal supplies were low, and in 1947 rebuilt in bronze. It remains at the Tokyo train station to this day. But the Japanese are not alone in their love of dogs: 40 million American households have dogs (and 34 million have cats). Oddly enough, the everlasting loyalty of a pet provides a good model for deep friendship.

FINALLY, MAKE HUMANITY YOUR FRIEND

We've evolved to care for each other over time. The evolutionary biologist David Sloan Wilson, author of *Darwin's Cathedral*, has developed a novel theory of altruism that features such valuable traits as loyalty. David has made a strong case for group selection of altruism—that is, if we help others in our group, we will fare better. This idea goes all the way back to Darwin himself, who thought that tribes whose members were prepared to help one another would be more cohesive and successful. This idea became known as group selection. When David first sculpted this group selection theory in graduate school, he says, "I can't even express how excited I was. Just imagine, there I was, just a graduate student, but I was so excited, I called up the great naturalist E. O. Wilson, and I said, 'I must come to you and tell you about my theory of group selection! I want you to publish it in the *Proceed-*

ings of the National Academy of Sciences.' And he said, 'Well, okay.' And I drove there, and that's basically how I published my first paper."

Though an individual might benefit from selfish behavior, individuals in groups benefit from helping each other. Wilson sees social groups as organisms trying their best to survive. It's a fascinating viewpoint. And it would go a long way toward explaining traits like loyalty, and why they are so important. It makes complete sense, says Wilson, that traits like altruism and loyalty would evolve *because* they're good for us.

Yet we all know that group loyalty has a dark side. Loyal love can lead to an exclusivity that wraps the chosen few in the warm buffer of our affections, but is indifferent or even hostile to those outside that haloed circle. This is referred to as in-group loyalty and out-group hostility. According to the psychologist Marilynn Brewer of Ohio State University, who studied thirty different ethnic groups in East Africa, out-group hostility may arise when resources are scarce. As Brewer notes, when in-groups regard other groups with contempt, we end up with conflict and even "ethnic cleansing."

We need to be loyal to our shared humanity. As proof of our innate ability to do so one of IRUL's funded researchers, the psychologist Arthur Aron of Stony Brook University in New York, has demonstrated that we can expand our circle of loyalty to those outside our social group. As Aron said to me, "Positive feelings toward other groups does not *need* to diminish loyalty for one's own. In fact, sometimes working together with one's own group to help another group increases both in-group *and* out-group loyalty."

Art has found in his new research that it is possible to create positive feelings toward an out-group while maintaining loyalty to an in-group. "We've experimentally created friendshiplike connections with a member of another group, and in our studies we make people aware that one is a member of one group, and the other of another group. Thanks to a grant from IRUL in January 2003, we studied a practical intervention to promote caring and generosity between members of different racial and ethnic groups. In our first laboratory experiment, we took pairs of strangers from different racial or other groups. In a forty-five-minute task, they shared personal concerns, discovered the things they had in common, and did a series of structured tasks that gradually escalated in their personal nature.

We already know from previous studies that these kinds of activities bring strangers close, feeling very intimate. This effect does diminish over time, but is still present even months later." Feeling close to one person from an out-group tended to increase a person's overall sympathy and admiration for that person's group as a whole. "Thus," says Art, "a connection with one single individual can facilitate sympathy beyond that individual to their entire group."

Fewer and fewer people on this earth are out of sight and out of mind. Some scholars and thinkers would even say that hatred has outlived its usefulness. The neuroscientist Antonio Damasio, author of *Looking for Spinoza: Joy, Sorrow, and the Feeling Brain*, points out that hatred had far greater evolutionary value when we were cloistered into small tribes. And another major thinker, Robert Wright, author of the provocative book *Non-Zero*, suggests that as our economies and technologies progress toward a common humanity, we'll simply be unable to annihilate other cultures—and won't even wish to, because our exchanges with them will be so important. A self-described materialist, Wright sees a grand arc of history toward greater and greater cooperation. Our global community, he predicts, will be shaped by win-win scenarios. In my own field of bioethics and unselfish love, I can say that there is definitely a drive toward integration across all disciplines. So, in a world united by Black-berries and blogs, with camera cell phones that can beam photos to our friends and family anywhere instantaneously, we have an opportunity to broaden our loyalties. Here's how:

❧   *See yourself as part of a whole.* The first astronauts who catapulted into space and looked back at our blue and green earth were deeply moved by its small, perfect wholeness—our home. Pause now to realize how much we need each other, every human. Expand your feeling of loyalty to the entire human race, to every fragile and marvelous person who populates this planet, which is one among billions of planets orbiting billions and billions of stars in the universe.

❧   *Reach out to someone different.* Find an individual who comes from a very different background and engage that person in conversation, or perhaps a shared activity. You most likely will find yourself naturally extending the great power and beneficence of loyalty in an ever-widening circle, like ripples of water on a calm lake on a spring day.

⚜   *We do better together.* Group selection gives us a very strong explanation for the cooperation, warmth, and loyalty that has evolved in our species.

Your Loyalty Score

It's time to answer the questions on the loyalty section of your Love and Longevity Scale. We have divided responses into percentiles, or fifths. These are general guidelines; you may score right near the cutoff between percentiles, so please keep this in mind and use the scale as a friendly tool. Remember:

There are two steps to determining your score. First, determine which items need to be "reverse-scored" (denoted with the ® symbol). For reverse-scored items, see the chart below for how to score.

If you score a . . .	. . . assign yourself a score for that item of:
1	6
2	5
3	4
4	3
5	2
6	1

The second step is to add the scores for individual items *after* the reverse-scored items have been reverse-scored. Take the quiz now, and take it again if you wish after you've finished this book and begun practicing the art of loyalty in your daily life.

Using the scale provided, please circle the one number that best reflects your opinion about whether or not each statement below describes you or experiences that you have had. There are no correct answers, so please respond as honestly as possible to each one.

1. I make sure that what's important to my family is important to me too.
    **1=strongly disagree   2=disagree   3=slightly disagree   4=slightly agree
    5=agree   6=strongly agree**

2. Members of my family know that they can always depend on me, rain or shine.
    **1=strongly disagree   2=disagree   3=slightly disagree   4=slightly agree
    5=agree   6=strongly agree**

3. My family can always count on me as if I were a "teammate."
    **1=strongly disagree   2=disagree   3=slightly disagree   4=slightly agree
    5=agree   6=strongly agree**

4. I think it's no big deal to move away from family for greener pastures.[®]
    **1=strongly disagree   2=disagree   3=slightly disagree   4=slightly agree
    5=agree   6=strongly agree**

5. I can think of lots of legitimate reasons for skipping chores or my family responsibilities.[®]
    **1=strongly disagree   2=disagree   3=slightly disagree   4=slightly agree
    5=agree   6=strongly agree**

6. Keeping my friends' welfare in mind is important to me.
    **1=strongly disagree   2=disagree   3=slightly disagree   4=slightly agree
    5=agree   6=strongly agree**

7. Friends know that they can always depend on me, rain or shine.
    1=strongly disagree 2=disagree 3=slightly disagree 4=slightly agree
    5=agree 6=strongly agree

8. When friends have problems, I don't really want to hear about it.[®]
    1=strongly disagree 2=disagree 3=slightly disagree 4=slightly agree
    5=agree 6=strongly agree

9. If I stop going to a club, a gym, or some other activity, I don't
    worry about whether I'll still have time for the friends I met
    there.[®]
    1=strongly disagree 2=disagree 3=slightly disagree 4=slightly agree
    5=agree 6=strongly agree

10. I make myself available to help my friends mostly when it suits
    me.[®]
    1=strongly disagree 2=disagree 3=slightly disagree 4=slightly agree
    5=agree 6=strongly agree

11. I am more concerned about how I could help a coworker or
    neighbor than about how much effort it could cost me.
    1=strongly disagree 2=disagree 3=slightly disagree 4=slightly agree
    5=agree 6=strongly agree

12. Neighbors or coworkers can depend on me, rain or shine.
    1=strongly disagree 2=disagree 3=slightly disagree 4=slightly agree
    5=agree 6=strongly agree

13. People in my neighborhood or at work can always count on me
    like a "teammate."
    1=strongly disagree 2=disagree 3=slightly disagree 4=slightly agree
    5=agree 6=strongly agree

14. I mostly help coworkers or neighbors when it benefits me too.[®]
    1=strongly disagree 2=disagree 3=slightly disagree 4=slightly agree
    5=agree 6=strongly agree

15. I make myself available to help my neighbors or coworkers mostly when it serves me.[®]
    1=strongly disagree   2=disagree   3=slightly disagree   4=slightly agree 5=agree   6=strongly agree

16. I try to make decisions about what to buy and how to spend my time according to what is good for humanity.
    1=strongly disagree   2=disagree   3=slightly disagree   4=slightly agree 5=agree   6=strongly agree

17. I think of the human race as a team of which we are all members.
    1=strongly disagree   2=disagree   3=slightly disagree   4=slightly agree 5=agree   6=strongly agree

18. I am more concerned about how I could benefit society than about how much effort the activity could cost me.
    1=strongly disagree   2=disagree   3=slightly disagree   4=slightly agree 5=agree   6=strongly agree

19. I would not feel bad if I'm too busy to volunteer my time to organizations or activities that are good for society.[®]
    1=strongly disagree   2=disagree   3=slightly disagree   4=slightly agree 5=agree   6=strongly agree

20. I just don't feel much loyalty to people, especially ones I don't know.[®]
    1=strongly disagree   2=disagree   3=slightly disagree   4=slightly agree 5=agree   6=strongly agree

YOUR LOYALTY SCORE

High Giver (80th percentile)	94 or higher
Giver (60th percentile)	87–93
Moderate Giver (40th percentile)	79–92
Low Giver (20th percentile)	71–78

Eleven

The Way of Listening:
Offer Deep Presence

In 1979, listening saved Daniel Gottlieb's life. That was the year this family therapist's cervical spine was severed in a near-fatal automobile accident, leaving him quadriplegic, paralyzed from the chest down. "I was surrounded with love," he says. "I had two kids, a career, a job I could go back to, yet I was suicidal. I suffered an exquisite alienation. I felt that I was different than the rest of my species. One night I was lying in intensive care staring at the ceiling, wishing I could go to sleep and never wake up, when a nurse approached me. She asked if I was a psychologist. I nodded yes. She then asked me, 'Does everybody feel suicidal at some point in their lives?' She didn't know that, at that very moment, I was suicidal. I told her it was not unusual and asked if she wanted to talk about it."

The nurse pulled a chair over to Gottlieb's bed and spoke for a few hours about her life and struggles. "After she left," says Gottlieb, "I realized, 'I can do this. I can live as a quadriplegic.' That nurse saved my life. The knowledge that I could still help another person saved my life. And I don't think that's unique to Dan Gottlieb." After a year of rehabilitation, Gottlieb began to see a few patients at home on a volunteer basis, and several years later, as his health stabilized, he resumed his career. Since 1985, Gottlieb has been hosting *Voices in the Family*, an award-winning mental health call-in radio show, and writing a regular column for the *Philadelphia Inquirer*.

As a quadriplegic, says Gottlieb, his world became much quieter. He was a man without the use of his legs, and people treated him differently "My practice changed dramatically. There was a new silence inside me, and in the silence I was able to hear people's hearts. We can only hear with our heart when the noises of the ego are quiet. That's when we're open. And when we're open, we attain the kind of security everybody longs for—the security that people build fences to find, buy guns to find, marry each other to find. It can be found when we listen with our hearts. I listen to people's words, but I hear their vulnerability, fear, trepidation, and longing."

Why is listening so powerful? "We need someone to witness our lives, because being witnessed diminishes the solitude we all live with," says Gottlieb. "As the Bruce Springsteen song says, 'Everybody has a hungry heart.' Alienation and prejudice are the greatest sources of suffering in our world. The first step toward healing this pain is eye contact. The second is compassion. These are both part of listening with our hearts. A woman came to me years ago and said, 'I feel like my soul is a prism, but everyone I know sees only one color.' The definition of a good therapist, parent, lover, or friend is to see the prism of someone else's soul. All the colors. Bearing witness like that can help make someone whole. The most generous question you can ever ask someone is simply, 'What is it like to live inside your skin?' Ask that question, and you've given another person a gift. Then sit down and listen."

In a moving newspaper column of December 2004, Gottlieb wrote a letter to his four-year-old grandson, who had asked why his legs didn't work. Imagining his grandson listening quietly, Gottlieb describes what it is like to live inside *his* skin: "Twenty-five years ago today, I kissed my wife and my two daughters (your mother) goodbye and walked across a newly frozen lawn to my car to go to work. Those were the last steps I ever took. Two hours after that walk across the lawn, the wheel of a tractor-trailer hit my car. In that moment I became a quadriplegic. . . . When I had my accident, my greatest pain was that I couldn't figure out who I was or where I belonged. I was now different from my friends, family and colleagues. And when I heard a doctor refer to me as a 'quad,' I realized I now belonged to a group I didn't want to be in. Sam, this sense of not belonging caused me terrible pain. . . . Since that day, I learned that almost everyone could point to a single event that permanently changed his or her life. It could be a divorce, a diagnosis, or the sudden death of a loved one, but at those moments, lives are forever changed. . . . And inevitably when that happens, we all want the same thing; we want what we had yesterday."

But, says Gottlieb, what he learned was precious: "I grew to understand that the help I gave my patients had nothing to do with my ability to walk; it was about my heart and mind. And in that work, I found my connection to the larger world."

Just as important as bearing witness to others, says Gottlieb, is bearing witness to yourself. Each morning Gottlieb practices mindfulness meditation. "I just sit and listen to my breath and myself, and watch when my own thoughts get intrusive. Be compassionate with yourself. Tolerate your emotions. Be present to yourself above all."

Genuine Presence Is Deep Listening

To listen to another is to honor their deepest being. In this chapter, you will learn how simply being present, with loving attention, is one of the most life-altering forms of love, and you'll learn why it's good for you as well as others. The philosopher Gabriel Marcel called this kind of listening "real presence." The psychoanalyst Theodor Reik wrote of "listening with the third ear," the title of one of his most famous books. Listen with your third ear, said Reik, and you can catch what people do not say, but what they truly feel and think. When we truly absorb another's story, we are saying, "You count. Your life and feelings and thoughts matter to me. And I want to know who you really are." We all crave just this—this opening out from our solitude.

By listening, we participate in the full spectrum of another's life experience. We give the gift of radical receptivity. Suddenly we are transported into what Martin Buber called the "I-thou" relationship—in which it is the "between" that matters. Listening is marked by a profound and quiet atten-tiveness that is the epitome of love. The mere act of listening, even though it seems to contain no action, often liberates others to move on with their lives.

When we are listening, our silence is a more potent expression of love than our speech. Think of it this way: memorable music always has rests, caesuras, moments of nonsound, and these empty, silent spaces help render the music beautiful. The same is true of listening. It renders love beautiful.

At Case Western School of Medicine, we often take medical students to the hospital, where we may all crowd into a single patient's room to in-terview them. One day we were interviewing the mother of a child with mild Down's syndrome. The boy also had a sinus infection at the time and was very unsettled. Chris, the student who'd been assigned to conduct the patient interview, was extremely compassionate. He asked thoughtful ques-tions of the mother, but her child was so unruly that after about fifteen minutes Chris simply stopped, turned to the boy, and said, "Why don't you walk around the table and say whatever you want to each of us?" The boy surprised us all by responding, "You need to ask me questions, not just my mom!" Then he went around the conference table, from chair to chair, and said to each person, "You need to listen to me too." So the whole group chimed in and began to interview this little boy, who did amazingly well as he explained how much he struggled with infections and how much he loved his family. The boy was almost serene by this point. One student was so impressed that she went into special-care pediatrics just to work with such children.

Here are a few gifts of listening, according to new studies:

Listening activates the part of our brains hardwired for empathy. New re-search shows that through specialized neurons, we are able by watching and listening to experience a bit of what others experience. Because we're a so-cial species, listening is crucial to our survival. It's the glue of connection.

When we listen to others in pain, their stress response quiets down and their body has a better chance to heal. In fact, according to Greg Fricchione, assis-tant chief of psychiatry at Massachusetts General Hospital, empathy is like a powerful drug in its ability to change a person's neurochemical ecology.

When we listen and are listened to, we begin to feel secure in our relationship with another, and confident that that person will provide loving care in times of need. Research shows that the person who is listened to is more likely to offer support to someone else in need.

Love, in the form of listening, is vitalizing for the spirit. In one remarkable study by Carolyn Schwartz, five sufferers of multiple sclerosis who offered support by listening to other patients over a period of two years experienced a dramatic change in how they viewed themselves and life. Depression was lifted, and self-confidence and self-esteem improved markedly among these givers.

Listening works because we're hardwired to include others with whom we bond in our sense of self—even if they are different from us. Once you form an intimate bond, the other becomes part of your definition of yourself, and then you can't help but extend that person care and compassion. In a few different and equally remarkable studies for IRUL, Arthur Aron of Stony Brook University in New York found that facilitating a bond by listening to others can reduce prejudice within less than an hour's time—and that this effect lasts for months.

The future of our world may literally depend on listening, and it starts at home. Attentive presence plays a huge role in a young child's life. Scientific research has shown again and again that a playing baby looks back at the mother to be sure she is still present. That kind of presence on the part of a parent is the key to secure attachment—and a healthy child who becomes a healthy, giving adult.

The Simple Beauty of Listening

Last week a student named Janet came into my office in tears because she had been refused a scholarship for graduate study at another university. For about half an hour, I listened quietly as she cried and gave voice to her concerns. When she had finished, I reflected back those concerns to be sure I was perceiving them accurately and then suggested that she call the admissions officer at the university, express her needs as clearly as she had with me, and ask whether they could possibly reconsider the scholarship. She did this, and the university gave her a teaching assistantship. Most of what I offered Janet was the gift of listening, along with one small suggestion.

Our urgent need for a patient listener is beautifully evoked in Anton Chekhov's *Misery*, written in 1886. Iona Potapov, an ordinary coachman, has suffered the death of his son. As he drives his horse-drawn carriage through the snowy streets, he tries to share his grief with anyone who will listen, but nobody has time. Finally, at the end of a long day, he sits in the stable and pours out his grief to his mare, who listens and breaths on Iona's hands. At last he's freed from the loneliness of his despair.

A good listener is so vital that without one we feel an existential aloneness, like the psalmist in the Bible who cries out, "No man cared for my soul." This has led some scholars to call the God of the Psalms a God of listening. Our need for a listener is an inherent aspect of all prayer. God, in whatever form we see him/her/it, is the ultimate fellow traveler offering deep, listening companionship on life's journey.

Opportunities to listen are woven into our days minute by minute and hour by hour—all we really need to do is be quiet and offer an ear. A student stops me in the hallway to discuss an upcoming exam, my neighbor motions me over to tell me about the raccoon that overturned his garbage can, a colleague chats with me in the elevator, my wife spills out a story about a flare-up among the children at the preschool. When we listen to such small stories, we are actually affirming the other's essential worth. Even the most casual greeting in the office or on the elevator—"Good morning, how are you?" then the pause to hear a response such as, "Fine, thanks, and you?"—is meaningful. Without these simple interactions, the lubrication that allows us all to mesh and get along would disappear. We would all eventually begin to worry about whether we are accepted, welcomed, and appreciated by others.

Sometimes we listen by attending to another's body language, tone, and facial expression. This is especially true with the very young and the elderly. Listening at the bedside of the dying was a special skill of Dame Cicely Saunders, who founded the world-renowned St. Christopher's Hospice in 1967 as the first research and teaching hospice and served as an international adviser to the Institute. Until her death in 2005, Dame Cicely would spend hours a day simply listening to the dying with empathic presence. She said her chief role in life remained the same through the decades: providing an attentive presence that allowed those on their journey out of life to express their fears and hopes. In medieval Europe, a hospice was a covered area attached to a monastery where travelers could sleep the night. Cicely Saunders saw dying similarly and appropriated the word *hospice* to depict the hospitality we give to those on that final journey. Listening is indeed a kind of profound hospitality—a form of hospice. You may recall the story about Helen Keller, as a blind and deaf child, frantically pulling the buttons off her grandmother's dress, and only Helen's mother was able to enter into Helen's world deeply enough to understand that she wanted her rag doll to have eyes. After two buttons were sewn onto the doll's face, Helen became peaceful and calm. Helen's mother listened to her as deeply as any priest listens to a confession, any psychologist listens to a client's story, any lover listens to the peaceful breathing of the sleeping beloved.

My personal favorite family story of listening goes back to the 1970s. At the time, my older brother was openly gay and a contributing editor for *New York* magazine. My sister had married a man about my father's age, and as for me, well, I was thrilled by almost any new philosophy or worldview that I ran across and tended to do a fair amount of talking about it to my dad. One day he asked me what I would suggest he do to help him deal more effectively with his children. I suggested he make an appointment with Albert Ellis, whose rational emotive therapy was in its heyday. Dad actually went into New York City to have a session with Dr. Ellis, and the next time I was home I discovered him doing his morning jumping jacks in the living room while repeating, with my brother's friends in mind, "they're all my buddies." He said that ten times. More jumping jacks and then, with his son-in-law in mind, "He's my boy." A little more breathlessly, but ten times. More jumping jacks and then, almost entirely out of breath, with Stevie in mind, "Just listen." Dad said he was following the good doctor's recommendation. He repeated the words, "Just listen," ten times, and then finally his morning exercises had concluded. I was touched, but I had a good laugh too. Albert Ellis has always been known for his irreverence.

Lessons from the Frontiers of Research

The love in listening is this accessible: just pause and attend. This easy act reverberates through another's being—and almost miraculously, through your own. When you allow yourself to be still and present, you find yourself able to enter another's space and to feel what they feel. Listening is a source of genuine empathy. I have always wondered about the mysterious bond that arises through listening, and I'm excited to report that new science on special neurons in our brain suggests why listening is powerful. These neurons actually allow us to essentially experience what another is feeling. I believe they are a key to the power of listening.

LESSON ONE: MIRROR OTHERS

"Listening is a miraculous ability," says Greg Fricchione, whose clinical research examines the connection between our brain's evolution and our spirituality. Fricchione is a consultant to the Institute who helps us determine the best projects to fund. "It evolves out of empathy, and we're learning more and more each day about where empathy resides in the brain."

The word *empathy* emerged in the 1890s, and it literally means "feeling into"—from the Greek *empatheia*. "Talking and listening are part of our evolutionary heritage as mammals and social organisms," Fricchione explains. "Through the miracle of language, we are linked even though separate. And we are able to understand the feelings and perceptions of others through specialized neurons called mirror neurons."

Mirror neurons are the subject of a whole new wave of research these days. They go a long way toward explaining why and how empathy may be wired into our neurocircuitry. Here's how mirror neurons work. Any kind of pain—whether a broken leg or the emotional agony of watching someone die—is processed in a part of the brain called the anterior cingulate cortex. "Let's suppose," says Fricchione, "that we pass by a mother sobbing on the side of the road because her child has been run over by a truck. If I were to take pictures of that mother's brain with functional magnetic resonance imaging, her anterior cingulate would just be exploding, the neurons firing wildly, because she is experiencing such deep, severe pain. As passersby, our mirror neurons will respond, and we will have similar explosions in our brain." Through our mirror neurons, explains Fricchione, we are able to experience a bit of what others experience, and since we're a species that relies on social attachment to survive, this capacity is crucial. It is also the underpinning of good listening. As we hear others' stories, watch their faces, and listen to their voices, our emotions are activated.

"As empathic listeners, we are evolved to feel and then soothe the suffering of our fellow human beings, precisely because of the neurological endowments we have evolved as a species," says Fricchione. Listening can heal in part because it does soothe the pain of the person speaking—thus quieting down the overactive brain. "Suppose I'm a cardiologist, and my patient has just had a heart attack and is in physical pain," says Fricchione. "I sit down by his hospital bed and listen as he says, 'Doctor, I'm only forty-five, and my father died when he was fifty from a massive heart attack. I have two young children at home, and I'm scared.' The doctor who listens empathically is going to help that person heal, in part because that person's cardiac pain *and* his emotional pain are being processed in the same part of the brain, the anterior cingulate cortex." In addition, pain triggers a cascade of hormonal and chemical signals called the stress response. If we reduce both emotional and physical pain, the stress response quiets down and the body has a better chance to heal. That's why cardiac patients with low social support are more likely to have another heart attack.

But we aren't just talking about physical pain. Most of the world's suffering is that of the heart. As Mother Teresa said, "Loneliness is the most terrible poverty." Listening and empathy lift us out of loneliness. "If you have a genetic vulnerability to major depression and you suffer any kind of pain," says Fricchione, "empathy is going to act on you like a powerful drug in terms of its ability to change your neurochemical ecology. This is a very important equation for health." According to the psychologist Stephanie Preston of the University of Michigan, "in order to understand how someone is feeling, you try on the feeling yourself. It's a kind of contagion model."

Fricchione and his colleagues hypothesize that reducing the stress response may release chemicals, such as nitric oxide, that help reduce overactivation in the immune, vascular, and nervous systems. Just as interesting is the fact that the so-called motherhood hormone—oxytocin, which facilitates labor, breast-feeding, and a mother's bonding with her child—seems to be released in response to social interaction. In one 2003 study, this hormone was paired with social support and given to thirty-seven healthy men who were then exposed to a social stress test. The combination of oxytocin and social support was linked to increased calmness, reduced anxiety, and lower levels of the stress hormone cortisol in the saliva.

When we listen, we also tend to look. New neurologic research indicates that our brains have evolved to monitor facial expressions; as we do so, there is a measurable increase in blood flow to an area.

So, how might you mirror another through listening?

❧   *Listen with the whole self.* Quietly sit with someone, in silence, eyes locked. In the silence, let yourself listen to your own body and "feeling" state and "feel" what you sense in the other person. Do this for ten minutes, just being present, and then afterwards talk about what you felt. You may realize you have sensed, through a mysterious process of empathy, much of what was going on inside the other person, even without words. You will also find that just clearing the space for being attentively, silently with each other allows connection and warmth to arise.

❧   *Slow down and wait.* This exercise comes from Sally Ollerton, coordinator of the Early Stage Program for the Alzheimer's Association of Cleveland. Slow down. Ask the person, "What do you want to tell me?" Look at the person as if he or she is the only person in the world. Pause and respectfully wait. You are not in a hurry. You are not task-oriented. You are simply affirming another being's worth. Now you have established a truly caring connection.

❧   *Switch perspectives.* This exercise comes from Leah Green, founder and director of the Compassionate Listening Project. The exercise is best done with a partner but can also be done alone. Describe a conflict you are having with another person. Don't try to solve it, just talk about what is happening and how it feels. Now, introduce yourself as the person you are having a conflict with and tell the story as you might imagine it from that person's perspective. You may be surprised by what you learn about how the other person sees you and what your own role in the conflict might be.

LESSON TWO: EXPAND WHO YOU ARE

Listening to others can help us to understand and like them. This can be a challenge, however, when we feel we don't already share common traits and values with the other person. Stephanie Preston notes that the elderly are often ignored for this very reason: "They're considered different, and so people don't take them seriously," says Preston. "They may move at a much slower speed than younger people, and they may also speak more slowly or repeat themselves, and that mere physical difference causes us to regard them as separate. We see ourselves as people who have control over our lives, whereas they don't. It takes an effort to listen patiently to what they say. The animal kingdom is organized by hierarchy, and so are we."

Listening to others may be just the medicine we need in our personal, social, and cultural lives because it may help reduce our spontaneous tendency to feel prejudice, says Arthur Aron of Stony Brook University. Art has been studying close relationships for the last twenty years, developing a theoretical model that once you form an intimate bond, the other person becomes part of your definition of yourself and then you can't help but extend them care and compassion. In one fascinating study, Art asked individuals to rate themselves and then their partner for specific traits—such as anxious, ambitious, or artistic. Then, in a follow-up study, these individuals were asked whether these traits were true of themselves. "When a trait is true of themselves, they say 'true.' When it's true of their partner but not themselves, they also tend to say 'true,' but their reaction time is slower. In other words, they hesitate, because it's both true and not. It's not their own trait. But to the extent that they view their partner as part of themselves, it is indeed their own trait." Aron has performed special neuroimaging studies that show this as well. "You're in the fMRI scanner and you hear your own name, the name of another person you know, and the names of strangers." It turns out that the parts of the brain that light up when you hear your own name and the name of someone you know are more similar to each other than to those parts that light up when you hear the name of a stranger. This is fascinating evidence that there is a neurological basis to the way we identify another as self.

Often, genuine listening allows terrible differences to begin to melt away. Leah Green of the Compassionate Listening Project tells the story of an American Jewish woman whose parents were survivors of Auschwitz. "We went one day to listen to a former SS soldier," recalls Green. "He had begun having nightmares when he turned sixty. It took him that long to really let himself feel what he had done. And listening to him was really, really hard for this woman, as you can imagine. She had visited Auschwitz herself. She broke down in tears after the soldier finished talking to us, and he came over to her very slowly and asked permission to be with her. I thought she might hit him, but she agreed, and he apologized to her in such an amazing way that it seemed as if she were liberated for a brief time from pain she had carried her whole life. And as we listened to the circumstances of his own difficult childhood, and how and why he became a Nazi, I could almost put myself in his shoes. It was the first time I myself had experienced that level of empathy while hearing someone's personal story." Green says that in listening you provide a trusting container for the storyteller. "I've listened to people who we call terrorists and who call themselves freedom fighters. I listened for an hour to the personal story of a terrorist who had spent many years in prison, and though I could not empathize with his actions, I could begin to understand the intensity of his anger: he had watched his father, uncles, and friends killed right in front of his eyes as a child. I started to feel what it must be like to live his life. And he was so moved that he'd been listened to that he began to listen to us about the possibility of nonviolent change."

Green says that her work in listening and in teaching others to listen compassionately has left her with a feeling of profound gratitude. "I often get cards from those I have taught, and they will say that at last they have a tool to shift relationships in their lives, especially ones that had seemed permanently broken. It's quite an honor to be able to help people this way."

Bonding with someone in a different group—such as another racial or religious group—may actually lessen prejudice. "Say I'm white," says Aron, "and I have a good friend who is black. Well, to some extent then, I myself am black. So just as I extend empathy to myself, I extend it to those who are part of myself and my identity—and inevitably, I extend it to the group they are in."

In one study sponsored by IRUL, Aron had two strangers spend up to four hours together to create a sense of connection. Forty such pairs of individuals were tested. Paired either with someone of their own race or with someone of another race, these individuals were given a set of exercises to create closeness and then questioned regarding their positive, compassionate emotions toward members of that other racial group. Aron found that empathic listening built closeness. "The way you become connected naturally in a friendship is doing things with another person, but most important of all, you self-disclose. You reveal things in a gradually escalating pattern. If you were to reveal too much too quickly, it might scare the other person away. If you don't reveal enough, the bond won't form. It's a bit like a dance." Most important, says Aron, is the fact that as you talk about yourself the other person listens and accepts. It's listening and acceptance that matter so much. With this insight, Aron has created a series of tasks that gradually increase closeness. "It's quite dramatic," says Aron. "In just forty-five minutes, people can get a sense of genuine closeness. And over four hours when we also integrate activities where people work together, that closeness can actually last for a little while."

The optimal way of achieving closeness, says Aron, is to bring a pair together for an hour once a week for four weeks. First they self-disclose; then they play games and puzzles together and compete together against other pairs. In the third week, they discuss their identification with their own group and with other groups. The findings are exciting: people who were paired with a member of another racial group showed more compassion for that group as a whole than did people paired with a member of their own racial group. Aron plans to repeat the study with most of the several thousand incoming freshmen at Stony Brook to get a much more robust indication of this effect. He also plans a study of police in Palo Alto, California, who live in a mixed ethnic community. In fact, Aron found himself permanently changed by working with police in a pilot study. "One of the first things the police said to us was, 'People in our community think of us as fat, doughnut-eating, lazy, aggressive folks,'" and I realized I had similar stereotypes. I made sure, when we served them refreshments, not to serve donuts. Spending time with policemen on my own made me able to see the world from their perspective, especially as someone who grew up in the 1960s and participated in demonstrations.

"Listening to those who are not like you is important for your personal growth and development," says Aron. "It helps you challenge your own views and expand your sense of life. It's also very good for society, in a world that is increasingly interdependent. If we're going to live in harmony, we need to feel compassion for members of all groups." Listening is the beginning of creating a more diverse tapestry in our own lives and a more harmonious world in general.

How can you listen as a way of bridging differences? Arthur Aron has developed an effective exercise for his studies that guides individuals in easy ways to share information so as to quickly create a bond. Here are some questions from Aron's guidelines that you can ask anyone, no matter how different they are from you:

- Given the choice of anyone in the world, whom would you want as a dinner guest and why?
- What would constitute a perfect day for you?
- Name three things you and your partner in this exercise seem to have in common.
- If you could wake up tomorrow having gained any one quality or ability, what would it be?
- What do you value most in a friendship?
- What do you like about me?
- Your house catches fire. After saving your loved ones and pets, you have time to make a final dash inside to save just one item. What would it be? Why?

After sharing questions and answers, notice if you are feeling warmer toward this person who may seem very different from you. Are you sensing a shared humanity under all the differences?

LESSON THREE: LISTEN AND FEEL BETTER

New research shows that listening can transform your sense of self and improve your life—even when you are ill. In a remarkable and highly publicized two-year study published in the journal *Social Science and Medicine*, Carolyn Schwartz studied 137 patients who were ill with multiple sclerosis. The bulk of the study examined 132 participants who were offered two different approaches to their illness: eight weekly meetings in which they would be taught coping skills, or monthly phone calls in which someone else with MS would give them listening and support.

The hidden gem in the study turned out to be the five MS victims who were trained by Schwartz to offer compassionate listening and support over the phone. "I met with these five people monthly," recalls Schwartz. "That allowed me to continue the training so that by the end of two years this group of five people were very good at listening compassionately to others."

When Schwartz applied scientifically rigorous data analysis to the total group of 137, she found that *giving* support improved health more than receiving it. Those five MS sufferers who offered support felt a dramatic change in how they viewed themselves and life. Depression, self-confidence, and self-esteem improved markedly among these givers. Giving, in the form of listening, was vitalizing for the spirit. "These people had undergone a spiritual transformation," says Schwartz, "that gave them a refreshed view of who they were."

This study is unique in two important ways. When we examine studies on giving and health, we may often wonder, "Which came first, the generosity or the well-being?" It's hard to tease out an ultimate proof, although strong correlations are certainly regarded as significant evidence across the sciences. But in this study we have people who are already ill and yet giving transformed their lives. This is very provocative. Generous behavior may not have catapulted them out of a wheelchair, but it brought them an inner sense of meaning and joy that is the essence of a life well lived.

The study also reveals the power of listening to others. Study participants made comments like, "There's a quietness in the soul when I'm listening to someone," "It's tough to get depressed when you are helping someone," and "I could still feel valuable . . . because I had something to give."

Carolyn offers specific advice from her training sessions with MS patients:

✿ *Learn to listen in a nondirective and supportive way.* This suggestion is based on the research of the psychologist Carl Rogers. The supporter reflects what the participant says, and does not give advice. You tell me, "I'm feeling sad," and I say, "I hear that you're feeling sad. What makes you sad? Can you tell me more?" You focus on the most emotional word in the person's sentence and repeat it in some way and ask for more. You probe in an empathic way, without judgment.

❧ *Refrain from talking about yourself.* "We live in what I call a dyadic monologue culture," says Schwartz. "I tell you what's bugging me, and you say, 'Gee, that's too bad, let me talk about what's bugging *me*.' It becomes a ping-pong match. In empathic listening, you simply listen and encourage the other to talk. You'll know it's working because the conversation will flow, become intimate, you'll feel close to the person, and as a listener you'll start to feel a kind of helper's high. It feels good when someone opens up and tells you what's important to them."

❧ *Set limits.* "Occasionally, our listeners would have problems with someone who wanted to monopolize their time," recalls Schwartz. "We'd set a fifteen-minute boundary for sessions, but one patient would talk for forty-five minutes. We had to train his helper to be more assertive about getting off the phone and setting limits. You can't help another person if you're overwhelmed by his needs. So ten minutes into the conversation, she would say, 'I'm really enjoying talking to you and just want to let you know we have about five minutes left.' Then about a minute before the conversation was to end, she'd mention that. That kind of skill is very important if you're going to help others by listening."

Listening to others is good for them and good for ourselves. When we listen to others, it's as if we're all breezing downhill easily. When we refuse to listen to others, disharmony results and we're pedaling up a hill with difficulty.

Research shows that when we feel secure in our personal attachments to others and confident that they will provide loving care in times of need, we are more likely to offer our own support to someone else in need.

"People need to feel others care about and listen to them," says Preston. "People are less likely to let their health deteriorate if they feel valued and heard. And your ability to heal depends in part on your faith in your doctor, and that is dependent on whether you feel he or she really listens to you. Over and over again, people will report frustration with their doctors, not because they doubt the physician's expertise, but because they feel the doctor wasn't listening. It would be interesting if doctors were instructed, even for the first twenty seconds of a patient visit, to look into their patient's eyes and truly listen to what they're saying."

These gentle guidelines on listening that will help heal you as well as others come from the psychologist Bhita Ghafoori.

❧ *Learn the difference between open and closed questions.* Closed questions require specific, simple answers. "Did you graduate from high school?" is a closed question. "Is the headache on the left or right side?" is also a closed question. However, "Could you tell me what you'd like to talk to me about?" is an open question that encourages disclosure.

❧ *Encourage others to keep talking by repeating key words and restating longer phrases.* By echoing others in an encouraging way, you show that you understand what they are saying and feeling.

❧ *Reflect the other person's feelings in order to show empathy.* "It seems like you've been feeling very anxious lately," or, "You sound like you're feeling very sad about that."

LESSON FOUR: LISTEN WITH YOUR WHOLE BODY

"You're my friend, right?"

That's what Trent—a man who was both blind and on antipsychotics—said to Joan Eads, an assistant at L'Arche, an international federation of communities for people with learning disabilities and the assistants who volunteer to help them and sometimes live with them. Eads recalls: "Trent had been in an institution since he was a year old. Each night he went to sleep holding his radio in his arms really tight. He loved that radio, because people had always stolen it from him. I felt deep compassion for Trent." One night she was giving him his bath and towel-drying his back, and he said, "You're my friend, right?" "I realized that over the years many hundreds of strangers had bathed Trent without sensing the sacred life inside him," she recalls. "He had lived through hell, and yet he could still trust and love and ask someone to be his friend. He was able to do that in a way I myself never had. God was present to me in that moment." Eads notes that L'Arche's policy of sharing each person's sacred story is the core of the program's beauty.

Eads tells another story of listening to nonverbal communication from a L'Arche member named Ruth, who suffers from cerebral palsy and requires a communication device. "Her body is very broken," says Eads. "She and I would go swimming together. She loved it. Afterwards we'd go into the hot tub, and she'd be having a lot of muscle spasms. One time I saw two beautiful young women in the hot tub and thought to myself, *Oh, I'm so fat in comparison*. I was ashamed and self-conscious, but as we got into the tub Ruth, with her broken body, started splashing the water to get the two women's attention, and then pointed to me and made the sign language for "friend." She did this with a big smile, as if she were very proud, as if she were saying, 'I'm so happy to say to these young women that this is my friend Joan.' That was quite a humbling and amazing moment in my life."

"Listening is as nonverbal as it is verbal," says Kevin Reimer, an ordained minister and psychologist at Azusa Pacific University who runs a grant-funded research program that looks at compassionate care in L'Arche. "It's the power of presence, of listening and understanding expressed through touch or simple emotion. It may be dinnertime at L'Arche, and a core member who has the mental capacity of a three- or four-year-old may be hanging her head and crying a little. You'll see people pass the peas and put their arm around her. These moments are mundane as well as sacred, but they're imbued with affirmation. At L'Arche, there is almost an asymmetry of communication, because the members are disabled and so you enter into their space and end up discovering what's really important in life. We all tend to inflate our own importance." Listening and being present for another actually reveals the three lies that we often live by and that cause us pain, says Reimer: the lie that we are what we have, the lie that we are what other people say about us, and the lie that we are what we do for a living. In listening, we reveal deeper truths about the primary force in relationships: today I trusted someone. Today someone trusted me. Today I was able to give something significant to another.

How can you listen in this deeper way—a listening that is not just about the voice but about the heart and the essence of another? Give someone you love a gentle backrub and "listen" to their sighs of pleasure as their body relaxes. "Listen" to the way they lean in toward you. Take someone's hand and "listen" to how they clasp yours in return. Give someone a hug and let the hug last more than just a moment. "Listen" together to your bodies as they reaffirm closeness and warmth.

LESSON FIVE: LOOK TO THE VERY YOUNG

We can learn from the young, because they are spontaneous. "When a six-week-old baby smiles, that smile is so full of joy and so unfettered by negativity," says Stephanie Preston. "It's a beautiful thing, and when I first experienced that in my own children, I decided that my overriding goal would be to maintain that feeling in them. A child's happiness is precious, and I'll do anything not to spoil it. My own capacity for love has changed so much since experiencing it in my children. It is they who have taught me to be empathic and loving."

As our children teach us, so we can teach and protect them. The psychologists Ilse de Koeyer-Laros and Alan Fogel, both of the University of Utah, have been studying empathy in babies and young children. "We started when the babies were just a year old, and we study them every year," she explains. She and her colleagues look for an activity they call co-regulation. "We believe when you look at real communication, even if one is talking and one is listening, you are both active and creating the conversation, second to second, in real time. You are continually influencing each other. If I started to talk and you were silent all of a sudden, I'd have the sense that you were truly listening to me, and that would help me shape what I say. You can see this in mother-baby interactions." When a mother and her child are interacting, they often gaze intensely at each other, play together, laugh together. Even when a baby is very involved with a toy and not looking at the mother, says Koeyer-Laros, the mother quietly watches her baby play and offers help if needed. During active co-regulation, there is more positive emotion and communication.

"Attentive presence plays a huge role in a young child's life," says Koeyer-Laros. "Even when babies are very young, you can listen to their small signals. We know, for instance, that when a baby is playing, it will look back at its mother to be sure she is still present. A baby will explore its world but always come back to this patient, secure parent who is waiting there for them. It will turn to its parents when upset and start to know that, no matter what, Mom or Dad is going to take care of me."

When parents are truly present for their children through positive and negative experiences, the children are able to explore the richness of their own emotions safely. For instance, research has shown that securely attached children will give more elaborate answers about their whole range of emotions than children whose parents' style did not lead to secure attachment. One pattern, called "chase and dodge," often occurs with parents who have emotional difficulties themselves, such as depression, Koeyer-Laros explains. "This mom might feel rejected if her baby looks away. In one of our studies, we had a mom who kept calling her baby's name, tapping his head, grabbing his chin to turn his head back to her in a high chair. We know that some parents become very anxious and want to know, 'Are you still there? Are you still seeing me? What's wrong?' " That's the opposite of empathic presence and listening. These parents are not able to let the baby be who he or she is at that moment. These parents may also not be able to handle their children's negative emotions and may refuse to acknowledge them. In contrast, "when Mom listens closely to her child and attends empathically through all experiences, the child begins to be able to do the same for him- or herself," says Koeyer-Laros.

One IRUL-funded researcher, James E. Swain of Yale University, studies the neurobiological aspects of parental care, especially in mothers. Parental "engrossment" in the child and preoccupation with creating a safe environment for the child make perfect evolutionary sense. Parents are clearly hardwired to be excellent listeners when it comes to the newborn child. In fact, their listening has an almost obsessive quality. An attentive love that listens even to the tone of a cry with great care is vital in providing a child with resiliency and protection against psychiatric problems in later life and is generally thought to have enduring consequences. So attachment early on is formative and shapes the future of the child in ways that, even if not entirely determinative, are highly influential.

Stephanie Preston has experienced the power of listening in raising her own daughter. "If she says, 'I want to put on my own shoes,' and I'm rushed and say, 'We don't have time,' and put them on her myself, I may have tantrums for the next two hours. But if I wait patiently for the three minutes it takes her to put on her shoes, she's much happier. It takes effort in this moment for me to pay attention and listen to her, but in the long term I minimize behavioral problems. If a child doesn't feel they're being listened to, you may spend the whole day fending off temper tantrums. If you take an extra minute every twenty minutes to check in with them and see what it is they feel and want, life becomes much easier. You don't resent your child. Your whole life becomes more positive, and the atmosphere in your home is peaceful. Listening to your child allows you to pedal with the wind, not against it."

Try this exercise with your own child:

❧ *Love your child by listening.* Try to set aside a significant period of time each day to invite your child to speak from the heart. Listen to the words as well as the emotions. Imagine it is the first time you have ever truly listened to your child. Make the experience new. Children feel worthy and loved when their parents listen. This simple exercise comes from Laura Janusik: At the end of the day, when you tuck your child into bed, ask him or her, "What was the worst part of your day? And what was the best part of your day?" Janusik says you will gain invaluable information about the individual personality that is emerging in your child. You can also apply this exercise to friends and family, students, neighbors, and colleagues.

The Gift of Empathy

In children, empathy emerges in the second year of life, when they develop self-awareness. Though newborns can cry in response to other babies' cries, this is not a universal response, and we are not sure if it is a kind of conditioned response or if it reflects a primitive form of empathy. Preston believes it is a form of empathy.

By the age of six months, babies tend to react to the distress of others by seeking comfort for themselves. By nine months, babies start to respond to the emotional signals of others. For instance, one study found that babies will echo their mothers' sadness with negative facial expressions. By age two, toddlers can experience empathic concern for others and may try to comfort them in their distress. As they develop language, their empathic repertoire expands.

Good listening is good nurturing. Those who deeply listen to us are the ones we move toward. Today's listening is the basis for tomorrow's love.

Your Listening Score

It's time to answer the questions on the listening section of your Love and Longevity Scale. We have divided responses into percentiles, or fifths. These are general guidelines; you may score right near the cutoff between percentiles, so please keep this in mind and use the scale as a friendly tool. Remember:

There are two steps to determining your score. First, determine which items need to be "reverse-scored" (denoted with the ® symbol). For reverse-scored items, see the chart below.

If you score a . . .	. . . assign yourself a score for that item of:
1	6
2	5
3	4
4	3
5	2
6	1

The second step is to add the scores for individual items *after* the reverse-scored items have been reverse-scored. Take the quiz now, and take it again if you wish after you've finished this book and begun practicing the art of true presence and listening in your daily life.

Using the scale provided, please circle the one number that best reflects your opinion about whether or not each statement below describes you or experiences that you have had. There are no correct answers, so please respond as honestly as possible to each one.

1. I am careful to give my undivided attention to family members who are talking with me.
   1=strongly disagree   2=disagree   3=slightly disagree   4=slightly agree
   5=agree   6=strongly agree

2. When one of my loved ones needs my attention, I really try to slow down and give them the time they need.
   1=strongly disagree   2=disagree   3=slightly disagree   4=slightly agree
   5=agree   6=strongly agree

3. My loved ones know that if they have concerns, they can come to me and I'll give them the attention they need.
   1=strongly disagree   2=disagree   3=slightly disagree   4=slightly agree
   5=agree   6=strongly agree

4. It's hard for me to slow down and listen when my family members need to talk to me.[®]
   1=strongly disagree   2=disagree   3=slightly disagree   4=slightly agree
   5=agree   6=strongly agree

5. I sometimes fail to notice my family members' needs and concerns because I don't take time to pay attention.[®]
   1=strongly disagree   2=disagree   3=slightly disagree   4=slightly agree
   5=agree   6=strongly agree

6.   I listen attentively when a friend needs to talk with me.
     1=strongly disagree 2=disagree 3=slightly disagree 4=slightly agree
     5=agree 6=strongly agree

7.   When one of my friends needs my attention, I try to slow down and give them the time they need.
     1=strongly disagree 2=disagree 3=slightly disagree 4=slightly agree
     5=agree 6=strongly agree

8.   My friends feel comfortable sharing their problems with me.
     1=strongly disagree 2=disagree 3=slightly disagree 4=slightly agree
     5=agree 6=strongly agree

9.   It's hard for me to slow down and listen when my friends need to get my advice or share their feelings.®
     1=strongly disagree 2=disagree 3=slightly disagree 4=slightly agree
     5=agree 6=strongly agree

10. My friends would probably agree that I'm not the world's best listener.®
     1=strongly disagree 2=disagree 3=slightly disagree 4=slightly agree
     5=agree 6=strongly agree

11. People in the neighborhood or at work seek me out to talk about what is bothering them.
     1=strongly disagree 2=disagree 3=slightly disagree 4=slightly agree
     5=agree 6=strongly agree

12. My neighbors and coworkers know that they can come to me if they need to share their feelings with someone.
     1=strongly disagree 2=disagree 3=slightly disagree 4=slightly agree
     5=agree 6=strongly agree

13. I am known in my neighborhood or workplace as someone who makes time to pay attention to others' problems.
     1=strongly disagree 2=disagree 3=slightly disagree 4=slightly agree
     5=agree 6=strongly agree

14. I probably would not notice if a neighbor or coworker had a problem that they wanted to discuss with me.[®]
1=strongly disagree   2=disagree   3=slightly disagree   4=slightly agree
5=agree   6=strongly agree

15. Few, if any, of my coworkers or neighbors would come to me for advice or sympathy if they had a problem.[®]
1=strongly disagree   2=disagree   3=slightly disagree   4=slightly agree
5=agree   6=strongly agree

16. I try to give people time and attention when they need to talk to somebody, even if it's a complete stranger.
1=strongly disagree   2=disagree   3=slightly disagree   4=slightly agree
5=agree   6=strongly agree

17. I try to really pay attention to problems that are going on in the world.
1=strongly disagree   2=disagree   3=slightly disagree   4=slightly agree
5=agree   6=strongly agree

18. I'm usually in such a rush that I can't take time to talk with strangers.[®]
1=strongly disagree   2=disagree   3=slightly disagree   4=slightly agree
5=agree   6=strongly agree

19. Frankly, I don't have the time to try to understand problems occurring around the world.[®]
1=strongly disagree   2=disagree   3=slightly disagree   4=slightly agree
5=agree   6=strongly agree

20. I'm so distracted by all of the things I have to do that I can't take time to understand the problems of strangers.[®]
1=strongly disagree   2=disagree   3=slightly disagree   4=slightly agree
5=agree   6=strongly agree

Your Listening Score

High Giver (80th percentile)	99 or higher
Giver (60th percentile)	93–98
Moderate Giver (40th percentile)	86–92
Low Giver (20th percentile)	78–85

Twelve

The Way of Creativity:

Invent and Innovate

On a blazingly clear autumn afternoon in 1997, the fashion photographer Rick Guidotti's life irrevocably changed course. He was a few blocks from his office when he saw a twelve-year-old waiting for the bus with a friend.

"She had no pigmentation in her hair, skin, or eyes, and she was gorgeous," says Guidotti. "Before I could stop to ask her to take a photo, she was gone. So I went to Barnes & Noble around the corner and began to read up on albinism. And every photo I found was in a medical textbook, alongside other genetic conditions. You'd see children and adults in their underwear up against walls in doctor's offices with a black bar across their face to protect their anonymity. Each picture was an image of despair, misery, and hopelessness, all in the context of disability. And I said to myself, 'Wait. This is so different than that glorious girl giggling and laughing on the street with her hair blowing in the wind.' "

Guidotti contacted the National Organization for Albinism and Hypopigmentation (NOAH) and arranged with them to let him "show the world the beauty of albinism. I remember the first woman I photographed. She came into my studio with her head down and her hair in her face. She'd been teased and tortured her whole life. I put on music and took photographs and within minutes it was almost like I'd held up a mirror and for the first time she saw what I saw: this amazingly glorious, beautiful creature. It was electrifying. I knew the kids would still tease her, but they would never have quite the same impact again."

After the pictures were published in *Life* magazine in June 1998, other organizations centered on genetic difference contacted Guidotti. Soon he had abandoned fashion photography entirely, and his new organization, Positive Exposure, has become a worldwide effort to erase stigma. His co-director, epidemiologist, and psychiatrist, Diane McLean, has been video-taping the life stories of many of the individuals Guidotti photographs. "There's a universal message here," he says. "It's about celebrating difference, looking at the beauty in difference. I rememebr the day this work grabbed hold of my heart really tightly and wouldn't let me go. A twenty-five-year-old boy said to me, 'The hatred and abuse I experience every day will never disappear, but what has disappeared is the hatred I felt for myself.'

"Another time a woman with Marfan's syndrome, which can cause a curvature of the spine and very long arms and legs, came up to me at one of my exhibits. I'd photographed a boy with Marfan's, without his shirt, and it was a beautiful portrait. This woman said to me, 'My dad and I both have Marfan's, and neither one of us has ever been to the beach in a bathing suit. Now that I've seen this portrait, I am buying a bikini.' Once there's a shift in your perception of beauty or difference, it never shifts back." Guidotti's photographs are so powerful and beautiful that just looking at them, one undergoes a sea change. "A man who runs an institute on genetics came to visit the studio, and he walked in and looked around and said to me, 'This is like motherhood. I get it. What do you want me to do for you?'"

Today, says Guidotti, he's no longer traveling first-class with an entourage and sleeping at the Four Seasons Hotel. He's traveling coach, sleeping on people's couches, and photographing only people with genetic disorders—changing their lives, showing them their own beauty. As one portrait subject, Katherine, said, "In the photos that Rick took of me, I did not see my disease. I did not see devastation, limitations, or deficiencies. I saw a human being."

Creativity, like love itself, is a gift that simply by its expression benefits those who express it and those who receive it. Rick Guidotti has taken his creativity a step further, turning it into a calling shaped by love.

Creativity: The First Mover

From the chrysalis of a caterpillar to the compass of the cosmos, from a star system to a soufflé, from King Lear to Harry Potter, from the gleaming fins of the Sydney Opera House to the honeycombed symmetry of a beehive, creativity brings new forms into being. We all share in this every day of our lives. We need to know it deep in our bones—deep in our stem cells!—and feel ourselves as part of a divinely inspired, unfolding tapestry.

The first hexagram of the *I Ching*—the classic book of Chinese philosophy and divination—is called "Ch'ien," the creative. "Creativity" is the *I Ching*'s word for the primal power of the universe. The *I Ching* is not alone in this view. The Harvard theologian Gordon Kaufman has suggested that we think of God as creativity itself. "God is the ultimate mystery of things, a mystery that we have not been able to penetrate or dissolve—and likely never will," says Kaufman. We can marvel at the thrilling evolution of star systems and planets, the sumptuous, sublime diversity of life on earth, the emergence of human consciousness and the capacity to love—and yet, says Kaufman, we cannot quite picture or embrace the ultimate point of reference that we call God. He suggests that creativity itself is the divine mystery.

The diversity generated on our planet alone is a marvel. Somewhere between 10 million and 100 million species flourish on earth. Life is so hardy and inventive that some organisms can survive when frozen at temperatures of −70 degrees centigrade, while others thrive in deep-sea volcanic vents that gush black sulfurous water boiling at a hellish 700 degrees Fahrenheit. The best-selling author and scientist Rupert Sheldrake writes: "The whole cosmos is in creative evolution. And you get the impression that there's a kind of creativity for its own sake. It's not at all clear why there should be so many species of beetles, for instance." (It has been estimated that there are between 300,000 and 350,000 different species of bee-tles.) And all of this life is so interconnected, co-evolving, and balanced that the waste of one species becomes the food of the next. The whole is truly dependent on the interlocking parts. All around us and within us is what the nineteenth-century botanist Christian Ehrenberg called "the everywhereness of life."

So here you are, today, alive in the midst of all this aliveness, your brain's 100 billion neurons firing away. What does all this creativity mean to you, and how can you give creativity to yourself and others? "The universe produces novel, ordered, beautiful complexity, again and again," says the philosopher Philip Clayton, a visiting professor at Harvard. "It just grows more complex and interconnected and beautiful and amazing and awe-inspiring. What does it mean to view human existence in this context?" Clayton believes that we can learn about the meaning of human creativity by looking at the universe. "Once we recognize that we are microcosms of this macrocosmic process of unfolding novelty, that we are participants, we can look at our own lives with a sense of richness. I appropriate that sense of unfolding creativity, I joyfully participate."

"Creativity allows humans to survive," says the Harvard psychologist Shelley Carson. "We don't have the strength or speed to escape our predators, so we've survived by being creative and innovative. Creativity allows us to communicate across distance—with the telephone and Internet, but also across centuries, with poetry, art, and history. We're able to share our hopes, dreams, and frailties with people that lived before us, and we'll share our own with those who come after us." The psychologist Thomas Ward of Texas A&M University says much the same in a recent paper: "We are an enormously creative species. In a relatively short span of time, geologically speaking, we have gone from fashioning rocks into our first primitive tools to building spacecraft that allow us to retrieve rocks from other planets." Ward thinks the hallmark of human thinking is its creativity.

Though creativity can be described in many ways, I've assembled here a list of the most common traits and benefits that creativity researchers have uncovered.

Creativity is both novel and useful. "The scribblings of a two-year-old that a mom hangs on the refrigerator are creative in a sense, but ultimately they are not useful," says Shelley Carson, "so I don't define them as true creativity. True creativity must somehow be useful or beneficial to others."

Creative thinking is divergent. "Divergent thinking is not focused on one thing. It's associated with what we call defocused attention. Highly creative people use divergent thinking as their default," says Carson, "whereas most people only switch to divergent thinking by an effort." That means creative people are living on the edge cognitively. They're not living by a lot of rules. They're letting in a lot of different thoughts and experiences.

The personality trait most linked to creativity is openness to experience. Says Carson, "Openness to experience includes being imaginative, trying new things, being open to fantasy. It isn't that these people want to thwart convention, they simply don't pay attention to it."

Highly creative people are introverts who derive their greatest energy from inner stimulation. "They go inside themselves," says Carson, and that's where they find their energy. The creative person isn't shy, so when we say they're introverts, we mean they find strength and inspiration in solitude. They also have a *strong belief in what they're doing.* "They are simply doing their own thing. Now, when you look at teens who are dressing goth at school, they are purposely rebelling, they aren't doing that out of creativity. A creative kid might dress goth but then throw a bright red scarf around their neck. They don't follow any code, conventional or unconventional." In other words, to echo Thoreau, they follow the beat of a different drum—their own.

Discovery is a hallmark of creativity, and yet it may flow out of an individual proclivity for certain themes. The outpouring of artists and scientists alike is often guided by a deeply held picture or theme, according to Gerald Holton of Harvard University. The author of *Thematic Origins of Scientific Thought: Kepler to Einstein,* Holton believes that creative *thematas* persist over an entire lifetime's work. So creativity is both deeply held and organic—an expression of who we really are as well as sudden, original, and new.

The creative experience brings us into a state of "flow." According to Mihaly Csikszentmihalyi, author of *Creativity: Flow and the Psychology of Dis-*

covery and Invention and director of the Quality of Life Research Center at Claremont Graduate University in California, in a state of flow one feels outside of time, absorbed in the task at hand, and yet working with a sense of effortlessness that is deeply pleasurable.

According to Csikszentmihalyi's in-depth studies of creative individuals, they usually have *high physical energy*, *playful* and *flexible* styles, are comfortable with both solitude and company, are able to take risks, and are passionate about their work. They can hold paradox and polarity within the self.

Research by the Wellesley psychologist Paul Wink shows that creativity is linked to *healthy narcissism*, a positive self-regard: "I did my Ph.D. work on a famous cohort of 140 women from Mills College who had been studied by other researchers. At the time the study began, Mills College attracted women with artistic interests and those from prominent Hollywood families, so it was a very good way to study healthy narcissism and its link to creativity. I found that the women who were healthy narcissists were likely to be higher in creativity and *empathy* and to achieve high social status. They were open to experience, to joy as well as pain, and aware of the nuances and ironies of life. A sense of *vitality* characterized these women throughout their lives."

And finally, according to Shelley Carson, creative people are *curious*, prefer *complexity*, are *assertive*, and *self-assured*, prefer the *big picture*, are *driven*, and *independent*.

Creativity is linked with joy. It is also strongly predictive of the ability to self-actualize. It can help improve the mood and well-being of those who are physically ill, and it can lift self-esteem.

Lessons from the Frontiers of Research

The pure joy of a creative act moves us to play, explore, create, and integrate new views of ourselves. Creativity is a gift to our world. It is love for life itself and eminently worth cultivating. Research shows that, with practice and attention, we can all become more creative and joyful.

LESSON ONE: YOUR WORLD IS AWASH IN CREATIVITY

There are two kinds of creativity, according to Mihaly Csikszentmihalyi, and one of them is personal creativity, which "is very important for living a full life." We all participate in this kind of creativity, which Mihaly calls "Little C." In contrast, "Big C" is the kind of creativity that changes the world. We participate in that too, through deep appreciation. "If we think in terms of history and culture, something is only genuinely creative when it's made a difference to others," Mihaly says. "There has to be a conjunction between the work and the culture." He offers the artist Vincent van Gogh as one striking example. At first, van Gogh's work was ignored, but after World War I it suddenly became relevant. "People needed a new way to represent and cope with feelings they had because of the war. At that point, his work began to be noticed and taken up into the culture." For Mihaly, that was the moment when van Gogh became a "Big C" creator—one who has had a lasting impact on art and culture. "The great flowering of impressionism in Paris was due in part to the willingness of the new middle classes to decorate their homes with canvasses; this in turn attracted ambitious young painters from every corner of the world." So, says Mihaly, the creativity that wells up in any given field is partly inspired by the promise of recognition and appreciation.

Creativity is an interaction between the creator and the audience. And so I think of it as a form of love, of giving and receiving. Shelley Carson has a similar viewpoint about "big" and "little" creativity, but she divides creativity into *three* Cs, low, middle, and high. "Low C is what we all participate in every day," she says. "That is Scarlett O'Hara looking at the green drapes hanging in the living room and realizing she can make a dress out of them. Or the kid who uses bubble gum on the fender of his bike to keep the fender on because he doesn't have glue. This kind of activity is extremely creative and common. Middle C folks are those who actually make their living at a creative endeavor, whether it's designing wallpaper or creating art or writing. They are creative, but they are not yet changing the world. High C people are like Copernicus, Einstein, Picasso, Beethoven, Newton. They revolutionized their field and changed the world. I like to study all these forms of creativity, and what's interesting is that the kind of processing in all three forms seems to be the same." (Of course, as one researcher, Charles Lumsden, points out, it's really hard to know whether our most creative great minds would have dominated culture regardless of timing. Are there geniuses who are unknown because their creativity did not synchronize with the prevailing culture at the right time?)

We can take part in the "Big C" in the same way that Philip Clayton suggests we respond to the cosmos: "I joyfully participate." I grew up with a lot of creative people around me: my sister played the oboe, and my grandmother rented studios to painters like Robert Motherwell and Jackson Pollack. My father was a guiding hand in glass design at Steuben before he started his own design company. I learned early to partake in all that creativity through appreciation. We all benefit from the risks that Big C creators take: I think, for example, of Nobel Prize winner Barry Marshall, who swallowed a vial of the microbe h. pylori in order to prove to the world that ulcers are caused by an infection. He immediately got an ulcer, then gave himself antibiotics to cure it.

We are living in a cornucopia of Big C creativity. At any given moment, we can look around and realize we are awash in Big C, says the psychologist Mark Runco of California State University, editor of the *Creativity Journal*. And we can celebrate that with others. "As I talk to you now," Runco told me, "I'm in my library with a couple thousand books. All my CDs are over on the wall across from me. My television is on. I'm wearing a bright red shirt. I'm communicating with you over a distance because of the creativity of Alexander Graham Bell. Creativity is everywhere, and I'm not sure people realize just how much of it is actually around them."

❧ *Wallow in the bliss of Big C*. Look around you right now and tally up all the Big C marvels you are participating in. How did this book get into your hands? Well, if we want to talk about the book, it could not exist without the evolution of language—the most fundamental way that we share information with each other. This book also would not exist without the invention of the printing press, the creative work of the scientists I'm writing about, and advances in digital imaging and computers. And if we want to talk about your hands, which are holding this book, the opposable thumb is one of nature's marvelous inventions, without which we could not peel a banana, much less build a house. Then, of course, there is the eye gazing at the book—have you wondered how a nerve can become sensitive to light itself? One theory is that our eyes evolved from bacteria that were responsive to light. If that's true, says the science writer Carl Zimmer, "we gaze at the world with bacterial eyes."

❧ *Expose yourself to the Big C.* To enhance your own creativity, both Shelley Carson and Mark Runco advise exposing yourself to music, literature, and art. Make a point of going to museums and really looking at paintings. Study the life of a painter after viewing his or her work, read poetry, and go to poetry readings, art gallery openings, cathedrals, concerts. Read biographies of inventors or go to special science exhibits. Look up at the stars at night and contemplate the Big Bang or the way light comes in through your window in the morning. Wallow in the bliss of Big C creativity.

❧ *Plan a vacation around the life of a creative genius.* Join the ultimate play—a vacation—with an exploration of the life of a great creator. Retrace his or her physical life journey. For Georgia O'Keeffe, it might be New York, where she first met her husband, Alfred Steiglitz, and burst upon the New York art scene, and New Mexico, where her Ghost Ranch is immortalized and offers an inn to visitors. A vacation devoted to Mozart could follow his compositions and the places he traveled as he wrote and performed them. Mozart traveled even as a child on concert tours to Paris and London and later spent time in Salzburg, Italy, Munich, and Vienna. With his wife, he visited Prague three times.

❧ *Create your own retrospective.* Immerse yourself in your own self-designed retrospective of a favorite and great filmmaker, artist, writer, or any other creative individual.

Lesson Two: Creativity Is Pure Pleasure, So Do What You Love

"The soul is here for its own joy," wrote the poet Robert Bly, and in the same way, creativity is here for its own joy. There is a pure, visceral pleasure in creativity, no matter how "small." Shelley Carson studied one woman who was uneducated and went to work as a waitress in a restaurant. "She'd been there a few months," Carson recalls, "and she redesigned their menus and the food they were serving, put different tablecloths on all the tables, and rearranged the tables. That restaurant closed, and she went to work at Walgreen's. Before you knew it, she had redesigned how their counters were laid out and their holiday displays. She was driven to do these creative things. Like all creativity, it was intrinsically motivated. The reward comes from within."

This kind of daily creativity requires a willingness to break away from convention, and practicing it in small ways can have a profound effect on your personality. One yearlong study in 1981 followed nine women who began to meet once a week to work creatively on sewing, knitting, crocheting, weaving, and similar projects. They were encouraged to try out new ideas and to see the familiar in a new way. At the beginning of the year each woman was rated on personality traits by several of her relatives and close friends—none of whom knew the nature of the study. At the end of the year the women were again rated—and there was a significant change. They were judged more playful, less cautious, more independent and lively, more goal-oriented, more persistent, and less anxious in unfamiliar situations. Though this is a small study, it points in a remarkable direction—showing not only the beneficial impact of creativity but how easily it is within our reach.

In another 1988 study, a group of amateur jazz musicians were given a paper-and-pencil creativity test. They scored significantly higher than a control group on spontaneity, power of association, wealth of ideas, and willingness to take risks. The study concluded that making music, even in an amateur setting, may have released their creativity in general.

Research shows that creative people are physiologically sensitive and will rate an electric shock as more intense than a noncreative individual.

Creative people also take twice as long to "habituate" to a stimulus as non-creative people, indicating that they continue to notice and respond to it. (This can be measured by the electrical response of the skin, known as galvanic skin response.) This sensitivity must be pleasurable, because creative people seek novelty and stimulation. Mihaly Csikszentmihalyi feels that the strongest trait of a creative person is a constant curiosity—"an ever renewed interest in whatever happens around them."

❧ *Heighten your sensitivity.* Pay closer attention to sensation. Ask your partner or friend to give you a massage, but begin with the lightest touch possible. Attend to all the sensations. Notice your breathing. When something catches your attention, linger on it and observe its every detail. Focus on a single flower, or a single petal of a flower. Listen for the harmonies in a musical piece, the delicate weaving of a flute in a symphony, or the tremolo of an opera singer as she lingers on a note. Attend deeply and sensitively to your world.

❧ *Make the familiar new.* Try a novel approach to a familiar activity or routine. Render your garden all shades of purple this year. (Enjoy the comments from neighbors!) Prepare and eat a family meal backwards, starting with dessert. Garnish a salad with unusual delicacies, such as tropical fruit and caviar. Mix and match your clothes in new ways.

❧ *Let happiness be an inspiration.* In your happiest hours, pause to imagine all the new experiences you might invite into your life. In more neutral moods, willingly go out and choose some of those experiences you imagined.

Joy begets creativity, and creativity begets joy. As long ago as 1987, the psychologist Alice Isen of Cornell University found that three-quarters of individuals who were feeling happy and joyful (having just viewed a comedy or been given a gift) were more creative. They were more likely to see links between different words, solve problems, and come up with unusual associations. Four years later Isen also found similar results in third-year medical students, who were able to come up with solutions to complex medical problems sooner than their peers if they were in a joyful and positive state. Then, in 1999, Isen came up with a really interesting explanation for the link between happiness and creativity: she suggested that both positive emotions and creative thinking are mediated by the neurotransmitter dopamine—the "feel good" chemical.

Creativity, according to the psychologist Barbara Frederickson of the University of North Carolina, is a powerful "broaden and build" phenomenon based on positive emotions. When we're in a joyful state, we're more flexible and open to information. We are, in short, more playful. According to a 2004 study by Frederickson, negative emotions narrow our thoughts and actions toward survival. Positive emotions "widen the array of thoughts and actions that come to mind." Frederickson tested her theory by asking folks to view film clips that were neutral, ones that evoked joy, and ones that evoked fear and anger. Afterwards they were asked to list up to twenty things they'd like to do right then. Those who'd viewed joyful films wrote down twice as many things they'd like to do as those who'd seen films that evoked fear or anger.

Mihaly Csikszentmihalyi notes that most creative people refer to their work as play and say the equivalent of, "You could say that I worked every day of my life, or with equal justice you could say that I never did any work in my life."

❧ *Create an imaginary garden.* This exercise comes from Shelley Carson: Imagine yourself transported to a special garden. Visualize it in detail. Now, go look at pictures of flowers or go to a nursery and pick out specific flowers that you want in your garden next time you go there. Find pictures of stones or cobblestones and pick out exactly what kind of paths you want in your garden. Look at pictures of gazebos and add those to your garden. Work on your imaginary garden for months.

LESSON THREE: CREATIVITY IS MANY-SPLENDORED—KNOW YOUR STYLE

There are different types of creators, according to the Harvard researcher Howard Gardner, who is famous for his delineation of multiple forms of intelligence. (Dancers, for instance, have kinesthetic intelligence.) Gardner notes that creators fall into various types:

- Some like to *solve problems*. James Watson and Francis Crick, who discovered the double helix shape of DNA, were problem solvers.
- Others like to *build theories* that shed new light on reality so that we see it in a new way. Einstein, Freud, and Darwin were theory builders.
- Some of us *create works* based on internal imagery, crafting a creation that can be viewed, read, seen, or experienced again and again. This kind of creativity is introspective and strongly dependent on emotion. Writers and painters, from Shakespeare to Renoir, are examples.
- Another type of creator likes to *build a ritualized work* that is then performed. Choreographers like Martha Graham or directors of theater and movies are examples. Important aspects of the creativity lie in the *performance* itself.
- A fifth kind of creativity is in the social realm, where there is a *high-stake performance* in public that is intended to bring about social or political change. Gandhi and his followers are examples.

What type of creativity suits you best? Many of us favor one style, though some are nimble enough to engage in more than one style. Leonardo da Vinci is the example that usually comes to mind, and thus the apt cliché about a creative person being a "Renaissance man." For me, creativity really began to flower when I was asked to run an institute and to help build a network of colleagues and researchers with a common vision.

LESSON FOUR: THINK IN NOVEL WAYS

Creativity is powerfully linked with divergent thinking—the originality and flexibility of your thought processes. The divergent thinking in creativity is good for you. Marc Runco studied 115 individuals and found strong correlations between divergent thinking and self-actualization. The phrase "self-actualization" was coined by the psychologist Carl Rogers, who, says Runco, "described it as the ability to be spontaneous and authentic and creative. Rogers actually said that we can't tell the difference between creativity and self-actualization. They're inextricable." Shelley Carson agrees: "The more creative an individual can be, the richer their

life. We're going to appreciate beauty more, we're going to think in analogies more, we're going to seek out novel experiences more."

Divergent thinking is measured in a few different, fascinating ways.
One way scientists test divergence is the "remote associates" test, which
tries to measure the associations we make. Creative thinking usually links
different things together in novel ways. A lovely example comes from the
award-winning poet Anne Carson in her 1998 book *Autobiography of Red*.
She writes that poets "undo the latches of being." One way they do this is
by bringing together unlikely images in unforeseen and beautiful ways.
And then, as she writes in one of her remarkable poems, "all the substances
in the world went floating up. Suddenly there was nothing to interfere with
horses being hollow hooved. Or a river being root silver." What is a river
that is root silver? I imagine it glinting silver in a certain kind of daylight,
and yet because it is "root silver," I can see its "root," or riverbed, with
fish and mud and perhaps even the roots of plants and trees. I see its surface
and its depth. And I can feel its beauty, because a root silver river sounds
lovely. This is divergent thinking at its best.

In the remote associates test, people are presented with three words and
asked to come up with a fourth word that is connected to all three. To do
that they have to activate three different associational networks and find a
place where those networks overlap. For instances you are given the words
paint, *doll*, and *cat*. You might choose the word *house* as a fourth word because you can paint a house, a cat can be a housecat, and a doll can live in
a dollhouse. These tests can start out with simple and easy words with common associations and increase in difficulty. Those who do well on this test
are very good at divergent thinking. Says Shelley Carson, "Every once in a
while one of the individuals will come up with an association we hadn't
thought of before, but it's a good answer, so I add it to my list of possible
answers." Another test for creativity, called the Barron Welsh Art Scale,
presents different pictures in pairs to people and asks them to pick the one
they like best. "Highly creative people will always pick the more complex
picture," notes Carson.

Divergent thinking *is* associated with a deficit in what is known as "latent inhibition." This is our brain's filtering mechanism. While sitting at
the computer working, we are filtering out the fact that there are paintings
on our walls, trees outside the window, birds chirping, papers and books on

the desk. We're also filtering out memories and internally generated mental imagery. When Carson and her associates used brain imaging to look inside the brains of highly creative people, she found that the back parts of their brains lit up very strongly. "The areas that really lit up were the occipital and parietal lobes. In other words, there was increased activation of the right hemisphere, which is loosely associated with creativity. (The brain is, of course, more complex than simple geographical divisions.) And there was a relative deactivation of parts of the brain associated with inhibition."

Carson and her colleague Jordan Peterson studied latent inhibition in highly creative people and found that they don't filter stimuli as strongly as others: "They score more like schizophrenics, who also have a filtering deficit," says Carson. "Our studies show that if you have this deficit, you're going to allow a lot more external and internal stimuli into your consciousness. Now, if you simply go into overload with all these stimuli, you may feel confused and disoriented. At the extreme, it might even lead to psychosis. But if you have a higher level of cognitive processing available to you, you will actually be able to process this information more fully than others. That's what we think is happening with highly creative people. They have more stimuli to work with, and they can see analogies between very different concepts and stimuli. In fact, Einstein described this process. He said that he envisioned many things, or psychical entities, floating inside his head, and then he mentally manipulated these things and brought them together to form new concepts. Another quote that I love comes from mathematician Henri Poincare: 'Ideas rose in crowds. I felt them collide until pairs interlocked. . . . I had only to write out the results, which took but a few hours.' "

❧   *Use "brainstorming" to enhance creativity.* On your own or with a group, take a problem and simply give free rein to your imagination. Express all the ideas you can think of to solve the problem, no matter how strange or wild they are. Nobody is allowed to voice a single criticism during the brainstorming session.

❧   *Try "mind-mapping."* This technique, invented by the British psychologist Tony Buzan, is a form of "lateral thinking" that is actually visual. You take a big piece of paper and a lot of colored pencils or markers, and you draw a central image (representing the "problem") at the center, then begin to draw spokes out from that image, and spokes from those images. For instance, I might draw "love" at the center and think, *How can I write a book about love?* Then I begin to think of different ways of love and draw spokes from those. I use the colors that feel appropriate to draw my branches. Then I may think of instances of those and draw spokes from those. I end up with a huge, wildly branching tree of associations, and I can begin to connect disparate branches that are branches of branches of branches. This allows me to see new patterns in new ways.

The beauty of mind-mapping is that as each idea is connected to the branch to which it relates most strongly, you end up with a pattern. As Gordon Dryden, author of *The Learning Revolution*, says, "An idea is a new combination of old elements. . . . There are no new elements. There are only new combinations."

🌺   *Think of multiple uses for a single object.* Shelley Carson tells her students to sit down and write as many uses as they can think of for a paper clip and then share the answers. "They're always surprised by others' answers." Similarly, choose a word, any word, and try to think of associations. For instance, the most common association with *table* is *chair*, according to studies. But you might also think *food, meals, mission, shaker, oak, pine, steel chef's table*, "Let's be open and put it on the table," and so on.

🌺   *Imagine how two very different items are similar.* Take two completely dissimilar items and try to imagine how they're similar, says Carson. "How is a can of soup similar to blood?" Or randomly pick two words out of a dictionary and try to find how they're similar, not just physically but symbolically.

🌺   *Try the opposite.* You can also do the opposite exercise: take two very similar things and try to see how they are different—for instance, *small* and *petite*.

LESSON FIVE: CREATIVITY OPENS OTHER LIVES

Johanna Grussner is a Finnish jazz singer and the inspiring centerpiece of *Seven Days of Possibilities: One Teacher, 24 Kids, and the Music That Changed*

Their Lives Forever by Anemona Hartocollis. After emigrating from rural Finland and attending the prestigious Berklee School of Music in Boston, Grussner went to New York to sing and supported herself by teaching music to ten-, eleven-, and twelve-year-olds at PS 86, a public school in the Bronx with thousands of students. Without any special funding, Grussner formed a children's choir that ultimately traveled to her homeland to perform. The *New York Times* printed three front-page articles during the trip. "My hometown elementary school had sixty students and three teachers," Grussner recalled in an interview with KALW radio in San Francisco. In contrast, in the Bronx public schools there were thousands of students and yet not a single music room. "The kids hadn't had music," she said. "I walked from class to class with my guitar on my back. I squeezed in a thousand students a week for one semester, and then switched my schedule the next semester to teach the other thousand. The children had so much energy that when they got to sing, they put everything into it. They sang with their entire bodies and all of their hearts." Grussner taught the children gospel because it was catchy and rhythmic and allowed them to move and clap. The children often had problems with attention and concentration in their classes, but as they learned to sing, says Grussner, "they finally had one subject they were special in, and they could feel good about themselves. When we sang in Finland the experience was so emotional that we all cried during the singing."

Creativity can help heal us physically and emotionally. In my work with dementia patients, I've been amazed to see how quiet and stable these individuals become when they begin to paint. At the Fairhill Center on Aging, where I have held focus groups for the Alzheimer's Association, I have marveled at the work of these older adults, which is so free in color and form that it almost seems to benefit from the disinhibition of dementia. Today the Alzheimer's Association produces yearly calendars that feature art by those with dementia. Instead of abandoning them because of the painful erosion of their self and memory, this celebration of their art engages them through creativity with what still remains. The abstract expressionist painter Willem de Kooning painted his way through much of his struggle with Alzheimer's, and national magazines featured his artwork. Even the Museum of Modern Art held an exhibition after his death that contained only the paintings he created during his final years with dementia. The art critic Kay Larson wrote, "The erosions of Alzheimer's could not eliminate the effects of a lifetime of discipline and love of craft . . . when infirmity struck, the artist was prepared . . . he knew what he loved best, and it sustained him." It's almost as if creativity is at the core of us all, deeper than rational thought.

A 2006 study of cancer patients by the psychologist and nurse Judith Paice of Northwestern Memorial Hospital found that art therapy significantly reduced patients' symptoms after just an hour. Fifty patients were studied over a four-month period; art therapy sessions reduced their pain, tiredness, depression, anxiety, drowsiness, lack of appetite, and shortness of breath. "Art therapy provides a distraction that allows patients to focus on something positive, and it gives patients a sense of control." Any creative act, whether dance, music, or art, can help people express themselves and can be very therapeutic, says Shelley Carson. "Just the act of writing is mood-altering," she adds.

Singing can also be therapeutic, according to a long-term study cosponsored by George Washington University and the National Endowment for the Arts. Begun in 2001, the project follows participants in community arts programs who are age sixty-five to one hundred, like the Senior Singles' Chorale. Compared to a control group of the same age, the singers feel physically healthier, visit the doctor less often, have fewer falls, and are more involved socially, less depressed, and in better spirits. "It's extraordinary that they actually improved," says Gene Cohen, director of the Center on Aging, Health, and Humanities at George Washington University. According to Eric Roter, an emergency room physician and master cellist, not only is singing creative, but "it's a very physical process, and when you're making music, your body responds as if you were giving it a physical workout." At other centers in the study, seniors participate in writing or creating visual art. One participant, eighty-year-old Walter Peach, says he had never touched a paintbrush and had to be "dragged" to the first class, but after going, "I felt so good about myself," he says. "I'm really proud of my paintings. I have an entirely different outlook on myself. It increased my self-esteem so much."

The Chicago music therapist Louise Dimiceli-Mitran has used drumming in her healing work at Advocate Illinois Masonic Medical Center. "When you're in a drumming circle, it's as if all your body is in tune with a rhythmic orchestra," she says. Drumming in groups can boost the immune system, according to a study involving more than one hundred participants and published in the journal *Alternative Therapies*. According to the study leader, Dr. Barry Bittman, director of Meadville Medical Center's Mind Body Wellness Center in Pennsylvania, an increased number of infection-fighting immune cells was found in the drummers' bloodstreams. The drummers also had an improved ratio of dehydroepiandrosterone (DHEA) to cortisol, a hormone balance that is beneficial to immune function. A control group that simply listened to drumming but did not participate had no change in either measure. Changes in these immunity markers might be attributed to the stress-reducing benefits of self-expression and camaraderie as well as the rhythm of the drumbeat, speculates Bittman.

And according to Eric Roter, playing music for someone is full of humanity, a kind of humanity that heals. "If you go into an exam with your doctor, it's artificial and sterile. There's something about playing music, and being the recipient of that music, that is ineffable. It's as if you're transferring the psyche of one person to another. It's so personal and intimate, and even though you can't measure it, it's very beneficial for both people. A few months ago, I played for a lady who had cancer. She died a few weeks later. Playing for her was so amazing, and I feel indebted to her, because she brought out more in me than I could've brought out by performing alone. The audience brings out things in the performer. Also, when people make music, they breathe differently, they hold their bodies differently. In order to make good music, you have to be relaxed. You can't be stiff. So you learn to be relaxed and energetic at the same time, and that's healthy for you."

❧ *Indulge yourself more deeply in a creative hobby.* Turn to creativity to heal yourself and then others. Make a hobby an avocation—something more meaningful than an indulgence or a dabble. Seriously practice a musical instrument, take a course in calligraphy, painting, photography, boatbuilding, or garden design, and then practice your new skill with devotion.

❧ *Share the gift.* Pass that skill along as a gift to others by performing, exhibiting, teaching others, or throwing a party in your newly designed and planted garden next summer.

LESSON SIX: WED CREATIVITY TO SERVICE (BE A MORAL GENIUS)

The physicist Amit Goswami has suggested that creative freedom is fundamental to ethics. Sometimes dilemmas arise to which there are no logical solutions. As Goswami says, "When logic is insufficient to reach an ethical answer, it can only be reached by a creative quantum leap. The creative approach often yields a richer solution that actually revolutionizes the context of the problem itself. Ethics in essence seems to involve inner creativity."

Creativity in the moral realm can transform itself into a kind of genius. Only a few of us are overcome by this profound sense of calling. These are the folks we call extreme altruists: they are the Bachs and Beethovens of the moral world, the ones who are so single-minded and focused that they willingly make great sacrifices. This kind of genius is like riding a fifteen-foot wave in a hurricane at Gilgo Beach in Long Island—I know this because I used to ride those waves as a teen. They surge and surge, and you simply have to hold on. For these folks, giving has a momentum of its own that is unstoppable.

Consider the life of Peace Pilgrim, who from the years 1953 to 1981 walked twenty-five thousand miles on foot, promoting peace along the way. She crossed the country seven times on foot and often walked until she was given shelter, and fasted until she was fed. The mission of her walk: international disarmament and peace among all individuals. She was a creative genius in the moral realm, inspiring others to give. Born in 1908, Peace Pilgrim—whose birth name was Mildred Norman Ryder—went through a kind of epiphany in 1938 after spending the night in the woods praying to discover her calling in life. "A great peace came over me," she later recalled. "I experienced a complete willingness without reservations whatsoever, to give my life to something beyond myself." She began "living to give, not to get." Years later she described her first experience of complete inner peace and bliss: "I did not seem to be walking on the earth . . . but . . . every flower, every bush, every tree, seemed to wear a halo. There was a light emanation around everything and flecks of gold fell like slanted rain through the air."

After hiking the Appalachian Trail, the idea of becoming a peace pilgrim, walking the country for peace, came to her: "I saw in my mind's eye, myself walking along and wearing the garb of my mission. . . . I saw a map of the United States with the large cities marked . . . coast to coast and border to border. . . . I knew what I was to do. I will talk to everyone who will listen to me about the way to peace."

Her epiphany and vision was as creative an act as a painting or a piece of music—it was what the psychologist Michael Piechowski calls moral creativity. He suggests that "if discovering a truth is a creative process, then discovering one's true self must be one too." Inner growth and transformation can be a way of creating a new self.

Millard Fuller, founder of Habitat for Humanity, is also a genius in the moral realm: he built a mission, an organization, and literally built homes. As I mentioned in chapter 2, at the age of thirty he was already a millionaire when he and his wife sold their business, gave their money away, and went to Koinonia Farm, a Christian community in Georgia. Fuller and Clarence Jordan founded "Partnership for Housing" in 1969, working together with fifteen other members of Koinonia. In mid-1976, after several years building houses in Zaire, Fuller and his wife Linda established Habitat for Humanity. Land would be donated to families without homes, and the community members would help build homes for them. By 2005, 200,000 houses had been built for 1 million people, and Habitat was operating in one hundred countries. The creative beauty here is that, no matter who we are and where we come from, we can all, as Fuller says, "pick up a hammer and begin to drive nails and build a house! Families have such strong feelings about their new homes."

Mahatma Gandhi is another astounding example of moral genius: his life and work mobilized others to service. His moral creativity led him to invent *satyagraha*, nonviolent resistance to injustice, which contains several stages:

- Persuading others through discussion and reason
- Persuading others through suffering (fasting)
- Nonviolent noncooperation, or civil disobedience

It may be that love—of humanity—allows creative geniuses in the moral realm to "discover" their unusual solutions to human suffering and inspire others to follow in their paths. Interestingly, research shows that, from an early age, gifted children show moral sensitivity and seem to demonstrate an advanced ability to think about justice and fairness and an increased desire to console others. Research into children with IQs over 160 found them to be far above their peers in conceptualizing fairness, justice, and responsibility toward others. One group of exceptionally gifted twelve-year-olds scored higher than the average college student on a test of moral reasoning and judgment.

I think as I write this of Thomas Edison, whose birthplace is about two hours west of Cleveland, not far from where I have lived for the last eighteen years. "I want to serve and advance human life, not destroy it," he once said. "I never perfected an invention that I did not think about in terms of the service it might give others. . . . I find out what the world needs, then I proceed to invent." With only three months of formal schooling, totally deaf in his left ear and 80 percent deaf in his right, this genius made more than ten thousand failed attempts before creating a filament for the electric lightbulb. He literally lit the world.

❧   *Contemplate moral genius.* Be inspired by history. Read biographies of Peace Pilgrim or Thomas Edison or the Reverend Martin Luther King Jr., whose nonviolent sit-ins were an act of moral creative genius. And so, in their own way, are walks like the March of Dimes walk, AIDS walks, and any other walk for a cause in which individuals find a novel solution to helping others. Maya Lin's Vietnam Memorial was an act of creative and moral genius, for the visceral, physical experience of walking it moves us, wrenchingly and unforgettably.

❧   *Participate in moral creativity.* Join in a walk for a cause, or get involved in a nonprofit foundation whose work seems creative and imaginative to you.

A Final Thought

I am deeply moved by the perspective of Buckminster Fuller, a visionary, architect, and inventor, creator of the geodesic dome, and author of twenty-eight books. He was deeply concerned with sustainability and the environment and over his lifetime was awarded twenty-five patents and many honorary doctorates. In the winter of 1927, at the age of thirty-two, bankrupt and jobless, "Bucky" had watched his daughter Alexandra die of pneumonia. He nearly committed suicide, but instead, at the last moment, he embarked on "an experiment, to find what a single individual can contribute to changing the world and benefiting all humanity." Of creativity, Bucky Fuller said this: "When I am working on a problem . . . I only think about how to solve the problem. But when I have finished, if the solution is not beautiful, I know it is wrong."

Creativity begins with trust. Trust yourself to invent and innovate, and dare to dream.

Your Creativity Score

It's time to answer the questions on the creativity section of your Love and Longevity Scale. We have divided responses into percentiles, or fifths. These are general guidelines; you may score right near the cutoff between percentiles, so please keep this in mind and use the scale as a friendly tool. Remember:

There are two steps to determining your score. First, determine which items need to be "reverse-scored" (denoted with the ® symbol). For reverse-scored items, see the chart below for how to score.

If you score a . . .	. . . assign yourself a score for that item of:
1	6
2	5
3	4
4	3
5	2
6	1

The second step is to add the scores for individual items *after* the reverse-scored items have been reverse-scored. Take the quiz now, and take it again if you wish after you've finished this book and become more creative in your daily life.

Using the scale provided, please circle the one number that best reflects your opinion about whether or not each statement below describes you or experiences that you have had. There are no correct answers, so please respond as honestly as possible to each one.

1. I enjoy using my creative skills to help family members with valuable projects.
    1=strongly disagree   2=disagree   3=slightly disagree   4=slightly agree
    5=agree   6=strongly agree

2. I think it's important to help family members develop skills so that they can be original.
    1=strongly disagree   2=disagree   3=slightly disagree   4=slightly agree
    5=agree   6=strongly agree

3. I'm good at finding matches between family members' abilities and potential opportunities for them.
    1=strongly disagree   2=disagree   3=slightly disagree   4=slightly agree
    5=agree   6=strongly agree

4. I don't help family members much when it comes to figuring out good solutions.[®]
    1=strongly disagree   2=disagree   3=slightly disagree   4=slightly agree
    5=agree   6=strongly agree

5. I'm not good at helping family members figure out their strengths in life.[®]
    1=strongly disagree   2=disagree   3=slightly disagree   4=slightly agree
    5=agree   6=strongly agree

6. I get pleasure out of using my creative skills to help friends with valuable projects.
    1=strongly disagree   2=disagree   3=slightly disagree   4=slightly agree
    5=agree   6=strongly agree

7. Motivating friends to seek out awesome or motivating experiences is something that interests me.
    1=strongly disagree   2=disagree   3=slightly disagree   4=slightly agree
    5=agree   6=strongly agree

8. I keep a lookout for books or movies that might contribute to a friend's personal growth.
    1=strongly disagree   2=disagree   3=slightly disagree   4=slightly agree
    5=agree   6=strongly agree

9. I don't spend much time helping friends develop their goals or ways to reach them.[®]
    1=strongly disagree   2=disagree   3=slightly disagree   4=slightly agree
    5=agree   6=strongly agree

10. Coming up with ways for friends to create or find opportunities for themselves doesn't interest me.[®]
    1=strongly disagree   2=disagree   3=slightly disagree   4=slightly agree
    5=agree   6=strongly agree

11. Time does not matter when it comes to helping neighbors or people at work develop a creative idea.
    1=strongly disagree   2=disagree   3=slightly disagree   4=slightly agree
    5=agree   6=strongly agree

12. I like using my creative skills to help people at work or in the neighborhood with valuable projects.
    1=strongly disagree   2=disagree   3=slightly disagree   4=slightly agree
    5=agree   6=strongly agree

13. I keep an eye out for books or movies that might contribute to a neighbour's or colleague's personal growth.

    1=strongly disagree   2=disagree   3=slightly disagree   4=slightly agree
    5=agree   6=strongly agree

14. I'm not very helpful to people at work or in my community when it comes to figuring out good solutions.[®]

    1=strongly disagree   2=disagree   3=slightly disagree   4=slightly agree
    5=agree   6=strongly agree

15. Inspiring neighbors or coworkers to strive for important causes is not my strength.[®]

    1=strongly disagree   2=disagree   3=slightly disagree   4=slightly agree
    5=agree   6=strongly agree

16. I try to motivate people to nurture the important relationships in their lives.

    1=strongly disagree   2=disagree   3=slightly disagree   4=slightly agree
    5=agree   6=strongly agree

17. I encourage strong, positive attachments and relationships in life, whether it is with pets, crafts, or good causes.

    1=strongly disagree   2=disagree   3=slightly disagree   4=slightly agree
    5=agree   6=strongly agree

18. I am not interested in helping children develop goals and ways to reach them.[®]

    1=strongly disagree   2=disagree   3=slightly disagree   4=slightly agree
    5=agree   6=strongly agree

19. Coming up with ways to create opportunities for other people doesn't interest me.[®]

    1=strongly disagree   2=disagree   3=slightly disagree   4=slightly agree
    5=agree   6=strongly agree

20. Figuring out good solutions to help others is not particularly motivating for me.[®]

1=strongly disagree   2=disagree   3=slightly disagree   4=slightly agree
5=agree   6=strongly agree

YOUR CREATIVITY SCORE

High Giver (80th percentile)	99 or higher
Giver (60th percentile)	92–98
Moderate Giver (40th percentile)	83–91
Low Giver (20th percentile)	73–82

※

Thirteen

※

Doing Good, Living Well:
Your Life Program

So here we are, you and I. If you recall, I asked you in the first chapter to take my hand and find the fire, the secret of giving.

The fire warms the words of "Dr. Frat," the former director of the Comprehensive Burn Center in Cleveland: "My work has filled me with a peace and joy that surpasses all understanding," he said, "and I can never put into words." I feel that fire in the voice of Christina Noble, "mum" to every street child in Vietnam, who told me, "I know that love is absolutely beautiful, an incredible gift, and to share it is even more beautiful." Pastor Otis Moss found the fire in Martin Luther King Sr.'s promise: "For the rest of my days I will not hate. I will not hate. I want to go on record that I will not hate." That flame flickers in the heart of quadriplegic therapist Daniel Gottlieb: "The knowledge that I could still help another person saved my life. There was a new silence inside me, and in the silence I was able to hear people's hearts." I carry with me, right now and always, the gentle light of Jean Vanier, founder of L'Arche: "We are all broken in some way.

The only answer is to love each other." And the response of one L'Arche assistant: "Here there is a very pure love you don't experience in other places in society. Here you learn that innocence is beautiful, that the disabled can be like living prayers." I can still feel the epiphany of the head of a genetics institute who, when he saw the photographs of Rick Guidotti, said simply: "This is like motherhood. I get it. What do you want me to do for you?"

You've encountered the work of many scientists in this book who have studied generous love. The science backs up our intuition, again and again. From Stephanie Brown's research showing that giving to others reduces mortality . . . to Neal Krause's work showing that even the simple act of praying for others slashes the impact of health difficulties in older folks . . . to Paul Wink's remarkable study showing that giving protects us across an entire life span, over a period of fifty years . . . science shows that giving shifts our psychology and our biology, no matter what our age, experience, or walk of life. Some of our scientists have looked at lives, and others at molecules—we've begun to understand the calculus of the hormones triggered when we give, hormones like oxytocin, and we've watched the parts of the brain that light up in states of deep compassion. We're mapping a new terrain of neurocircuitry that one scientist calls the "calm and connect" axis—the opposite of fight-or-flight.

The science now gives me confidence to say what I've always felt: a loving life is the only credible way of life. Though science can never capture the mystery of love, it is a powerful pathway to truth, and it's telling us that if we give to others, we will benefit enormously.

There is no contradiction in my view. At a moment like this, a few evolutionary biologists might pop up, like a jack-in-the-box, saying, "But of course! Nature made sure giving feels good, because we're all selfish! Scratch any altruist and watch an egoist start to bleed!"

I sometimes wonder what they really mean by this. Are they suggesting that there is no such thing as real giving, because real giving has to be unselfish—it can't benefit the giver at all? In this view, if we care for our children or our kin, it's because they share our genes, not because we are in any way innately good, and not because we simply, powerfully, unconditionally *love* them.

Think of the single cell in the primordial soup so long ago. When that cell joined together with other cells, they began to integrate and cooperate, even taking up different specialities. They evolved into multicellular organisms. The magnificent variety of life, the cornucopia of creative diversity, is due in large part to this cooperation. As David Sloan Wilson says, "We have said since millennia—in fact, this has been a fundamental tenet of religion—that if you do good things, it will reflect back to you, not immediately, not every time, but in general. This is a deeply entrenched notion. In contrast, some of the assumptions of scientists are actually a little bit shocking from this perspective." In fact, David's research has shown that altruism flourishes best in a context of altruism. In other words, a healthy society is a giving society.

We seem to have a compelling need to *explain* generosity—we seem utterly mystified by it at times. This was more than evident in a 2002 conference I participated in on game theory and love at the Institute for Advanced Studies at Princeton. Game theory focuses on how groups of people interact in an effort to achieve their own goals; it creates mathematical models for these interactions and tries to test them both in real groups and in computer simulations. The conference was sort of like a wrestling match: we threw together game theorists, theologians, and philosophers. The program was co-chaired by Dr. Martin Nowak, head of a new center in theoretical mathematics at Harvard. Nowak is justly famous for a rendition of game theory called "Generous Tit-for-Tat," which suggests that most of us enter relationships in an initial state of trust and benevolence, but when people are uncooperative or betray or harm us, we simply turn away from them eventually and focus our generosity and trust on someone else who will return it. Generous Tit-for-Tat is a revision of another equally famous and elegantly simple equation called Tit-for-Tat, invented by Robert Axelrod, who won a MacArthur genius award for his work. He asked people all over the world to submit mathematical formulas by which an individual might best survive and survive in this world. Many formulas were extremely complex, but the most robust one was one of the simplest, and it beat all the others. Called Tit-for-Tat, it went like this: You start out willing to trust and cooperate. If your partner betrays you, you punish him back—once. Then you are ready to cooperate with him again—in a sense, you have held your own, but have also been forgiving in the big picture.

And yet one more model comes from the biological anthropologist Chris Boehm of Stanford University, who is also on the leading edge of human evolutionary theory. Boehm has a truly beguiling idea: if doing good is good for us and our species, our genes may evolve over time in a less selfish and more giving direction. In other words, evolution might just be on the side of giving. This jibes with the work of Robert Wright, author of the best-selling classic *The Moral Animal* and, more recently, *Non-Zero*. Wright thinks that as we become a truly interdependent, global society, we will cooperate more and more and become a global organism.

I remember sitting in a restaurant in May 2005 with Dr. Jerome Kassirer, who for many years was the editor of the *New England Journal of Medicine* and is now on the faculty at Case Western Medical School, with an appointment in my own Department of Bioethics. We spent two hours speaking about the human capacity for unselfish love. I pointed out to Jerome that he devotes hours each day to the careful reading of research papers by junior scholars in order to help them get published. He is an emblem of the way of the nurturer. When I told him this, he said, "I'm doing this because it makes me feel great, so how could it be love? I only believe in egoism." I said to him that his intense happiness was the whole point.

And so I say, more of such selfishness! Feel good when you give. Have you ever seen a statue of the Buddha in which he was not fat and grinning from ear to ear? I have absolutely no desire to champion love that doesn't bring the giver joy and happiness. Enjoy giving to the "breadth and depth of your soul" and take the simple message of this book to heart: Give and be happier. Give and be healthier. Give and live longer.

Daily Giving: Your Personal Program

We're all different—a truism if there ever was one—and that means that the way you give to others is ultimately your own choice. That's the whole point of this book: to delineate the richness of giving, and the many ways we can do it. Edison was a great inventor—and he spent much of his time alone working. Mother Teresa was rarely alone—she was constantly at the bedside of the poor and dying. There couldn't be two more different people, but both were world-class givers.

Giving is a simple act. Shifting your life begins now, with one simple act. Most of us score high on at least a few ways of giving. I don't want to prescribe too rigid a program for anybody, but here are some useful ways you can work with this book:

❧ *Choose one way of love in one sphere each day.* Offer one act of giving that day. With ten ways and four spheres, there will be forty different ways. Experiment over forty days and notice what you're good at and what feels good—small acts? Large acts? Giving in the family? Giving to strangers?

❧ *Start with the way of love you scored highest on.* Practice acts of giving in that way for a week. Then try the way you scored second-highest on for another week. Focus on each way for a week, down to the way of love you scored lowest on, for a total of ten weeks. Again, notice what feels best and what is most rewarding. If you want, test yourself on the ways you scored lower on to see if they've changed after you've created a shift in your style of giving.

❧ *Focus on the domains of giving rather than the ways.* Choose a domain, such as family, and each day practice a different way of giving in that sphere. Then move to the next sphere. This will take about forty days.

❧ *Do what you love.* If you feel passionate about one of your domains or ways and just love it and feel deeply rewarded by it, then stay there and focus on it even more.

At the end of eight to ten weeks, try answering the questions on the Love and Longevity Scale again. But remember, the scale is just a tool. Even more important is your feeling about life—your inner life, your real life—and the ways in which you feel more enlivened, more appreciated, happier, more valued and valuable after giving. Remember the inspiring words of Gandhi: "The difference between what we do and what we are capable of doing would suffice to solve most of the world's problems."

On the Way to Milesburg

It's late on a hot summer night, and I'm on the broken bus to Cleveland—
I'm on the bus home. I'm trying to sleep but I can't, because the young man
behind me keeps tapping me on the shoulder. I'm thinking back to the
words of Stephanie Preston: "It is my children who have taught me to be
empathic and loving." I'm smiling at the memory of Ronald Reagan, who,
shot and in danger of dying, instantly set the emergency room doctors at
ease by quipping, "I hope you're all Republicans." I'm remembering Korey
Thompson, the Alzheimer's clown, telling me, "One time I just held my
two hands out to a person with dementia and imagined that in the center
of my palms was the softest, most tender love, and she looked up at me and
smiled." The words of Cass Forkin echo in my mind: "We sent a man with
only six weeks to live on a barge down the Mississippi. It's never too late to
make a difference."

That's what I want to tell you now. It's never too late to make a difference. Are we home yet? George Bennett is home—a man who nearly died
in an accident that burned his entire body, and who says of his wife: "Because of her loyalty, I began to realize I was going to make it, whatever it
took. My relationship with her keeps improving. It's just better and better."
And Vivian is surely home too: "I can't imagine what I would do without
him. Who could I ever be with? He's my one and only."

The young man on the bus to Milesburg was a stranger, and yet he taps
at my shoulder always. I hear him asking me, "Are we there yet?" It's the
question we all ask. The answer is love. Love is for you, from you, and because of you. Just give it.

Acknowledgments

I have been blessed to know a visionary ninety-three-year-old man from rural Tennessee who went to Yale and to Oxford as a Rhodes scholar, and who would have become a Presbyterian minister if he hadn't discovered a talent for investing that made him one of the most successful men of his generation: Sir John Templeton. Sir John and I first met in the lobby of a Washington, D.C. hotel in 1994. The one idea he was always most passionate about was the energy of generous love in our lives, and without his support, entire new fields of research into forgiveness, gratitude, and love would never have emerged as convincingly as they have. Without this inspiring and courageous man, who has donated much of his fortune to the study of these and related ideas, and whose generous grant birthed the Institute for Unlimited Love, this book would never have existed.

Many talented visionaries at the John Templeton Foundation have been immensely helpful along the way, including the ever-inspiring Pamela Thompson; the remarkable Judy Marchand, whose loyalty and practical wisdom have been hugely important; Arthur Schwartz, who always thought-fully asks what more might be accomplished; Charles Harper, Jr., whose passion and brilliance set the necessarily high standards for excellence that love research deserves; and John M. Templeton, Jr., a marvelous physician who has been a warm friend, and who exemplifies giving as a source of happiness. Linda Kelly has been a valuable helper as well.

And then there is Cleveland, where I've lived for nearly two decades. I have been lucky to stumble across so many absolutely amazing Clevelanders who have contributed to my life's work in every way that people possibly could. Judy and Dick Watson have guided me in every endeavor with a reflective wisdom and generous philanthropic support, and have recently endowed a Professorship in Science and Religion at Harvard University's Divinity School. Cathy and John Lewis have done more good for more people in this city than I can keep track of, and their guidance with the Institute has been invaluable. Taken together, these four remarkable individuals are real-life proof that it's good to be good.

Other Clevelanders who have contributed resources and ideas to the work of the Institute include Maria and Samuel H. Miller, Audrey and Albert Ratner, Jeanette Grasselli Brown, Kathy and James Pender, Vic Gelb, Ed Combs, Dorothy Hovorka, Lindsay and David Morgenthaler, and Jeff Lucier. I have been blessed by the people of Cleveland, and by the School of Medicine of Case Western Reserve University, where our former Dean, Nate Berger, an oncologist who understands the connection between emotions and healing, saw fit to allow me to locate the Institute at the school. I see Nate every few days in the hallway and he always asks me, "So, how's that love stuff doin'?" And I proceed to tell him the latest news. He is an especially good man, and his deeply joyful wife Suzy keeps him that way.

Every Institute advisor has been a great conversation partner for me over the years, including the late Dame Cicely Saunders of London, who invented the modern hospice movement; Herbert Benson, founder of the Mind-Body Institute at Harvard Medical School, who has shown me how much a little courage can achieve; Don Browning of the University of Chicago, a mentor and conversation partner since I began studying the idea of love in 1978; Rosalyn Carter, who has been so generous with her time and friendship; Robert M. Franklin of Emory University, and Reverand Otis Moss Jr., who over the years have deepened my understanding of *agape* love and nonviolence in the African-American Christian tradition; Millard Fuller, who sets the standard for "doing unto others" through building houses for the homeless.

John F. Haught of Georgetown University, Timothy Jackson of Emory University, and Tom Oord of Northwest Nazarene University have been theological thinkers always ready to ask the "Big Picture" questions about love and meaning in the universe. Seyyed Hossein Nasr of George Washington University and Jacob Neusner of Bard College have, with clarity and great erudition, kept the Islamic and Jewish traditions in the forefront of my mind over the years; Samuel Oliner, a Holocaust survivor who was rescued by a courageous German Christian family, has been a tremendous pioneer of the lifelong study of altruism; Olayemi Omatade has worked for years with children with AIDS in Africa and inspired a great many to take up that cause; Edmund Pellegrino of Georgetown University is a truly caring physician who has kept beneficence and compassion in the center of professional ethics in a time when it has been imperiled; Margaret Poloma of the University of Akron has been an extremely insightful conversation partner in the sociology of giving; Sidney Callahan, a writer and psychologist, has been a student of the moral sentiments and a model of goodness; Steven C. Rockefeller has exemplified for me the meaning of giving in the philanthropic tradition of a great family; Lynn Underwood, formerly of the Fetzer Institute and now of nearby Hiram College, has been my closest partner in developing the study of compassionate love in the research community; George Vaillant, of Harvard Medical School, has often energized me with his scientific acumen and warm smile; and Susan Wentz, among everyone I know in the medical profession, most exemplifies attentive listening and compassion.

The Fetzer Institute, the William T. Grant Foundation, and the Ford Foundation, with the help of Mike Edwards, have all contributed to ongoing Institute projects. Renee Rizzo, whom I have never actually met, is an actress who called me out of the blue five years ago when she first heard of the Institute, and has been a friend and contributor. Sanford N. McDonnell, a CEO emeritus of McDonnell Douglas, has taken a special interest in my work and provided support.

Others who have been colleagues and friends in the study of love and giving are Joan Campbell of the Chautauqua Institution, Greg Fricchione,

Julie Norman, Jeff Levin, Byron Johnson, Jeffrey P. Schloss, Mike McCullough, Julie Exline, Solomon Katz, William Grassie, Robert L. Haynie, Vincent Jeffries, Bill Kramer, Susan S. Larson, Doug Lawson, Donald Lehr, Martin E. Marty, David Myers, Lee Conklin, John Witte, Orien Reid, Holmes Rolston III, David S. Wilson, Harold Koenig, Esther M. Sternberg, Isabelle Paul, Robert Thurman, Stuart J. Youngner, and Dave Katz. All have all been important conversation partners along the way.

Arielle Eckstut of Levine-Greenberg Literary Agency and Kristine Puopolo, our editor, have both made many essential contributions along the way. Kris devoted so much of her valuable time to carefully reading and re-reading every section of the book, making invaluable contributions throughout. Both Jill Neimark and I feel indebted to these two fantastic women.

Finally, a special thanks to my wife, Mitsuko, who takes such good care of us all, to my daughter, Emma, for being such a good friend to so many, and to my son, Andrew, who is a gift to our entire family.

Index

About the Authors

⁂

Stephen Post is Professor of Bioethics and Family Medicine in the School of Medicine, Case Western Reserve University, and served as a Senior Research Scholar in the Becket Institute at St. Hugh's College, Oxford University. He is also President of the Institute for Research on Unlimited Love—Altruism, Compassion, Service, which was founded in 2001 with a generous grant from the John Templeton Foundation. Dr. Post has published over 130 articles in peer-reviewed journals such as *Science*, the *International Journal of Behavioral Medicine*, *Annals of Internal Medicine*, the *Journal of Religion*, the *American Journal of Psychiatry*, the *Journal of the American Medical Association*, and the *Lancet*. He has written seven scholarly books on love and eight other books, including *The Fountain of Youth: Cultural, Scientific & Ethical Perspectives on a Biomedical Goal* and *Altruism and Health: An Empirical Approach*, both published by Oxford University Press. He is also editor-in-chief of the definitive, five-volume *Encyclopedia of Bioethics*. Dr. Post received the Distinguished Service Award from the National Board of the Alzheimer's Association. He has chaired nine national conferences in his field. He lives in Shaker Heights, Ohio, with his wife, Mitsuko, and their two children, Emma and Andrew.

Jill Neimark is a widely published science writer living in New York City. Her novel *Bloodsong* was a Book-of-the-Month Club selection, published in hardcover and paperback and in five foreign countries. Her poetry has appeared in the *Cimarron Review*, the *Massachusetts Review*, and *Borderlands*. She has published three children's books, one of which, *I Want Your Moo*, with coauthor Marcella Bakur-Weiner, has been in print for over a decade. She is a former features editor at *Psychology Today*.